SOUTH AMERICAN AND LATIN AMERICAN ECONOMIC HISTORY

Edited by
Stuart Bruchey
Columbia University

Editorial Consultant
Herbert S. Klein
Columbia University

A GARLAND SERIES

ECONOMIC STRUCTURE AND DEMOGRAPHIC PERFORMANCE IN JAMAICA 1891–1935

Richard A. Lobdell

GARLAND PUBLISHING, INC.
New York & London 1987

Library of Congress Cataloging-in-Publication Data

Lobdell, Richard A.
Economic structure and demographic performance in Jamaica, 1891–1935.

(South American and Latin American economic history)
Bibliography: p.
1. Jamaica—Population—History—19th century.
2. Jamaica—Population—History—20th century.
3. Agriculture—Economic aspects—Jamaica—History—19th century. 4. Agriculture—Economic aspects—Jamaica—History—20th century. 5. Jamaica—Economic conditions. I. Title. II. Series.
HB3553.L63 1987 304.6′097292 87-8345
ISBN 0-8240-1365-4 (alk. paper)

All volumes in this series are printed on acid-free, 250-year-life paper.

Printed in the United States of America

ECONOMIC STRUCTURE AND DEMOGRAPHIC PERFORMANCE IN JAMAICA, 1891 - 1935

by

Richard A. Lobdell

PREFACE TO THE GARLAND EDITION

It is now nearly a dozen years since the bulk of this dissertation was written. In the interval a number of scholarly works on Jamaican economic and demographic history have been published; there have also been significant reassessments of both the staple theory of growth and the plantation interpretation of colonial economic development. In light of this recent literature, I was pleased to receive Garland's request that my dissertation be published in its original form.

As I worked through the text to correct typographical errors and infelicities of style, it became clear that the original dissertation would have been strengthened if the results of recent studies had then been available. Most notable in this regard is the absence of any discussion of dependency theory as it might have applied to Jamaica during this period. My attempt to blend the staple theory of growth with the plantation interpretation of economic underdevelopment might be read as a version of dependency theory, but at best it is incomplete and lacks the unity of theories which have been more recently developed. What passes for "econometrics" in the text is also a matter of some embarrassment. The tests of the hypotheses are certainly elementary; the use of recently developed statistical techniques would have made the results more persuasive and compelling, if no more true. Finally, much more is now known about the patterns of demographic performance in Jamaica during the early nineteenth century. The incorporation of those findings would have been extremely helpful in establishing patterns of continuity and change over a much longer time period.

These deficiencies notwithstanding, working through the text has confirmed my earlier belief in the dissertation's strengths. Firstly, an attempt has been made to test empirically a set of economic-demographic relationships which previously had been the subject of descriptive analyses. Secondly, the empirical analysis centres on small geographic areas, the administrative parishes of Jamaica, rather than on Jamaica as a national unit. Finally, the study illustrates the wealth of economic and social data that exist for Jamaica and her parishes during this period. In these three respects time has not eroded the dissertation's contribution to an understanding of Jamaican economic and demographic history during the late nineteenth and early twentieth centuries.

Financial support for the original dissertation was generously provided by the Canada Council and by McGill University's Centre for Developing-Area Studies. Professors Harold Wright, George Grantham, Allen Fenichel, and John Iton were members of my dissertation committee at McGill and each offered much sound advice and constructive criticism. I am grateful to Jeannine Watson and Pat Buchanan who helped prepare the text for the Garland edition. Most of all, I am pleased to acknowledge my profound debt of gratitude for the kind and helpful counsel consistently offered over the years by R. B. Sheridan, D. G. Hall, and my wife Judith Lobdell.

Winnipeg, Canada

August 1985

CONTENTS

LIST OF TABLES AND FIGURES

Chapter I

INTRODUCTION

Once the most prized of Britain's tropical colonies, Jamaica had receded into the shadows of the empire during the late nineteenth and early twentieth centuries. The principal source of the island's former wealth and influence, the cultivation of sugar cane, had been in difficulties since the promulgation of free trade in Britain at mid-nineteenth century. With the appearance of bountied European beet sugar in British markets following 1883, the Jamaican sugar industry suffered even further decline.[1]

It is true that the sixty year period ending in 1940 witnessed occasional periods of modest prosperity. The meteoric rise of the banana staple export industry in the 1890's and the years of buoyant metropolitan demand for tropical produce during and immediately following the First World War were the principal causes of such modest prosperity.[2] Moreover, the essentially subsistence economy of Jamaican small settlers provided some measure of relief during the worst periods of depression in the staple export sectors.

As viewed by the Colonial Office and the landed oligarchy of Jamaica however, the period 1880-1940 was an era of generally unrelieved economic depression and potential social disintegration.[3] The decline of sugar exports seemed to threaten the existence of plantations, especially since bananas could be cultivated efficiently on small peasant plots. Moreover, with the increased importance of U.S. markets for Jamaican banana exports, the influence of Americans in Jamaica's economic and political affairs was unavoidable and was viewed with great suspicion by Whitehall and the local plantocracy.[4] Finally there were unmistakable signs of social unrest as the economy stagnated and as countless emigrants returned to Jamaica. In June of 1897 some 30,000 Jamaicans gathered in Kingston to hail Victoria's Diamond Jubilee; in May of 1938 an even larger crowd gathered to cheer Alexander Bustamante's demands for better wages and self-government.[5]

During these fitfull years the shapers of public policy were primarily concerned with three separate but closely related aspects of these distressing conditions. Not unexpectedly the first and foremost concern was to ensure "the good government of the colony". In addition to the application of normal police powers, the colonial government regularly reported to London on the behaviour of individual political and social activists, monitored the activity of political movements, and detailed the activities of U.S. citizens and companies in Jamaican economic and political affairs.[6] Apart from these efforts to maintain law, order and loyalty, the good government of the colony presupposed the efficient collection of taxes and the judicious disbursement of public revenues. The successive appointment of special commissions of enquiry into the financial affairs of the colonial government indicates that such attempts at fiscal responsibility were far from successful in the eyes of the Colonial Office.[7]

Secondly, public policy was explicitly concerned with the expansion of the island's staple exports. Transport services were reorganized and expanded to facilitate the movement of staple export crops to the various ports of the island, and irrigation schemes were undertaken to encourage large scale cultivation of sugar and bananas. In addition, direct government subsidies were paid on sugar exports and were given in aid of central sugar factories. Political as well as financial assistance was provided to banana exporting producer co-operatives in an effort to break the monoposony position of the United Fruit Company.[8]

Thirdly, official public policy was obsessed with the so-called "Labour Problem". Jamaican wage labourers, it had long been argued by the planters, were unreliable in their willingness to work and were indifferent in their quality; hence, the expansion of staple exports was impossible in the absence of more "reliable" labour supplies.[9] In part this "Labour Problem" was the result of a viable alternative for wage labourers: namely, self-employment on small subsistence plots. In part, it was thought to be somehow related to the obvious predilection of Jamaicans to migrate abroad or to the towns. In any case, the extensive plantations were chronically unable to attract what was judged to be sufficient labour to expand or even maintain the level of staple exports.

That these three areas of concern were interrelated was obvious to most informed observers at the time. It was widely understood that both the volume of employment and the financial position of the colonial government--hence the ability to maintain the established social order--depended critically upon the overall level of economic activity and upon the prosperity of staple exports in particular.[10] The success of the staple export sector in turn depended upon the availability and quality of the wage labour force, the nature of public expenditure on transport and production subsidies, and the prices of exports in various international markets.[11] In brief, public policy began with the postulate that staple exports had to be maintained and if possible expanded.

Although the level and composition of economic activity was seen to be at least partly dependent upon the nature of the labour force, few contemporary observers seemed to appreciate the possibility that the so-called "Labour Problem", and the underlying demographic forces which largely determined that phenomenon, might be influenced systematically by the level and composition of economic activity itself. A few astute observers did recognize that migration patterns were somehow related to perceived economic opportunity.[12] On the whole, however, there was little appreciation that other features of demographic performance might be determined by economic or social structure.

It is the purpose of the present study to enquire into this latter possibility. That is, the present study examines possible relationships between socio-economic structure and demographic performance among the individual administrative parishes of Jamaica during the late nineteenth and early twentieth centuries. In Chapter II the relevant literature concerning Jamaican historical demography is reviewed. Particular care is taken to assess the strength and weakness of this scholarly literature.

In Chapter III, a causal model of the demographic consequences of socio-economic structure is presented. Special attention is paid to the differential influences of the organization of economic activity (plantation vs. peasant production) and of the composition of output (staple export crop vs. domestic crops) on the pattern of parish demographic performance. A set of specific hypotheses is derived from this model.

The structure of the economy during the period 1880-1940 is described in Chapter IV, and the patterns of demographic performance during the same period are discussed in Chapter V. In both chapters particular care is taken to examine activity at the individual parish level. By so doing, it is possible to generate statistical data suitable for an empirical test of the various hypotheses derived in Chapter III.

This empirical test is the subject of Chapter VI. Following a discussion of operational definitions of the variables involved, the data on parish demographic performance and parish socio-economic structure are subjected to multiple regression analysis. An interpretation of the results and their implications for the tenability of the specific hypotheses are presented. In Chapter VII the general approach and significant findings of the study are reviewed and comments are offered concerning the possibilities of further research.

ENDNOTES TO CHAPTER I

[1] R. W. Beachey, The British West Indian Sugar Industry in the Nineteenth Century. (Oxford: 1957); W. Root, The British West Indies and the Sugar Industry. (Liverpool: 1899); Richard A. Lobdell, "Patterns of Investment and Sources of Credit in the British West Indian Sugar Industry, 1838-97", Journal of Caribbean History,Vol. IV (May 1972), pp. 31-53.

[2] Gisela Eisner, Jamaica, 1830-1930. (Manchester: 1961); Lord Olivier, Jamaica: The Blessed Island. (London: 1936).

[3] Sir David Barbour, Report on the Finances of Jamaica. (H.M.S.O.: 1899); Report of the West Indian Sugar Commission. (H.M.S.O.: 1930); G. St.J. Orde-Browne, Labour Conditions in the West Indies. (H.M.S.O.: 1939).

[4] Wilson to Amery, Confidential Dispatch of May 24, 1925, C.O. 137/777.

[5] O. Phelps, "Rise of the Labour Movement in Jamaica", Social and Economic Studies, Vol. 9, No. 4 (December 1960); George Eaton, "Trade Union Development in Jamaica", Caribbean Quarterly, Vol. 8, No. 1 and 2 (June 1962).

[6] Hemming to Chamberlain, Confidential Dispatch of October 16, 1899, in C.O. 137/604; Johnstone to Milner, Confidential Dispatch of August 14, 1919, in C.O. 137/733; Wilson to Amery, Confidential Dispatch of May 29, 1925, in C.O. 137/777; Denham to Ormsby-Gore, Confidential Dispatch of March 22, 1937, in C.O. 137/821.

[7] Sir David Barbour, op. cit.,; Correspondence Relating to the Public Finances and Resources of the Island of Jamaica. (H.M.S.O.: C. 9177, 1899); Annual Reports of the Governor of Jamaica, in C.O. 140.

[8] Lord Olivier, op. cit., Chapter XXXI, pp. 377-398; A. Hart, "The Banana in Jamaica: Export Trade", Social and Economic Studies, Vol. 3, No. 2 (1954), pp. 212-229; Memorandum of the West India Department, in C.O. 137/790; Slater to Beckett, Private Letter of September 11, 1933, in C.O. 137/798; Memorandum of the West India Department, in C.O. 137/806.

[9] Lord Oliver, op. cit., pp. 290-310; Oliver to Crewe, Dispatch of October 10, 1910, in C.O. 137/679; Manning to Long, Dispatch of September 1, 1917, in C.O. 137/722.

[10] Hemming to Chamberlain, Dispatch of September 30, 1903, in C.O. 137/636; Annual Report of the Governor of Jamaica for 1909, in C.O. 140; Manning to Law, Dispatch of September 27, 1915, in C.O. 137/710; Probyn to Long, Dispatch of August 21, 1918, in C.O. 137/727; Stubbs to Secretary of State, Private Dispatch of

September 14, 1930, in C.O. 137/790; Jelf to Cunliffe-Lister, Dispatch of July 31, 1934, in C.O. 137/801.

[11] The problem of international market prices continually exercised planters and colonial officials. See, for example, the lengthy correspondence regarding the Brussels Sugar Agreement which was intended to improve the price of cane sugar in internationl markets: Swettenham to Elgin, Dispatch of October 5, 1906, in C.O. 137/652; Swettenham to Elgin, Dispatch of February 23, 1907, in C.O. 137/656; Manning to Long, Dispatch of May 11, 1918, in C.O. 137/726.

[12] Mr. Grindle, an official of the Colonial Office in London, thus noted on Probyn to Milner, Dispatch of December ?, 1920, in C.O. 137/743: "The reasons for the exodus of West Indian labour are patent--higher wages elsewhere. The reasons for higher wages elsewhere are, probably, cultivation on a larger scale with larger capital and consequently more efficient machinery. The reasons for larger cultivation elsewhere are the subject of political dispute."

Chapter II

ISSUES IN JAMAICAN HISTORICAL DEMOGRAPHY

This brief review of the literature on Jamaican historical demography has three main objectives. In the first place, it will serve to introduce an impressive body of research to the reader who may be unfamiliar with Jamaica. To this end, the review attempts to summarize the principal concerns and major findings of that literature. Secondly, this review indicates the most important unresolved issues in the field of Jamaican historical demography. Finally, the thrust of the present enquiry is placed within the context of the existing literature.

In common with the study of historical demography elsewhere, the literature on Jamaica has been primarily concerned with three broad problems. First of all, considerable effort has been directed towards detailed descriptions of demographic performance at selected points in time and during a variety of historical time periods. Concentrating on the patterns of mortality, fertility, and migration, descriptive studies have been conducted at the national, regional, parochial, and village level.

Secondly, the literature has attempted to assess the broader implications of Jamaican demographic performance over time. Attention has most commonly focused on the economic consequences of demographic performance, with special emphasis given to the changing character of the labour force. Some effort has also been directed to the evaluation of social consequences of demographic performance. In this respect, the literature is particularly concerned with the overall implications of migration and urbanization.

Thirdly, the literature has taken some interest in the identification of the socio-economic determinants of Jamaican demographic performance. Although migration has claimed the greatest share of this interest, a relatively small number of studies have pursued the correlates and determinants of mortality and fertility. Almost invariably these enquiries have been directed at demographic performance in villages or in the administrative parishes.

Research into these three broad areas has been undertaken by a wide variety of scholars employing different methodologies and exploiting varied sources of information.[1] Such diversity notwithstanding, the principal findings of this literature may be conveniently summarized with respect to the components of demographic performance: mortality, fertility, and migration.

MORTALITY

Jamaican mortality performance has been well-documented for the years following 1878 when compulsory civil registration of vital events began.[2] A survey of the literature yields comprehensive data on infant and general mortality over time, as well as careful estimates of mortality for specific groups differentiated on the basis of age, sex, race or class, and place of residence.[3] Attempts have been made to characterize the patterns of mortality before 1878, but severe data limitations have restricted this effort to easily identifiable groups such as military personnel or to individual plantations for which detailed data have survived.[4]

This impressive body of data indicates that the late nineteenth and early twentieth centuries were characterized by variable but generally declining mortality rates. Although limited by deficiencies in the original data on cause of death, most demographic analyses suggest that declining mortality after the turn of the century was critically influenced by improved preventive and curative health services. It is also clear that extreme fluctuations in general mortality were largely the consequence of epidemic disease, prolonged drought or severe flooding, and the general chaos which accompanied hurricanes or earthquakes.

Analyses of these data tend to confirm the general patterns of differential mortality observed elsewhere. Thus, male mortality rates were significantly higher than female mortality rates for every age group; mortality rates were much higher in urban than in rural areas; general mortality appears to have been extremely sensitive to variations in infant mortality; mortality seems to have been inversely related to socio-economic status of different groups.[5]

Relatively little study has been devoted to the identification of the determinants of Jamaican mortality during these years. Thus, many interesting empirical observations have not been pursued analytically. It is known, for example, that certain parishes persistently exhibited abnormally high mortality rates. Even when account is taken of differences in the age- and sex-composition of parish populations, the diversity in mortality experience is striking. Such variation has been partially explained by inter-parish differences in climate, available health services, and the veracity of the vital statistics.[6] Occasionally one encounters the suggestion that inter-parish variability in mortality experience may have been linked to differences in social and economic conditions among the parishes,[7] but careful investigation along these lines is noticeably lacking in the literature.

Rather more attention has been given to the consequences of Jamaican mortality experience. Most commonly, mortality experience has been viewed as one of the critical influences on the size and composition of the labour force.[8] Moreover, by its influence on the rate of population growth, mortality experience is frequently seen as an important determinant of migration and as exerting an inevitable influence on standards of living.[9] Considerably less study has been directed to the possible consequences of mortality experience on the level of fertility or the structure of social relationships.

By way of summary, the literature on Jamaican mortality has been primarily concerned with the compilation of accurate data and the detailed description of mortality performance over time and among specific sub-national groups. While some effort has been made to explore the underlying causes and broader consequences of mortality performance, it is fair to conclude that analysis has been subordinate to description.

FERTILITY

Jamaican fertility performance has been fairly well documented for the years following compulsory registration of births in 1878. The literature contains comprehensive information on national fertility performance over time as well as careful estimates of the fertility performance of women differentiated with respect to age, race or class, and place of residence.[10] Broad inferences on differential fertility may be drawn from more recent anthropological surveys of micro-populations,[11] although the relevance of such inferences is obviously diminished when applied to other times or larger populations. Similarly, enquiry into fertility performance before 1878 has been limited to available data on specific plantations.[12]

Analysis of the resulting data provides a description of Jamaican fertility performance which in many ways coincides with fertility performance elsewhere.[13] For example, urban fertility rates have been significantly lower than rural fertility rates since the beginning of civil registration. Among rural areas fertility performance varied considerably, although the degree of variation tended to diminish over time. As compared with mortality rates, variation in fertility rates over time are markedly low, although they were clearly subject to extraordinary short-term fluctuations during periods of natural catastrophe. Not surprisingly, completed fertility of individual women varied directly with the length of time during which they were at risk of pregnancy. Finally, incomplete and partial analysis suggests that completed fertility was related to socio-economic class status.

At least one feature of fertility performance in Jamaica differed significantly from the experience of most other non-Caribbean countries. Beginning with the registration of births in 1878 and continuing to the present day, between 60% and 75% of all births were formally illegitimate.[14] This is the direct result of the widespread social acceptability of bearing children out of legal wedlock. This important social convention has greatly diminished the usual significance of marital status and of variations in the marriage rate as indices of fertility or as explanations of observed fertility across households.

In an attempt to understand variations in household fertility, a good deal of the existing literature has been concerned with the classification of households on the basis of mating behaviour. The most common approach is to categorize households on the basis of formal marriage, stable common-law union, or informal visiting arrangements between the partners.[15] As might be anticipated on the basis of exposure to risk, completed fertility appears to have been inversely related to the "permanency" of the union; that is, married women generally exhibited the highest, and women in visiting unions the lowest, fertility.[16]

Given this body of descriptive literature, it is somewhat surprising that enquiry into the general determinants of fertility performance has been so limited. Much of the descriptive literature does suggest possible lines of enquiry, but seldom are these pursued analytically. Consider, for example, the useful finding that household fertility appears to have been systematically related to the nature of household mating patterns. This naturally leads to the problem of the determinants of mating patterns which did in fact vary considerably from parish to parish. It has been suggested that mating patterns were influenced by the system of land tenure, by the level and security of male income, and by the general nature of social relationships in the parish.[17] And yet, these propositions have not been systematically investigated.

As might be expected, the literature has devoted much attention to the broader implications of Jamaican fertility performance. The most common approach has been to assess the impact of fertility performance on the size and composition of population both over time and across parishes. Since parishes exhibiting high rates of fertility usually experienced relatively low rates of overall population growth, it is often concluded that differential fertility performance across the parishes was an important factor in the direction and volume of migration, which in turn altered the age and sex composition of parish population and hence influenced the nature of the labour force.[18] Somewhat less attention has been paid to the long-term social and political implications of fertility performance, although these are mentioned in most studies relating fertility performance to patterns of migration and urbanization.[19]

In conclusion, the literature on Jamaican fertility performance is particularly strong in the marshalling of reliable data and in the detailed description of fertility patterns over time, across parishes and among specific groups of women. On the other hand, the literature is less well-developed with respect to the underlying determinants of differential fertility performance.

MIGRATION

The study of migration represents a disproportionately large share of the literature on Jamaican historical demography. This is so partly because migration was highly visible and thus attracted the attention of contemporary writers, who were convinced that massive numbers of Jamaicans were migrating during the late nineteenth and early twentieth centuries. Given the tremendous amount of contemporary comment, it is natural that later scholars would be attracted to the study of internal and external migration patterns.

A second factor encouraging a large body of migration studies is the virtual absence of reliable statistics concerning the movements of Jamaicans. Apart from some highly doubtful annual estimates of emigration, the colonial government collected no direct data on migration during this period. Thus, much of the existing literature has been devoted to the indirect estimation of migration flows within the island and to foreign destinations.[20] It is hardly surprising that the resulting estimates, which must be derived through manipulation of census data, are crude and incomplete.

However inexact even the best estimates may be, the literature has made clear the general features of migration during these years. Although apparently not as massive as contemporary observers believed, emigration to foreign countries was substantial during the late nineteenth and early twentieth centuries. Between 1881 and 1921 net emigration was at least 146,000. Although the period 1921-1943 witnessed net immigration into the island as former emigrants returned, the volume of net emigration was at least 120,000 during the whole period 1881-1943.[21] Since these estimates are of minimum net emigration, the flow of Jamaicans to foreign destinations was certainly greater and at times must have been enormous.

Available estimates of inter-parish migration tend to support the impressions formed by contemporary observers. Between 1911 and 1921 at least 50,000 Jamaicans changed their parish of residence.[22] During the period 1921-1943, it is estimated that "one-fifth of the island's native-born population were involved in internal migration."[23] Given that these are minimum estimates only, one can hardly doubt the size and significance of internal migration during these years.

A number of studies have been suggestive of possible determinants of migration flows. Not unexpectedly, suggested determinants fall into two categories: factors acting to 'push' migrants from place of origin, and factors acting to 'pull' migrants toward destinations.

Descriptive studies seem to imply that conditions in Jamaica may have provided an incentive for overseas migration. Thus it has been observed that an unusually high proportion of emigrants came from the urban parishes and from a few rural parishes wherein fertility rates and rates of natural increase were exceptionally high.[24] This is interpreted as evidence of a 'push' factor in emigration. Nonetheless, a propensity to emigrate cannot usually be exercised in the face of perceived distress abroad. Hence, it is widely supposed that the 'pull' of perceived economic activity overseas was the more influential determinant of the timing, destination, and volume of emigration.[25] Formal testing of these propositions has not been undertaken for the period 1881-1943, although enquiries into more recent emigration flows are supportive of the determinants advanced.[26]

Detailed description of internal migration has also been suggestive of determinants of these flows.[27] Available data indicate that the principal flow of internal migration was from rural areas to the urban centre of Kingston and St. Andrew. Secondary flows into the town of Montego Bay in St. James and into a few rural parishes have also been identified. On this basis, it is generally supposed that internal migration was largely the consequence of a 'pull' by urban centres and by certain rural parishes wherein employment opportunities were believed to exist. In so far as a 'push' operated with respect to internal migration, it was the result of chronically high rates of natural increase of population in certain rural parishes. As with emigration, however, these determinants of internal migration have not been subjected to careful analysis during the years 1911-1943.[28]

Although generally oblivious to the implications of demographic performance, most contemporary observers were greatly exercised by perceived consequences of migration during the late nineteenth and early twentieth centuries. On the one hand, they generally feared that rural out-migration would lead to stagnation in agriculture through a reduction in the wage labour force upon which the prosperity of plantations depended. At the same time, commentators of the time were distressed over the perceived impact of rural-urban migration on urban economic and social conditions, and many decried the urban "corruption" of rural migrants. Emigration was viewed favourably in so far as it relieved pressure on urban employment and resulted in substantial remittances from overseas Jamaicans. But emigration also acted to reduce the agricultural labour force and the treatment of Jamaicans abroad was a source of considerable concern.

Most scholarly studies of migration tend to avoid such troublesome social and economic implications and focus instead on the demographic consequences of Jamaican migration. The most common approach has been to describe in some detail the impact of migration on population growth within the individual parishes.[29] Thus, it has been established that the rapid rate of population growth in the urban centre was almost exclusively the consequence of net in-migration. Conversely, the relatively low rates of population growth in most rural parishes, and the absolute decline of population in a few, were clearly the consequence of net out-migration rather than a failure of natural increase.

It is clear that the composition of parish population was also greatly affected by internal and external migration during these years.[30] The two urban parishes of Kingston and St. Andrew recorded an extraordinarily high proportion of females and an exceptionally low dependency ratio at each of the censuses of population. Considerable diversity was apparent in the composition of rural parish populations, but in general the dependency ratios were markedly higher and the proportion of males significantly greater than in the urban centre.

These and other demographic consequences of migration must have held important implications for economic performance and general social behaviour. Apart from some casual discussion of the impact of migration on urban employment, housing, and social unrest, the existing literature has not systematically explored the broader implications of internal migration. Nor has much attention been given to the implications of emigration from rural parishes.

In conclusion, the general features of Jamaican migration during the late nineteenth and early twentieth centuries have been adequately described in the literature. Much less well understood are the complex socio-economic determinants of migration. Descriptive studies have been suggestive in this respect, but careful analysis has not yet been undertaken.

SUMMARY

This brief and no doubt cursory review has emphasized the two major areas of strength in the existing literature. Firstly, the literature has been devoted to the accumulation and verification of reliable data on mortality, fertility, and migration during the period 1878-1943. Secondly, the literature contains detailed and extremely useful descriptions of demographic performance over time, among parishes, and across particular sub-national groups of people.

Out of this literature there emerges a fairly complete picture of Jamaican demographic performance during the late nineteenth and early twentieth centuries. Although additional data and more detailed description will no doubt be useful in filling in that picture, it is not likely to be significantly altered through further research along these lines. Data collection and detailed description have, in short, been pushed to the point of diminishing returns.

Beyond the generation of data and the careful description of demographic performance, the literature is less well developed. Considerable attention has been given to the consequences of demographic change, although much of the discussion has been confined to the subsequent demographic and economic implications. Much useful work remains to be done with respect to the social and political consequence of Jamaican demographic performance. Nonetheless, although clearly incomplete, the treatment of the broad consequences of demographic performance has been adequate.

The outstanding unresolved issues in Jamaican historical demography are encountered in an attempt to explore systematically the underlying determinants of observed demographic performance. In the best tradition of descriptive studies, the existing literature has carefully documented a striking variety of demographic performance over time and among the several parishes. In addition, some highly suggestive propositions have been advanced to explain such variations. But on the whole these propositions have not been well developed or empirically explored.

Within the general field of historical demography, local variations in demographic performance are commonly investigated with respect to local variations in economic and social conditions. The present study attempts to apply this general approach to the case of Jamaica during the late nineteenth and early twentieth centuries. That is, variations in demographic performance from one parish to another are viewed as arising out of differences in the economic and social conditions which characterized the several parishes. More specifically, the present study investigates the influence of parish socio-economic structure on the observed patterns of parish mortality, fertility, and net out-migration. The present study will thus shed some light on the underlying determinants of Jamaican demographic performance during the late nineteenth and early twentieth centuries.

ENDNOTES TO CHAPTER II

[1] Lambros Comitas, Caribbeana, 1900-1965: A Topical Bibliography. (Seattle: 1968); M. G. Smith, "Introduction" in Edith Clarke, My Mother Who Fathered Me. (London: 1972), pp. i-xliv.

[2] A careful analysis of the reliability of these vital statistics may be found G. W. Roberts, The Population of Jamaica. (Cambridge: 1957), pp. 22-28. See also, G. W. Roberts, "A Note on Mortality in Jamaica", Population Studies, Vol. IV, No. 1 (June 1950).

[3] G. W. Roberts, The Population of Jamaica. (Cambridge: 1957), Chapter 6, pp. 165-215; M. Tekse, Population of Jamaica in Numbers, 1844-1965. (Kingston: 1966); Government of Jamaica, Census of Population. (Kingston: 1943); Annual Reports of the Registrar-General for Jamaica, 1878-1943, in C.O. 140.

[4] A. M. Tulloch and H. Marshall, Statistical Report on Sickness, Mortality, and Invaliding among Troops in the West Indies. (London: 1838), as discussed in G. W. Roberts, The Population of Jamaica. (Cambridge: 1957), pp. 165-171; G. W. Roberts, "A Life Table for a West Indian Slave Population", Population Studies, Vol. V, No. 3 (1951); Michael Craton, "Jamaican Slave Mortality: Fresh Light from Worthy Park, Longville and the Tharp Estates", Journal of Caribbean History, Vol. 3 (1971), pp. 1-27.

[5] G. W. Roberts, The Population of Jamaica. (Cambridge: 1957), pp. 165-215.

[6] Ibid., pp. 191-193.

[7] Ibid., pp. 190-191.

[8] Ibid., pp. 165-215.

[9] G. Eisner, Jamaica, 1830-1930. (Manchester: 1961).

[10] G. W. Roberts, The Population of Jamaica. (Cambridge: 1957), Chapters 7 and 8, pp. 216-306; Annual Reports of the Registrar-General for Jamaica, 1878-1943, in C. O. 140

[11] Edith Clarke, My Mother Who Fathered Me. (London: 1972); G. E. Cumper, "The Jamaican Family: Village and Estate", Social and Economic Studies, Vol. 7, No. 1 (March 1958); L. Alan Eyre, Geographic Aspects of Population Dynamics in Jamaica. (Boca Raton: 1972).

[12] B. W. Higman, "Household Structure and Fertility on Jamaican Slave Plantations: A Nineteenth Century Example", Population Studies, Vol. 27, No. 3 (1973), pp. 527-550.

[13] A comprehensive analysis is provided in G. W. Roberts, *The Population of Jamaica*. (Cambridge: 1957), pp. 216-306.

[14] *Ibid.*, p. 290.

[15] *Ibid.*, pp. 263-269, 294-306; M. G. Smith, *op. cit.*; G. E. Cumper, "The Fertility of Common Law Unions in Jamaica", *Social and Economic Studies*, Vol. 15, No. 3 (September 1966); Edith Clarke, *op. cit.*; M. G. Smith, "Community Organization in Rural Jamaica", *Social and Economic Studies*, Vol. 5, No. 3 (September 1956).

[16] G. W. Roberts, *op. cit.*, pp. 294-306.

[17] Edith Clarke, *op. cit.*

[18] G. W. Roberts, *supra*, pp. 152-164.

[19] *Ibid.*, pp. 158-164; G. E. Cumper, "Population Movements in Jamaica, 1830-1950", *Social and Economic Studies*, Vol. 5 (1956), pp. 261-280.

[20] G. W. Roberts, *supra*, Appendix III, pp. 339-340; M. J. Proudfoot, *Population Movements in the Caribbean*. (Port of Spain: 1950); G. W. Roberts and J. A. Bryne, "Summary Statistics on Indenture and Associated Migration Affecting the West Indies, 1834-1918", *Population Studies*, Vol. XX, No. 1 (1966).

[21] G. W. Roberts, *op. cit.*, p. 139; W. F. Maunder, "The New Jamaican Emigration", *Social and Economic Studies*, Vol. 4, No. 1 (1955), pp. 38-63.

[22] G. W. Roberts, *supra*, p. 149.

[23] *Ibid.*, p. 152.

[24] *Ibid.*, pp. 138-141; W. F. Maunder, *op. cit.*

[25] G. W. Roberts, *supra*, pp. 134-138; W. F. Maunder, *op. cit.*; G. Eisner, *op. cit.*

[26] W. F. Maunder, *op. cit.*; G. W. Roberts and D. O. Mills, *A Study of External Migration Affecting Jamaica, 1953-55*. Supplement to *Social and Economic Studies*, Vol. 7, No. 2 (June 1958), pp. 1-126.

[27] G. W. Roberts, *The Population of Jamaica*. (Cambridge: 1957), Chapter 5, pp. 142-164.

[28] Studies of more recent internal migration do, however, tend to support these propositions. See, for example: N. A. Adams, "Internal Migration in Jamaica: An Economic Analysis", *Social and Economic Studies*, Vol. 19, No. 2 (June 1970), pp. 137-151; G. E. Ebanks, "Differential Internal Migration in Jamaica, 1943-1960",

Social and Economic Studies, Vol. 17, No. 2 (June 1968), pp. 193-228; R. N. Harris and E. S. Steer, "Demographic-Resource Push in Rural Migration: A Jamaican Case Study", *Social and Economic Studies*, Vol. 17, No. 4 (December 1968), pp. 398-406.

[29] G. W. Roberts, *supra*, pp. 142-164.

[30] See below, Chapter V; see also, G. W. Roberts, *supra*, pp. 62-76.

Chapter III

A MODEL OF ECONOMIC-DEMOGRAPHIC RELATIONSHIPS IN JAMAICA

The fundamental thesis of this enquiry may be stated simply: parish demographic performance was systematically influenced by the nature of parish socio-economic structure. It is of course possible that the nature of parish socio-economic structure was in turn conditioned by parish demographic performance over time. Nonetheless, the present study abstracts from this latter effect and focuses exclusively on the underlying socio-economic determinants of observed demographic performance.

In order to pursue this objective, an analytical framework is required. Hence this chapter develops an abstract model of economic-demographic relationships which is applicable to the individual parishes of Jamaica during the late nineteenth and early twentieth centuries. The principal objective of this model is to relate demographic performance to socio-economic structure in such a way as to yield potentially testable hypotheses.

AN OVERVIEW OF THE MODEL

At the outset it is well to stress the general spirit of the following model. Although frequently deterministic in form and language, the model is best viewed as a broad framework within which to investigate empirically the socio-economic influences on observed demographic performance. In essence, the model conceives demographic performance to have been an integral part of--hence, "determined by"--the nature of the socio-economic structure within which demographic events occurred. Thus the model is more empirical than analytical in its structure, and more indicative than deterministic in its hypotheses.

As illustrated schematically in Figure 3.1, the model consists of three principal components. First, an economic sub-model sets out the factors which give rise to the concept of parish socio-economic structure within an individual parish at some given point in time. Secondly, a simple demographic sub-model traces through the inter-relationships among several variables which collectively establish the pattern of demographic performance within an individual parish at some given point in time. The solid-line arrows in Figure 3.1 indicate the direction of influence between constituent elements within each of these sub-models.

The third component of the model is shown as a set of broken-line arrows which links the economic and demographic sub-models. These linkages, which will be called the economic-demographic relationships of the model, represent the principal hypotheses concerning the influence of socio-economic structure on demographic performance. It is the task of this chapter to elaborate the nature of these relationships. In order to do so, it is useful to consider in turn the economic and demographic sub-models and then to derive the nature of the economic-demographic relationships between them.

Fig. 3.1

THE MODEL IN SCHEMATIC FORM

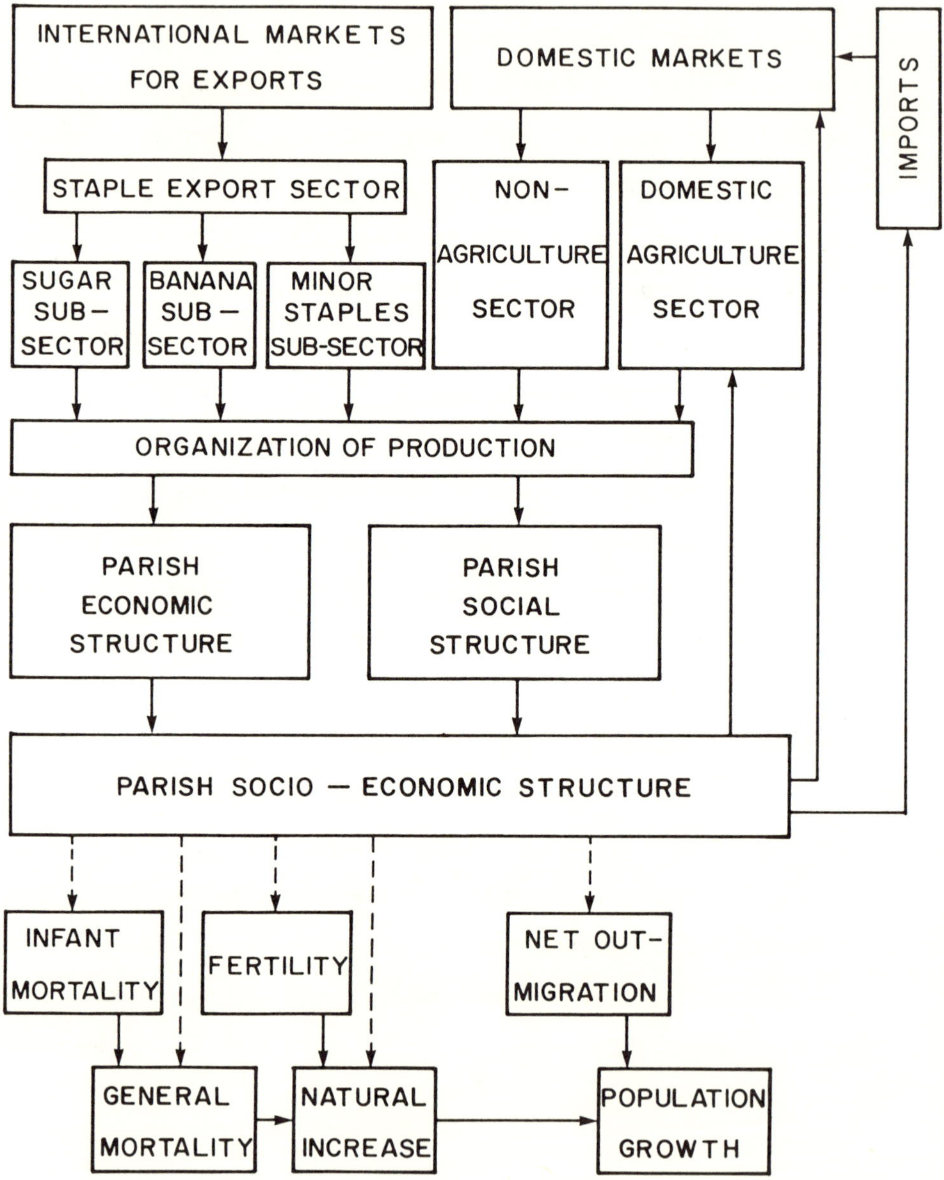

THE ECONOMIC SUB-MODEL

The economic sub-model illustrated in Figure 3.1 has a twofold purpose. Firstly, it identifies the principal sectors of the economy and thus provides a framework for the detailed description of economic performance with which the following chapter is concerned. Secondly, the economic sub-model formally introduces the concept of parish socio-economic structure, which in effect represents the independent variable of the overall model. Consequently, the present discussion deals primarily with the meaning, determinants, and characteristics of parish socio-economic structure.

The Concept of Socio-Economic Structure

The concept of parish socio-economic structure derives from two separate but related approaches to the study of Jamaican economic structure and hence to the interpretation of Jamaican economic history. It is therefore useful to review briefly the principal features of these two approaches which for convenience may be designated the "staples" and the "plantation" interpretations of Jamaican economic history.

Any staples interpretation of economic history is inevitably influenced by the early work of Harold Innis on Canada and of Douglas North on the United States.[1] More recent works by Melville Watkins, Johnathan Levin, Dudley Seers, and others have been instrumental in the extension of classical staples theory to tropical regions.[2] Much of the recent theoretical work on the so-called "open economy" is, in fact, heavily influenced by the general approach of the staples interpretation.[3]

Staples interpretations of economic history and economic development stress the economic implications of production for export as opposed to production for domestic consumption. In particular, these two types of production are viewed as having significantly different impacts on national income, employment, aggregate saving and investment, and the rates of change of these variables over time. Early writers appeared to be convinced that an expanding staple export sector is inevitably a source of economic performance far above that which could be expected if production remained domestically oriented.[4] If international trade were an engine of economic growth, then staple exports would be the fuel.

More recent practitioners of the staples interpretation have been less optimistic. Reflecting on the experience of staple exporting nations outside North America, many writers have come to argue that a staple export sector may actually inhibit economic growth and development. Countries may be placed in a "staples trap" which limits flexibility in the composition of output and hence lays the economy open to extreme fluctuations arising from precarious international market conditions.[5] Moreover, it is argued, the generation of surplus and its productive investment are two separate phenomena. In so far as staples-generated surplus is lost through imports, non-productive domestic investment, or the repatriation of profits to overseas residents, the staple exporting economy need not experience any growth.[6]

Detailed description and analysis of the export trade are indications of the extent to which Jamaican historiography has, until quite recently, been dominated by the staples approach. This is most apparent in the economic history literature which traditionally has put great stress on the export trade in sugar, bananas, and the minor staples. Even the literature dealing with political history and social conditions has tended to emphasize the impact of the staple exports on the economy and hence on the polity and society of the island.

In recent years, the plantation interpretation of Jamaican history has tended to supplant the earlier emphasis on staple exports. Reflected in the works of Robert Baldwin, Lloyd Best and Kari Levitt, and most recently in the studies by George Beckford, the plantation approach lays emphasis on the organizational forms of production.[7] In particular, a distinction is drawn between production organized by plantations and production organized by independent small farmers and peasants.

The manner in which production is organized is held to have both economic and social implications. Thus much discussion is given to the differential effects of organizational form on such economic variables as the distribution of income between and within factor classes, the propensities to save and to invest, and the nature of technological innovation. In addition, the plantation approach concerns itself with the impact of organizational forms of production on social variables such as class structure, labour relations, community organization, and the distribution of and access to political power.

Although diverse in their emphasis, the principal plantation interpretations of Jamaican history are generally agreed in their conclusions. Plantation production is invariably viewed as economically exploitative, socially elitist, and politically corrupt; in short, the plantation is a "total system" which positively constrains the processes of economic development in its widest sense.[8] At the same time there is an undeniable idealization and even romanticization of peasant organized production.[9] In the absence of a pure case of peasant production in the Caribbean, the literature has drawn on the experience of North America and upon detailed studies of Caribbean peasant communities during more recent times. The results have been intriguing if ambiguous. In general it is concluded that peasant organized production is more conducive to overall economic development because incomes are distributed in a more egalitarian fashion, because social stratification is less rigid, and because political institutions are more responsive to local needs.

Far from being antagonistic interpretations of Jamaican economic history, the staples and plantation approaches are highly complementary since each tends to emphasize different features of the same economic structure. It is hardly surprising therefore that advocates of the staples interpretation are also concerned with the organizational forms of production; similarly, proponents of the plantation interpretation pay considerable attention to the composition of output. Depending on the particular historical problem under study, one or the other of these features of economic structure may be given emphasis, but in general both must be considered simultaneously.

This suggests that any study of individual parishes should strive to combine the staples and the plantation points of view. In the first place, the structure of parish economy should be investigated with respect to (i) the composition of parish output and (ii) the manner in which parish production was organized. Secondly, the economic and social implications of parish economic structure should be interpreted according to the staples and the plantation approaches to the study of Jamaican economic history. These economic and social implications in fact represent the specific aspects of parish socio-economic structure with which the present sub-model is mainly concerned.

Composition of Output

The composition of parish output during any given time period depended upon the relative importance of the three major economic sectors shown in Figure 3.1. Although these sectors are examined in detail in the following chapter, it is useful to outline the nature of each here.

In the opinion of the colonial government and the local oligarchy, the most significant of these sectors was given over to the production of various staple export crops. Completely dependent upon and closely responding to conditions in international markets, producers in this sector undertook the cultivation and crude processing of two general types of staple exports. The major staples consisted of bananas and sugar products; the minor staples included spices, coffee, cocoa, citrus fruit, and logwood. Whatever the particular crop involved, activity within the staple export sector was commercially oriented and heavily dependent upon overseas markets.

The second broad sector of the economy was given over to the cultivation of agricultural crops for domestic consumption. Output of this sector included a wide variety of fruits, vegetables, ground provisions, and meat products. These commodities were either consumed directly by producers or were traded in purely domestic markets. Thus activity in this sector was influenced by, but not wholly dependent upon, conditions prevailing within domestic markets for foodstuffs.

All other economic activity has been included within the non-agricultural sector. Commerce, construction, transport, manufacturing, and the service industries represent the major components of this sector. The level of activity within this sector was primarily dependent upon the strength of domestic demand since virtually none of the sector's output was traded internationally.

It is of course obvious that these three sectors coexisted within any particular parish. Each agricultural parish typically produced export crops and domestically consumed crops; moreover, each possessed a non-agricultural sector if only in the form of domestic servants, petty commerce, and small scale construction activities. Similarly, the urban parishes of Kingston and St. Andrew, which were largely given over to non-agricultural production, nonetheless still produced agricultural commodities for export and for domestic consumption.

This heterogeneity of output is not an insuperable barrier to the classification of parish economic structure on the basis of composition of output. All that is required is an objective measure of the relative importance of these three sectors within a given parish during some specified time period. As shall be seen in Chapter IV, it is beyond dispute that non-agricultural production was concentrated in and clearly dominated the output of the parishes of Kingston and St. Andrew. Although the composition of output among rural parishes is not quite so straightforward, it may be approached indirectly by examining the use to which cultivated land was put. This is based on the plausible assumption that the composition of agricultural output depended upon the distribution of cultivated acreage across various crops. Hence, the larger (smaller) the proportion of cultivated acreage under staple export crops, the larger (smaller) was the composition of output dominated by staple export production.

Organization of Production

Responding to demand conditions in appropriate markets, entrepreneurs undertook to organize production in a variety of ways. Although the following chapter deals extensively with actual patterns of production organization, it is useful to outline the main features of each so as to indicate how the organization of parish production may be approached.

During the late nineteenth and early twentieth centuries, agricultural production was organized in four principal ways. The most studied form was of course the plantation. Regardless of the specific crops produced, plantation agriculture involved substantial acreage worked exclusively by wage labour complemented by a diverse and extensive stock of capital equipment. Plantations also enjoyed relatively easy access to a variety of credit sources through which their operations might be financed. Output was most frequently sold in international markets, although certain plantation produced commodities (e.g., beef and coconuts) were absorbed by domestic markets. In short, plantations were industrial enterprises characterized by specialization of labour, strict management of inputs, and production for cash sale.[10]

Small farms represented a second method by which agricultural production was organized. These small farms were characterized by moderate acreage worked partly by wage labour and partly by family members using relatively few purchased or capital inputs. The availability of credit to small farmers was extremely limited throughout the period. Although a portion of output was consumed directly by producers, the greater share was sold in domestic and international markets. Small farms were, in short, essentially commercial operations.[11]

The organization of agricultural production by small settlers ("peasants") was extremely widespread. Such production typically involved very small acreages worked exclusively by family labour using only the simplest cultivation tools. Credit facilities were completely unavailable to peasant producers except in times of natural disaster when government loans were occasionally provided. Output was principally consumed directly by the peasant household, but peasants did produce certain staple exports for sale internationally and surplus foodstuffs were marketed domestically.[12]

Finally, agricultural production was organized by individual households on tiny garden plots. Usually less than an acre in extent, these garden plots were worked by the part-time labour of family members. Capital equipment consisted of the ubiquitous machete, hoe, and fork; credit was completely inaccessible to these producers.

Output consisted exclusively of foodstuffs which were directly consumed by the producing household.

Production within the non-agricultural sector appears to have been organized in two ways.[13] Firstly, production was organized by self-employed individuals who owned the necessary means of production and who marketed output themselves. Individual craftsmen were responsible for much of the commodity output of this sector, personal and professional services were naturally organized by own-account labourers, and a large share of the retail trade was organized on the basis of family enterprise. On the other hand, business enterprise and the colonial government also organized production in the non-agricultural sector. This was most notable in transport, public utilities, wholesale trade, manufacturing, and of course the civil service. In these cases, production was organized along wage labour lines and output was marketed almost exclusively within the domestic economy.

The principal characteristics of these various organizational forms of production have been summarized in Table 3.1 below.

In one obvious sense, the organization of parish production depended upon the composition of parish output: the production of non-agricultural output could hardly be organized by agricultural forms of production. Hence, production within the urban parishes of Kingston and St. Andrew was organized along craft or industrial lines. Since it is impossible to distinguish these two organizational forms empirically, the urban parishes will hereafter be classified as "non-agricultural" with respect to output and to organization.

TABLE 3.1

CHARACTERISTICS OF ORGANIZATIONAL FORMS OF PRODUCTION: A SUMMARY

Feature	Plantation	Small Farms	Peasant Plots	Household Gardens	Craft Production	Industrial Production
Acreage	>100 Acres	10-100 Acres	1-10 Acres	<1 Acre	---	---
Labour Force	Wage Labour	Wage Labour Family Labour	Family Labour	Part time - Family Labour	Wage Labour Family Labour	Wage Labour
Capital Equipment	Cultivation Tools, Mechanical Transport, Processing Machinery, Fertilizers Improved Seeds	Cultivation Tools, Animal Transport, Limited use of Fertilizers	Cultivation Tools, Limited Animal Transport	Cultivation Tools	Tools of Trade Raw Materials	Tools of Trade Raw Materials Mechanical Transport Electrical and Mechanical Power
Credit Sources	Accumulated Savings; Commercial Banks Government Aid	Accumulated Savings; Limited Government Aid	Accumulated Savings	---	Accumulated Savings; 'Trust'	Accumulated Savings Commercial Banks 'Trust' Limited Government Aid
Disposition of Output	Export Markets Domestic Markets	Export Markets Domestic Markets Direct Consumption	Domestic Markets Direct Consumption	Direct Consumption	Domestic Markets Direct Consumption	Domestic Markets

Within agricultural parishes, however, the organization of parish production is not dependent upon the composition of parish output. This results from the fact that staple exports and domestically consumed crops may be produced by every form of production organization, with the exception of house garden plots. Hence the overall organization of parish production depends upon the relative importance of the various forms of production organization which actually existed during a particular time period.

The most obvious approach to this problem would be to examine the distribution of parish land under each alternative form of production organization. It is unfortunate, but hardly surprising given the interests of the colonial government, that available annual data refer only to acreage under control of plantations.[14] Thus, a characterization of parish economic structure on the basis of organization of production may be only approximate since distinctions can be made only between plantation and non-plantation forms of agricultural organization.

Some Aspects of Parish Socio-Economic Structure

The structure of parish economy has been characterized in terms of the composition of parish output and the organization of parish production. These two features of parish economy in turn hold important implications for the nature of parish socio-economic structure. These implications have their origins in the staples and the plantation interpretations of Jamaican economic history. Although some of these implications have not as yet been verified empirically for the late nineteenth and early twentieth centuries, all of them are rooted in persuasive theoretical arguments and many have been verified for more recent periods.

Four specific aspects of parish socio-economic structure are given prominence here: the level of income, the distribution of income, the stability of income over time, and the nature of social institutions which are associated with various economic structures. Each will be discussed in turn with a view to indicating the dependence of each on the structure of parish economy.

Income Levels: Staples interpretations of Jamaican economic history argue that the level of income accruing to an agricultural region depends primarily upon the composition of output. More specifically, it is supposed that staple exporting regions generally enjoy higher incomes than do regions in which production is geared to subsistence or to purely domestic markets. Plantation interpretations of Jamaican economic history also argue that the composition of output, rather than the organization of production, was the principal feature of economic structure determining the level of income.

Rigorous empirical evidence in support of this view is rather sparse for the pre-World War Two years. Most informed contemporary observers were of the opinion that income levels were highest in urban parishes, next highest in staple exporting regions, and inevitably lowest in areas given over to domestic agriculture.[15] Incomplete data for the late nineteenth and early twentieth centuries appear to confirm roughly this ordering of income levels.[16]

More recent studies also suggest that staple exporting regions enjoy higher money incomes than do regions given over to the cultivation of domestic crops, and that both have generally lower incomes than do regions in which non-agricultural production prevails.[17] Thus, although the evidence is far from conclusive, it would appear that the composition of output is a rough indicator of income levels enjoyed by parishes.

In terms of aggregate real income, however, it is uncertain that either non-agricultural or staple export parishes enjoyed a significant advantage over parishes given to the cultivation of domestic agricultural crops. Unlike the former parishes, the latter required little money income in order to fill consumption needs, especially for foodstuffs which represented the single largest item in household expenditures. In time of drought, flood, or other circumstances which tended to disrupt domestic agricultural output, those parishes dependent upon local markets for the purchase of foodstuffs experienced greatly inflated prices and absolute shortages since domestic agricultural producers understandably filled their own needs first. This relative independence of domestic agricultural parishes from the market for foodstuffs undoubtedly acted to raise their real income, though it remains uncertain whether the resulting level of real income exceeded that of other parishes. In any case, it is clear that the gap was substantially narrowed; domestic agricultural parishes may have been money poor, but were certainly food rich in comparison with other parishes.[18]

Distribution of Income: It is generally argued that the manner in which income is distributed among factors of production and across households depends upon the organizational forms of production. This is certainly the conclusion of plantation interpretations of Jamaican economic history and is implicitly accepted by most staples interpretations as well.[19]

Based largely on theoretical grounds, it is supposed that plantation production is generally characterized by a highly skewed distribution of household income which is a result of a factoral distribution of income that greatly favours the owners of land. Conversely it is supposed that non-plantation production is characterized by a more egalitarian distribution of income across households since the ownership of land is widely dispersed.[20]

Although generally not considered in the plantation interpretations, the distribution of income arising out of non-agricultural economic activity may also be expected to depend on the manner in which production was organized. Thus the more completely is such production organized along industrial wage labour lines, the more skewed will be the distribution of income across households as a result of the concentration of ownership of the means of production.

These theoretical propositions have been supported by scattered empirical evidence for the late nineteenth and early twentieth centuries. All will be discussed in Chapter IV, the factoral distribution of income under plantation production does appear to have been more favourable to land owners than was the case for agriculture in general.[21] Moreover, it is beyond dispute that the distribution of income across households was highly skewed for the island as a whole.[22] These data and the observations of contemporaries do not, of course, prove the case, but they are indicative and lend considerable credence to the general proposition that the organization of parish production is a rough guide to the distribution of income.

Stability of Parish Income: It is to be expected that the level of parish income will vary over time. The central issues here are the degree to which parish income varies over time, and the relationship between such variation and the structure of parish economy. For convenience, the phrase "stability of parish income" shall be used as a short-hand expression for the degree of variation of parish income over time.

On theoretical grounds it may be supposed that the stability of parish income arises out of the composition of parish output. More specifically, the cultivation of domestically consumed crops may for two reasons be expected to result in greater stability of parish income than will the cultivation of staple exports. In the first place, the production of staple exports typically involves one or two crops, while the cultivation of domestic crops is extremely diverse. Hence any variation in weather or the appearance of crop specific diseases may be expected to affect the volume of output more severely in the case of staple exports, and hence introduce marked variation in the level of income. Secondly, the international markets in which staple exports are sold are notoriously erratic with respect to prices.[23] Thus it is plausible to suggest that staple export production will in general be characterized by less stability of parish income than will domestic crop production.

There is some rather indirect empirical evidence to support this proposition.[24] Staple export crops do appear to have been particularly sensitive to adverse weather and botanical diseases which in turn generated considerable variation in the volume of staple exports over time. Moreover, staple export prices did show considerable variation over time. On the other hand, domestic agricultural crops were apparently less subject to severe fluctuations in output or to substantial variation in prices.[25]

With respect to parishes in which non-agricultural production prevailed, the stability of parish income is theoretically uncertain. It might be argued that such stability would be considerable since output did not depend on factor inputs of a seasonal type. Alternatively, it is possible that the stability of parish income was quite low since output was marketed domestically and was thus indirectly dependent on income generated in agriculture. There is no empirical evidence to resolve this problem and consequently the stability of income in non-agricultural parishes must be considered as undetermined.

<u>Parish Social Organization</u>: It is widely argued that the nature of social organization in Caribbean communities depends primarily upon the manner in which economic activity was organized.[26] Hence it is common to speak of "plantation society", "peasant society", and "urban society" as separate but co-existing types of social organization in Jamaica and throughout the Caribbean. Although these may be differentiated in any

number of ways, it is useful to consider how each is characterized with respect to only three aspects of social organization: the nature of social stratification, the manner in which individuals are integrated into the society, and the degree of social and economic mobility within the society.[27]

The nature of plantation society ultimately derives from the centralization of economic power in the hands of plantation owners. The virtual monopolization of arable land by the plantation effectively eliminates any alternative to wage employment and thus contributes to the skewed distribution of income typical of plantation economy. This in turn generates an extreme stratification of society along economic class lines; a stratification which is all the more rigid as a result of economic immobility derived from the concentration of land ownership. Individuals are integrated into plantation society through their role as employees and, consequently, social integration through friendship or kinship ties is especially weak. In short, the overall structure of plantation society is that of a "marked internal hierarchical structure approaching an internal caste system".[28]

The distinctive features of peasant society derive from the nature of peasant economy in general and the system of land tenure in particular. Land ownership and access to land through rental agreement are typically widespread in such economies and hence, as noted above, the distribution of income across households tends to be more nearly egalitarian. Social stratification certainly exists in such societies, but the criteria for status is ownership or access to land rather than income or wealth.[29] Consequently, social and economic mobility depends on the ability to acquire land through purchase or rental. In so far as certain "family land" is by custom inalienable, upward mobility is constrained while downward mobility of family members is all but eliminated. Individuals are therefore integrated into society through a strong network of kinship ties which are embodied within the institution of the extended family.[30]

Certain features of urban society are similar to those of plantation and peasant societies. For example, social stratification in urban society, as in plantation society, reflects the uneven distribution of economic wealth and income. Although the boundaries between urban social classes are sharply defined, the resulting social stratification is not normally as rigid as in plantation society.[31] Even more so than in peasant society, economic and social mobility in urban society is a distinct possibility through formal schooling and limited access to "desirable" (i.e., non-agricultural) employment. To be sure, such mobility is in reality quite limited for the vast majority of urbanites; nonetheless, mobility does occur and is likely more possible than in either plantation or peasant society.[32] Finally, individuals tend to be socially integrated through their roles as producers and consumers. Kinship and friendship ties do act as a means for social integration, but both are diminished in importance by the possibility of individual social mobility and by the disrupting influence of substantial migration into urban centres from rural areas.[33]

By way of summary, communities in which production is organized by plantations differ in social characteristics from communities in which production is organized by peasants; both these agricultural communities differ socially from urban communities in which non-agricultural production predominates.

As previous discussed, the organization of economic activity within any individual parish has always been simultaneously undertaken by plantations, peasants, and non-agricultural producers. Thus each parish will exhibit social characteristics associated with the "pure cases" of plantation society, peasant society, and urban society. The exact nature of parish social organization depends therefore on the relative importance of each organizational form of production within the parish. For example, parishes in which production is predominantly organized by peasants may be said to possess social features characteristic of peasant societies. Hence, inter-parish differences in the organizational forms of production may be used as a measure of inter-parish differences in social organization.

Summary and Implications

The major thrust of the economic sub-model is to establish that, during any particular time period, each individual parish is characterized by a unique socio-economic structure. On the one hand, the nature of parish socio-economic structure is given by such economic features as (i) the level of parish income, (ii) the distribution of parish income, and (iii) the stability of parish income over time. Simultaneously, the nature of parish socio-economic structure is given by such social features as (iv) the nature of social stratification, (v) the manner in which individuals are integrated into communities, and (vi) the degree of social and economic mobility within the parish. In so far as parishes differ in any of these six respects, they may be said to possess different socio-economic structures.

The classification of parishes with respect to their socio-economic structure would be greatly facilitated if each of these six features could be objectively measured. Given sufficient time and the appropriate historical evidence, there is no reason to suppose that such measures could not be derived. However, the difficulties encountered in the existing estimates of Jamaican national income for these years suggest that these specific features of parish socio-economic structure are not susceptible to statistical enquiry. Even if such an enquiry were possible, it is not clear that the results would justify the enormous research effort required.

A more realistic approach is to employ reasonable proxies for these six features of parish socio-economic structure. Arguing from the perspectives of the plantation and staples interpretations of Jamaican economic history, the present enquiry defines two such proxies: the composition of parish output and the manner in which parish production was organized. The composition of parish output serves as a proxy for the level of parish income and the stability of parish income over time. The organizational form of parish production serves as a proxy for the distribution of parish income and the characteristic features of parish social organization. As discussed above, these two proxies reflect the specific features of socio-economic structure among agricultural parishes in the following ways:

(a) The more completely is the composition of parish output dominated by staple exports (domestic crops), the higher (lower) is the level of parish money income, the lower (higher) is the level of parish real income, and the less (more) stable is parish income over time.

(b) The more completely is parish production organized by plantations (peasants), the more (less) skewed is the distribution of parish income and the more nearly are parish social features typical of plantation (peasant) society.

The nature of parish socio-economic structure has a number of interesting implications for economic performance and social behaviour. Among the economic implications are the level and composition of parish demand for imported and domestically produced commodities,[34] the propensities of the population to save and to invest, and the willingness to adopt new production techniques within the parish.[35] Among the social implications are the incidence and type of criminal behaviour within the parish,[36] the nature of partisan politics and the extent of trade union organization,[37] and the overall pattern of parish demographic performance.

It is this last implication that concerns the present study. Before describing the ways in which the nature of parish socio-economic structure may be expected to influence parish demographic performance, it is useful to discuss the demographic sub-model depicted in Figure 3.1.

THE DEMOGRAPHIC SUB-MODEL

The demographic sub-model sets out the relationships within a set of variables which collectively measures demographic performance for a given parish during some specified time period. The sub-model is thus primarily concerned with four demographic variables: infant mortality, general mortality, fertility, and net out-migration. From these four may be derived two additional variables: natural increase of parish population and overall change in population size.

These six demographic variables are related by definition and hence the sub-model requires only brief discussion. Infant mortality clearly influences general mortality since the latter incorporates the former. Natural increase of parish population is given by the arithmetic difference between total births and total deaths; hence, natural increase is dependent upon fertility and general mortality. Finally, overall change in population size is determined by the arithmetic difference between natural increase and net out-migration. These relationships are illustrated by solid-line arrows in Figure 3.1 above.

It is possible that certain demographic variables are linked in other ways as well. For example, in so far as net out-migration significantly altered the age- and sex-composition of parish population, it is possible that both parish fertility and mortality were indirectly dependent on net out-migration. Moreover, net out-migration may have been indirectly dependent on natural increase, especially in parishes where access to land was limited and alternative economic opportunities were scarce. Fertility and mortality may also have been related. It is possible, for example, that infant mortality had an indirect influence on subsequent fertility, and it is conceivable that fertility in turn influenced infant mortality. These and other possible interactions notwithstanding, the present sub-model concentrates exclusively on the linkages between demographic variables as set out in Figure 3.1.

THE ECONOMIC-DEMOGRAPHIC RELATIONSHIPS

The nature of parish socio-economic structure represents the independent variable of the overall model, and the patterns of parish demographic performance are taken as the dependent variables. These variables, and the two sub-models from which they are derived, are linked through five hypothesized economic-demographic relationships shown as broken-line arrows in Figure 3.1. Since these economic-demographic relationships are the hypotheses of the model to be tested, it is necessary to examine each in turn.

Before doing so however, it is important to recognize that parish demographic performance may have been influenced by a host of factors which the present model treats as exogenous. Among these are the random appearance of epidemic diseases, the religious and psychological predispositions of the population, and occasional natural calamities such as earthquake, hurricane, and prolonged drought.[38] Without denying the importance of these influences on parish demographic performance, they are nonetheless excluded from the present model.

The Infant Mortality Relationship

It is generally supposed that infant mortality is very sensitive to general socio-economic conditions.[39] This belief has become so widespread that infant mortality has recently enjoyed considerable status as a proxy for economic and social welfare.[40] The infant mortality relationship of the model is predicated on this view. In order to understand the manner in which parish socio-economic structure may be expected to influence parish infant mortality, it is useful to examine the features of parish socio-economic structure separately.

Evidence from other times and places suggests that in general infant mortality is inversely related to per capita real income. This is most obvious in comparative studies of national infant mortality experience.[41] Within any given nation or region, infant mortality appears to vary inversely with household income.[42] This suggests that overal infant mortality is influenced not only by per capita income, but also by the distribution of income across households. Thus, given some per capita income level, infant mortality is likely to be higher the less egalitarian is the distribution of income. In addition, there is some suggestion that infant mortality is indirectly influenced by the stability of income over time. Since the health of nursing mothers--and hence of infants--appears to depend on the regular availability of foodstuffs and other material items, it may be the case that unstable household income will tend to increase infant mortality.[43]

The features of social organization cannot be expected to influence greatly the level of infant mortality. There is little theoretical or empirical foundation to suggest that the degree of economic and social mobility affects infant mortality. Although infant mortality is normally expected to vary across social classes, this is more likely to be the result of differences in wealth and income rather than the nature of social stratification as such. It is possible that infant mortality is influenced by the nature of institutions through which individuals are integrated into a community. In so far as the nurture and protection of infants are at least in part community responsibilities, infant mortality may be expected to vary inversely with the extent to which individuals are integrated into the community. Although there is some indirect evidence to support this view in various village studies, its relevance for wider communities is uncertain.[44]

Against this background, it is reasonable to expect that parish infant mortality was influenced by the level, distribution and stability of parish real income, and possibly by the nature of social integration. More specifically, parish infant mortality is expected to vary inversely with (i) the level of parish real income, (ii) the degree to which parish income is distributed in a more nearly egalitarian fashion, (iii) the degree to which parish income is stable over time, and possibly (iv) the extent to which individuals are closely integrated into the community.

The first and third of these influences may be approximated by the degree to which parish output consisted of staple exports. The second and fourth may be approximated by the extent to which parish production was organized by plantations. Recalling the previous discussion of these proxies, the infant mortality relationship may be stated as two specific hypotheses:

(1a) During some specified time period, the more nearly is a parish dominated by the cultivation of staple exports (domestic crops), the higher (lower) will be parish infant mortality.

(1b) During some specified time period, the more nearly is a parish dominated by plantation (peasant) organization of production, the higher (lower) will be parish infant mortality.

The General Mortality Relationship

General mortality is obviously influenced by infant mortality since by definition general mortality measures the incidence of death in all age groups including infants. It is to be expected, therefore, that all socio-economic conditions influencing infant mortality will also influence general mortality. Although socio-economic conditions will influence both measures of mortality in the same direction, the strength of these influences on general mortality will be greater the larger is the proportion of infants among the total number of deaths.

Of course general mortality also depends on the incidence of death among age groups other than infants. Thus it is necessary to discuss briefly the manner in which parish socio-economic structure may be expected to influence parish mortality among these age groups.

The components of parish socio-economic structure may be expected to influence the mortality of non-infants in much the same way as they do the mortality of infants. Mortality of non-infants is expected to vary inversely with the level of real income per capita,[45] and is also expected to be higher the less egalitarian is the distribution of income. Non-infant mortality is not likely to be as affected by the stability of income over time, except perhaps among the aged and the infirm.[46] Finally, the features of social organization are not expected to influence substantially the mortality of non-infants for the same reasons as discussed in the case of infants.

In exactly the same manner as in the case of infant mortality, the general mortality relationship may be summarized as two specific hypotheses:

(2a) During some specified time period, the more nearly is a parish dominated by the cultivation of staple exports (domestic crops), the higher (lower) will be parish general mortality.

(2b) During some specified time period, the more nearly is a parish dominated by plantation (peasant) organization of production, the higher (lower) will be parish general mortality.

The Fertility Relationship

In recent years much research has been devoted to the socio-economic correlates of household, regional, and national fertility.[47] The result is a useful set of empirical observations relating fertility to a variety of factors, some of which are embodied in the nature of parish socio-economic structure. These findings thus provide an appropriate base from which to derive the expected relationship between parish socio-economic structure and parish fertility.

It is generally supposed that fertility is strongly influenced by the level of real income at the appropriate level of aggregation.[48]

Unfortunately there is much dispute as to the nature of that influence. On the one hand, there is evidence to suggest that fertility and real income levels are inversely related.[49] Such an inverse relationship is apparent in the very long period studies undertaken by scholars of the demographic transition.[50] During relatively short time periods, an inverse relationship is frequently observed when different socio-economic groups are compared: hence the common finding that urban residents, who typically enjoy higher incomes than do rural residents, normally have lower fertility rates.[51] Further, once the level of income exceeds substantially that required for bare subsistence, fertility is often observed to be inversely related to income regardless of social status.[52]

On the other hand, there is some empirical evidence to suggest that fertility and real income are directly related.[53] Thus within a given social class, it is often observed that household fertility (or family size) and household income are directly related. Moreover, at or near subsistence income levels, fertility and income are frequently observed to be directly related.[54]

In short there is no compelling theoretical argument or body of empirical evidence to suggest that fertility and real income are always related in the same way. The nature of this relationship appears to depend upon the length of the time period studied, the degree to which real incomes actually exceed some subsistence level of income, and whether individual households or some aggregate of households are examined. Since the present study deals with a relatively short time period during which real income was not far in excess of subsistence, it is perhaps not unreasonable to expect that parish fertility was directly related to parish real income.

The manner in which real income is distributed across households and the stability of parish income may also be expected to influence fertility.[55] Assuming that the real income-fertility relationship is positive at the household level, parish fertility may be expected to be higher the more nearly egalitarian is the distribution of income. The stability of parish income is likely to have some effect on fertility although the strength of that effect is probably not great. At income levels near bare subsistence, fecundity appears to be related to the diet of women.[56] The regular availability of foodstuffs in those regions enjoying stability of real income may thus have acted to increase fertility somewhat. There is also some evidence that stability of income was important in the formation of stable sexual unions which are known to have much higher fertility than more casual liaisons.[57]

Various studies of differential fertility in the Caribbean suggest that the nature of social organization is a far more critical determinant of fertility than are economic conditions within a community.[58] The way in which individuals are socially integrated into the community appears to be particularly important. Thus it has been argued that the extended family "is an institutional arrangement strongly conducive to high fertility".[59] An extended family reduces the costs of children to individual mothers in two ways: by guaranteeing a real income to both mother and child, and by sharing the time and effort of child rearing. Moreover, an extended family can be relied upon to help secure employment for children once they reach working age, thereby reducing an additional barrier to high fertility.[60]

Drawing these influences together, it may be expected that parish fertility was at least in part dependent upon the level, distribution, and stability of parish real income, and the nature of parish social organization. To be more specific, parish fertility is expected to vary directly with (i) parish real income, (ii) the degree to which parish income is distributed in a more nearly egalitarian manner, (iii) the degree to which parish income is stable over time, and (iv) the degree to which social integration is accomplished through extended families.

As discussed previously, the first and third of these influences may be approximated by the extent to which parish output consisted of staple exports. The second and fourth may be approximated by the extent to which parish production was organized by plantations. Thus, the fertility relationship of the model may be expressed in the form of two hypotheses:

(3a) During some specified time period, the more nearly is a parish dominated by the cultivation of staple exports (domestic crops), the lower (higher) will be parish fertility.

(3b) During some specified time period, the more nearly is a parish dominated by plantation (peasant) organization of production, the lower (higher) will be parish fertility.

The Natural Increase Relationship

By definition the natural increase in parish population is strictly determined by parish fertility and parish mortality performance during some specified period of time. Consequently there exists no direct link between parish socio-economic structure and natural increase in parish population. The natural increase relationship is therefore to be understood as the influence of parish socio-economic structure on parish fertility and parish mortality simultaneously. Given the fertility relationship and the general mortality relationship, the natural increase relationship necessarily follows and may be expressed in two hypotheses:

(4a) During some specified time period, the more nearly is a parish dominated by the cultivation of staple exports (domestic crops), the lower (higher) will be the natural increase in parish population.

(4b) During some specified time period, the more nearly is a parish dominated by plantation (peasant) organization of production, the lower (higher) will be the natural increase in parish population.

The Net Out-Migration Relationship

Parish net out-migration is defined as the arithmetic difference between gross migrations out of and into the parish during some specified time period. Since these gross migration flows are unknown for the late nineteenth and early twentieth centuries, parish net out-migration must serve as the sole measure of parish migration experience. In later chapters a distinction is made between net out-migration to other Jamaican parishes and net out-migration to foreign destinations. The present discussion makes no such formal distinction in the consideration of possible socio-economic determinants of net out-migration.

It is true that net out-migration is influenced by a number of factors not explicitly incorporated within the model. Among the more striking of these exogenous influences on net out-migration are the legal barriers to emigration or immigration, the degree of curiosity and venturesomeness of individuals, and the perception of a more amiable political, religious, or cultural environment in areas of destination as compared with region of origin.[61]

These and other exogenous factors notwithstanding, the nature of parish socio-economic structure may be thought to have exerted some influence on gross migration into and out of the parish, and hence on parish net out-migration. In order to understand the overall nature of that influence, it is useful to consider the separate influences of the components of parish socio-economic structure.

Perhaps the most common hypothesis in the general literature is that migration results from perceived differentials in income between places of origin and places of destination.[62] It is frequently the case that perceived and actual circumstances are at variance. In part this is the result of disguised differences in living costs; in part, it results from a miscalculation of employment opportunities. Although some Jamaican migrants no doubt appreciated these problems, it appears that many acted on the basis of perceived differentials in money income.[63] Thus it may be expected that parish net out-migration was inversely related to parish per capita money income.

Net out-migration may also be influenced by the manner in which aggregate income is distributed across households. Apart from the willingness to migrate, potential migrants require real resources with which to pay passages and sustain themselves during a period of resettlement. Thus, given some level of per capita income, the more nearly egalitarian is the distribution of income, the larger will be the number of persons who possess the capacity to migrate.[64] In the abstract an egalitarian distribution of income might serve to attract in-migrants. In the Jamaican case, however, such a distribution of income rested upon widespread ownership of land by individual families who were in general unwilling to alienate their holdings to non-family members. Thus, without access to land and in the face of little demand for wage labour, migrants will be less attracted to such areas than to urban areas or to rural regions in which wage employment is available.

The stability of income over time has an ambiguous influence on net out-migration. An individual migrant might be expected to favour a destination in which income stability was high relative to his place of origin.[65] However, there is some empirical evidence that migrants are often unaware of or tend to discount differences in the stability of income.[66] One possibility is that the stability of parish income affected parish net out-migration differently under different circumstances. During periods of relative prosperity, migration may have been largely unaffected by relative income stability between origin and destination; during times of economic distress, income stability may have been an important factor determining parish net out-migration.[67]

Parish social organization may also be expected to influence parish net out-migration. In particular, peasant society is more likely to encourage net out-migration than is plantation society. Since wage employment is very limited in peasant society, access to land provides the only effective means of employment for new entrants to the labour force. Family owned land might be a source of employment, but productivity cannot be indefinitely maintained as more and more labour is employed on fixed and relatively small plots of land. Consequently, migration from peasant society eventually becomes the only alternative for new entrants to the labour force.[68]

Pressure to migrate will also operate in plantation society since scarcity of land for individual cultivation is even more pronounced than in peasant society. Within plantation society there does exist an alternative to out-migration: namely, wage employment on the plantation itself. Hence although out-migration is typical of plantation society, it may be expected that net out-migration will be less than in peasant society.[69]

These separate influences may be summarized thus: Parish net out-migration may be expected to vary inversely with (i) parish aggregate money income, (ii) the extent to which the distribution of income is highly skewed, and (iii) the degree to which parish social organization is more nearly typical of plantation society. Stability of parish income has an uncertain effect on parish net out-migration, as noted in the preceding discussion.

As set out in a previous section, the first of these influences may be approximated by the degree to which parish output was dominated by staple exports. The second and third of these influences may be approximated by the extent to which parish economic activity was organized by plantations. In terms of these proxies, the net out-migration relationship may be expressed in two specific hypotheses:

(5a) During some specified time period, the more nearly is a parish dominated by the cultivation of staple exports (domestic crops), the smaller (greater) will be parish net out-migration.

(5b) During some specified time period, the more nearly is a parish dominated by plantation (peasant) organization of production, the smaller (greater) will be parish net out-migration.

Summary of the Economic-Demographic Relationships

A major purpose of this chapter is to derive a set of testable hypotheses relating parish demographic performance to the nature of parish socio-economic structure. For each component of demographic performance, discussion has centred on the expected influence of specific aspects of parish socio-economic structure: namely, the level, distribution, and stability over time of parish income, and the nature of parish social organization. Since statistical estimation of these variables is not feasible for the time period under study, the derivation of testable hypotheses requires the use of two proxies: the composition of parish output and the organizational form of parish production. Thus the hypothesized economic-demographic relationships of the model are all expressed in terms of these two proxies.

The specific hypotheses of the economic-demographic relationships may be verbally summarized as follows:

(6a) During some specified time period, the more nearly is a parish dominated by the cultivation of staple exports (domestic crops):

(i) the higher (lower) will be parish infant mortality;

(ii) the higher (lower) will be parish general mortality;

(iii) the lower (higher) will be parish fertility;

(iv) the lower (higher) will be natural increase parish population;

(v) the smaller (greater) will be parish net out-migration.

(6a) During some specified time period, the more nearly is a parish dominated by plantation (peasant) organization of production:

(i) the higher (lower) will be parish infant mortality;

(ii) the higher (lower) will be parish general mortality;

(iii) the lower (higher) will be parish fertility;

(iv) the lower (higher) will be natural increase in parish population;

(v) the smaller (greater) will be parish net out-migration.

These hypotheses may also be expressed in a manner which indicates the nature of the empirical testing to be undertaken in Chapter VI. Attention is focused exclusively on the agricultural parishes of Jamaica since urban parishes represent a socio-economic structure so different as to be better considered separately. For the i-th agricultural parish during some specified time period let

P_i be a numerical measure of the organization of parish economic activity;

X_i be a numerical measure of the composition of parish output;

V_i be a measure of parish demographic performance.

Suppose that the greater is the value of P_i, the more completely is production organized by plantations in the i-th parish; the smaller is the value of P_i, the more completely is production organized by peasants in the i-th parish. Further suppose that the greater is the value of X_i, the more completely is output dominated by staple exports in the i-th parish; the smaller is the value of X_i, the more completely is output dominated by domestically consumed crops in the i-th parish.

Thus, the basic postulate, that parish demographic performance during some specified time period depends upon the organization of parish economic activity and the composition of parish output, may be written as:

$$(6c) \quad V_i = v(P_i, X_i).$$

Parish demographic performance during any specified time period consists of parish experience with respect to mortality, fertility, and net out-migration. For the i-th parish during some specified time period, let

IM_i be a measure of infant mortality;

GM_i be a measure of general mortality;

FY_i be a measure of fertility;

NI_i be a measure of natural increase of population;

OM_i be a measure of net out-migration.

Each of the economic-demographic relationships illustrated in Figure 3.1 and described verbally above may be expressed as

(1c) $IM_i = a(P_i, X_i)$

(2c) $GM_i = b(P_i, X_i)$

(3c) $FY_i = c(P_i, X_i)$

(4c) $NI_i = d(P_i, X_i)$

(5c) $OM_i = e(P_i, X_i)$

The testable hypotheses of the model may be expressed in terms of the signs of the partial derivatives of the above equations, thus:

(1d) $\frac{\delta IM}{\delta P} > 0 \quad ; \quad \frac{\delta IM}{\delta X} > 0$

(2d) $\frac{\delta GM}{\delta P} > 0 \quad ; \quad \frac{\delta GM}{\delta X} > 0$

(3d) $\frac{\delta FY}{\delta P} < 0 \quad ; \quad \frac{\delta FY}{\delta X} < 0$

(4d) $\frac{\delta NI}{\delta P} < 0 \quad ; \quad \frac{\delta NI}{\delta X} < 0$

$$(5d) \quad \frac{\delta OM}{\delta P} < 0 \quad ; \quad \frac{\delta OM}{\delta X} < 0$$

These specific hypotheses are statistically tested in Chapter VI. In order to generate the data required for such a test, it is useful to examine in some detail the actual patterns of economic and demographic performance during the period 1890-1940.

ENDNOTES TO CHAPTER III

[1] H. Innis, Essays in Canadian Economic History. (Toronto: 1957); D. C. North, The Economic Growth of the United States, 1790-1860. (Englewood Cliffs, N.J.: 1961), especially pp. 1-16.

[2] M. Watkins, "A Staple Theory of Economic Growth", Canadian Journal of Economics and Political Science, Vol. XXIX (May 1963), pp. 141-158; J. Levin, The Export Economies. (Cambridge, Mass.: 1960); D. Seers, "The Mechanism of an Open Petroleum Economy", Social and Economic Studies, Vol. 13, No. 2 (June 1964).

[3] S. DeCastro, "Theorems of the Open Economy", Social and Economic Studies Vol. 19, No. 3 (September 1970); C. Kennedy, "Keynesian Theory in an Open Economy", Social and Economic Studies, Vol. 13, No. 1 (March 1964).

[4] H. Innis, op. cit.; D. C. North, op. cit.

[5] M. Watkins, op. cit.

[6] J. Levin, op. cit.; D. Seers, op. cit.

[7] R. E. Baldwin, "Patterns of Development in Newly Settled Regions", Manchester School of Economics and Social Studies, Vol. XXIV (May 1956); L. Best and K. Levitt, Export Propelled Growth in the Caribbean. (Montreal: 1968); G. Beckford, Persistent Poverty. (London: 1972).

[8] G. Beckford, op. cit.; C. Wagley, "Plantation America: A Cultural Sphere", in V. Rubin (ed.), Caribbean Studies: A Symposium. (Seattle: 1960).

[9] G. E. Cumper, "Dependence, Development and the Sociology of Economic Thought", Social and Economic Studies, Vol. 23, No. 3 (September 1974), pp. 465-482.

[10] G. Beckford, op. cit.; L. Best and K. Levitt, op. cit.; G. Eisner, op. cit.; M. Craton and J. Walvin, A Jamaican Plantation. (London: 1970).

[11] Lord Olivier, Jamaica: The Blessed Island. (London: 1936), pp. 311-327.

[12] Lord Olivier, op. cit., pp. 269-289; G. Eisner, op. cit., pp. 210-235; Report of the West India Royal Commission. (Cmd. 6077), pp. 35-50.

[13] G. Eisner, op. cit., pp. 168-180; Bluebooks of Jamaica, 1880-1938; Handbooks of Jamaica, 1880-1938.

[14] These data are presented in the annual Handbooks of Jamaica. From year to year, the criteria employed in order to designate a plantation appear to vary. In any case, farms in excess of fifty acres were uniformly judged to be plantations, and it is this criteria that the present study employs.

[15] Lord Olivier, op. cit.; W. M. Macmillan, Warning from the West Indies. (London: 1936); Sir David Barbour, Report on the Finances of Jamaica. (H.M.S.O.: 1899); G. St.J. Orde-Browne, Labour Conditions in the West Indies. (H.M.S.O.: 1939).

[16] G. Eisner, op. cit.; See also Chapter IV below.

[17] E. Clarke, My Mother Who Fathered Me. (London: 1966); K. Tekse, Internal Migration in Jamaica. (Kingston: 1967), Table 14, p. 24.

[18] G. Eisner, op. cit., pp. 378-379; Report of the West India Royal Royal Commission, op. cit., pp. 37-50.

[19) G. Beckford, op. cit., pp. 52, 202, 225.

[20] Ibid., especially pp. 3-52; R. E. Baldwin, op. cit.; H. Myint, The Economics of Developing Countries. (London: 1964), especially Chapter 4.

[21] G. Eisner, op. cit., pp. 209, 232.

[22] Report of the Nutrition Committee. (Kingston: 1937).

[23] G. E. Cumper, "Estimates of Jamaican Commodity Trade", _Social and Economic Studies_, Vol. 6, No. 3 (September 1957), pp. 425-430.

[24] See Chapter IV below.

[25] With respect to output, it was frequently supposed that "the average yield per acre may fairly be taken as much the same year by year" for domestically consumed crops. (See, _Annual Report of the Governor of Jamaica for 1897-8_.) The general stability of domestic crop prices is apparent in the price lists published from time to time in the _Handbooks of Jamaica_. See also, G. Eisner, _op. cit._, Appendix II, pp. 376-377.

[26] C. Wagley, _op. cit._; G. Beckford, _op. cit._; R. Redfield, _Peasant Society and Culture_. (Chicago: 1956); M. M. Horowitz, (ed.), _Peoples and Cultures of the Caribbean_. (New York: 1971).

[27] It may be supposed that the nature of social organization is also influenced by other phenomena such as racial composition and religious predisposition of the population. Since these phenomena did not vary across individual parishes in Jamaica, the present study abstracts from them.

[28] R. T. Smith, "Social Stratification, Cultural Pluralism and Integration in West Indian Societies", in S. Lewis and T. G. Mathews (eds.), _Caribbean Integration_. (Puerto Rico: 1967), p. 230.

[29] T. Shanin, (ed.), _Peasants and Peasant Societies_. (London: 1971); R. T. Smith, "Culture and Social Structure in the Caribbean: Some Recent Work on Family and Kinship Studies", in M. M. Horowitz, _op. cit._, pp. 448-475.

[30] E. Clarke, _op. cit._, pp. 60-69; W. M. Macmillan, _op. cit._, pp. 148-160.

[31] S. W. Mintz, "The Caribbean as a Socio-cultural Area", in M. M. Horowitz (ed.), _op. cit._, pp. 15-46.

[32] Lord Olivier, _op. cit._, pp. 200-214; W. M. Macmillan, _op. cit._, pp. 100-101; Olivier to Harcourt, Dispatch of April 21, 1911, in C.O. 137/684.

[33] S. W. Mintz, _supra_.

[34] G. St.J. Orde-Browne, _op. cit._, p. 19; See also, _Annual Reports of the Governor of Jamaica_, especially for 1896-7, 1899-1900, 1909-10, 1913-14, 1919-20.

[35] W. M. Macmillan, _op. cit._, pp. 85-87, 159; _Report of the West India Royal Commission_, _op. cit._, pp. 43-44.

[36] Hemming to Chamberlain, Dispatch of August 21, 1901, in C.O. 137/621; Swettenham to Secretary of State, Dispatch of November 8, 1905, in C.O. 137/647.

[37] O. Phelps, "Rise of the Labour Movement in Jamaica", *Social and Economic Studies*, Vol. 9, No. 4 (December 1960); R. Hart, *The Origin and Development of the People of Jamaica*. (Kingston: 1952).

[38] G. W. Roberts, *The Population of Jamaica*. (Cambridge: 1957); G. Eisner, *op. cit.*. especially pp. 136-140; See also, Chapter IV below.

[39] D. H. Wrong, *Population and Society*. (New York: 1961); A. Sauvy, *General Theory of Population*. (London: 1974), pp. 320-340; T. H. Hollingsworth *Historical Demography*. (London: 1969), pp. 181-184.

[40] Economic Council of Canada, *Economic Targets and Social Indicators*. (Ottawa: 1974), especially pp. 92-100.

[41] J. I. Clarke, *Population Geography*. (London: 1965), pp. 115-119; D. Nortman, "Population and Family Planning Programs: A Factbook", *Reports on Population/Family Planning*, No. 2, 6th Edition (December 1974).

[42] D. H. Wrong, *op. cit.*, pp. 31-34; A. Sauvy, *op. cit.*, pp. 260-262; E. A. Wrigley, *Population and History*. (London: 1969), p. 129.

[43] E. A. Wrigley, *op. cit.*, pp. 127-129; D. E. C. Eversley, "Population, Economy and Society", in D. V. Glass and D. E. C. Eversley, (eds.), *Population in History*. (London: 1965), pp. 52-53.

[44] E. Clarke, *op. cit.*, pp. 113-140; P. Deprez, "The Demographic Development of Flanders in the Eighteenth Century", in D. V. Glass and D. E. C. Eversley, (eds.), *op. cit.*, pp. 623-624.

[45] D. Nortman, *op. cit.*; P. Deprez, *op. cit.*

[46] E. A. Wrigley, *op. cit.*, pp. 168-169.

[47] See, for example, K. O. Mason and A. S. David, *Social and Economic Correlates of Family Fertility: A Survey of Evidence*. (Chapel Hill: 1971).

[48] J. L. Simon, *The Effects of Income on Fertility*. (Chapel Hill: 1971).

[49] *Ibid.*, pp. 42-50, 169-171; W. C. Robinson and D. E. Horlacher, "Population Growth and Economic Welfare", *Reports on Population/Family Planning*, No. 6 (February 1971), pp. 20-27.

[50] D. E. C. Eversley, op. cit., pp. 46-53.

[51] J. L. Simon, op. cit., pp. 77-93; D. H. Wrong, op. cit., pp. 70-71.

[52] Ibid., pp. 73-75.

[53] W. C. Robinson and D. E. Horlacher, op. cit., pp. 20-27.

[54] J. L. Simon, op. cit., pp. 42-50; E. A. Wrigley, op. cit., pp. 226-227.

[55] J. L. Simon, op. cit., pp. 95-97; A. K. Bhattacharyya, "Income Inequality and Fertility: A Comparative View", Population Studies, Vol. XXIX, No. 1 (March 1975), pp. 5-19.

[56] E. A. Wrigley, op. cit., pp. 66, 226-227; A. Sauvy, op. cit., pp. 348-351, 358-360.

[57] E. Clarke, op. cit., pp. 78-85, 116; G. W. Roberts, The Population of Jamaica. (Cambridge: 1957); G. E. Cumper, "The Jamaican Family: Village and Estate", op. cit., pp. 76-108.

[58] See the summary of evidence presented in M. G. Smith's "Introduction" to E. Clarke, op. cit., pp. i-xliv.

[59] K. Davis, "Institutional Patterns Favouring High Fertility in Underdeveloped Countries", Eugenics Quarterly, Vol. 2 (1959), as quoted in D. H. Wrong, op. cit., p. 63.

[60] E. Clarke, op. cit., pp. 90-112, 170-174.

[61] Olivier to Chamberlain, Dispatch of July 10, 1902, in C.O. 137/628: "The landless Jamaican labourer, with regular employment offering in the Island, goes abroad to Costa Rica, Ecuador and elsewhere, very largely because he enjoys the speculation, the travel, the experience and the excitement. . . ."

[62] See, for example, L. A. Sjaastad, "The Costs and Returns of Human Migration", Journal of Political Economy, Vol. LXX (October 1962), pp. 80-93; M. P. Todaro, "A Model of Labor Migration and Urban Unemployment in Less Developed Countries", American Economic Review, Vol. LIX, No. 1 (March 1969), pp. 138-148; J. R. Harris and M. P. Todaro, "Migration, Unemployment and Development: A Two Sector Analysis", American Economic Review, Vol. LX, No. 1 (March 1970), pp. 126-142; L. and J. MacDonald, "Motives and Objectives of Migration: Selective Migration and Preferences Toward Rural and Urban Life", Social and Economic Studies, Vol. 18, No. 4 (December 1968), pp. 417-434.

[63] "[Emigrants] bases their calculation on the cost of foodstuffs in Jamaica and were not informed of the very heavy cost of living in

Ecuador": Hemming to Chamberlain, Dispatch of April 9, 1901, in C.O. 137/618. Internal migrants appear to have been similarly influenced: see, for example, G. St.J. Orde-Browne, _op. cit._, pp. 84-85; _Report of the Unemployment Commission_, (Kingston: 1935), in C.O. 137/725.

[64] L. A. Eyre, _Geographic Aspects of Population Dynamics in Jamaica_. (Boca Raton: 1972), pp. 26ff.

[65] L. A. Sjaastad, _op. cit._

[66] J. R. Harris and M. P. Todaro, _op. cit._

[67] This point is explored in more detail in Chapter V below.

[68] E. Clarke, _op. cit._, pp. 170-177; S. Brunn and R. N. Thomas, "Socio-Economic Environments and Internal Migration: The Case of Tegucigalpa, Honduras", _Social and Economic Studies_, Vol. 21, No. 4 (December 1972), pp. 463-473.

[69] G. Beckford, _op. cit._, pp. 86-87, 97.

Chapter IV

JAMAICAN ECONOMIC STRUCTURE, 1880-1940

While retaining an essentially agricultural nature, the Jamaican economy underwent subtle changes during the late nineteenth and early twentieth centuries. In particular the principal staple exports of the island were open to considerable fluctuation both with respect to composition and total value. Closely associated with these changes were variations in the level and composition of employment, aggregate income, domestic agricultural production, and non-agricultural economic activity. Not only did the level and composition of output vary across these years, but in addition the manner in which agricultural production was organized varied considerably from place to place and from time to time. This chapter examines the impact of these changes on the economic structure of the island as a whole, and on the economic structures of the individual parishes.

It is convenient to divide the discussion into a number of sections. In the first, the changing patterns of overall economic performance during the period are surveyed. Part two enquires into the structure of the individual sub-sectors of the economy. Particular attention is paid to the changing patterns of output, the organization of production, and the spatial distribution of production in each of these sub-sectors. Patterns of employment are described in part three;

in part four, the patterns of income distribution are discussed. The chapter concludes with a short summary of Jamaican economic structure during these years.

OVERALL PATTERNS OF ECONOMIC PERFORMANCE

Changes in the level and composition of economic activity over time may be conveniently summarized with reference to national income accounts. The compilation of such accounts is a highly specialized and often vexatious undertaking, especially for historical periods during which the collection of relevant data was far from systematic and comprehensive. It is fortunate therefore that the national income of Jamaica for selected years during the nineteenth and early twentieth centuries has been estimated by two experts in the field.

In a study of remarkable ingenuity, Gisela Eisner[1] has compiled national income accounts for the years 1832, 1850, 1870, 1890, 1910, and 1930. Phyllis Deane's[2] earlier study, which served as a guide to Eisner's enquiry, provides comprehensive national income estimates for the year 1938, and somewhat less thorough estimates for each year in the period 1929-1937. Although these two studies employ different assumptions and definitions which tend to limit their comparability, they nonetheless provide a fairly reliable indication of the patterns of economic performance for the period under study.

The overall growth of the economy may be seen in Table 4.1. Gross Domestic Product (GDP) valued at current prices is estimated by Eisner to have increased by 128% between 1890 and 1930. The period 1910-1930 appears to have been characterized by the highest rate of growth of money GDP. Once adjustment is made for price changes, however, a somewhat different picture emerges. Although real GDP doubled between 1890 and 1930, the rate of growth of real GDP was nearly equal in the two twenty-year periods, 1890-1910 and 1910-1930. Thus in spite of wide variation in money GDP, real output was growing at an approximately constant rate during the whole period 1890-1930. It will also be seen in Table 4.1 that per capita real GDP increased slightly less than 27% over this forty year period.

TABLE 4.1

GROSS DOMESTIC PRODUCT, JAMAICA, 1870 - 1930

YEAR	G.D.P. CURRENT PRICES (£'000)	G.D.P. 1910 PRICES (£'000)	PER CAPITA G.D.P. 1910 PRICES (£)
1870	5676.9	6006.0	11.9
1890	8746.6	7925.3	12.4
1910	11361.9	11361.9	13.7
1930	19951.6	15969.5	15.7
		% GROWTH	
1870-1890	54.1	32.0	4.2
1890-1910	29.9	43.4	10.5
1910-1930	75.6	40.6	14.6
1870-1930	251.5	165.9	31.9
1890-1930	128.1	101.5	26.6

SOURCE: G. Eisner, Jamaica, 1830-1930, Tables 8.1, 8.11, LVI.

Phyllis Deane's estimates of national income for the period 1929-1938 are summarized in Table 4.2. These estimates are not strictly comparable with those of Eisner, since these two scholars have employed different price indices in order to estimate real output. Although the text is unclear, it seems likely that the Deane estimates are unadjusted for price changes. On this basis it appears that Net Taxable Output (NTO) in real terms increased by about 42% between 1929 and 1938, with the period of most rapid growth occurring between 1933 and 1938. When adjusted for population growth, the per capita real NTO is estimated to have increased by 23% over the period 1929-1938.

TABLE 4.2

NET TAXABLE OUTPUT,JAMAICA, 1929-1938

YEAR	NET TAXABLE OUTPUT CURRENT PRICES (£'000)	PER CAPITA NET TAXABLE OUTPUT CURRENT PRICES (£)	NET TAXABLE OUTPUT 1938 PRICES (1) (£'000)	PER CAPITA NET TAXABLE OUTPUT 1938 PRICES (2) (£)
1929	19187	19.5	14319	14.5
1930	19053	19.0	14885	14.9
1931	18339	18.0	15674	15.4
1932	17177	16.6	15759	15.2
1933	16391	15.6	15463	14.7
1934	16553	15.5	16389	15.3
1935	17147	15.8	17677	16.3
1936	17474	15.8	19416	17.6
1937	19420	17.3	19039	16.9
1938	20319	17.8	20319	17.8

(1) Deflated by General Price Index as reported in P. Deane, _op. cit._, Table 104, p. 141.

(2) Population estimated by procedure described in Appendix.

SOURCE: P. Deane, _op. cit._, Table 104, p. 141.

Treating the data presented in Table 4.1 and Table 4.2 with care it is possible to summarize the overall performance of the economy during the period 1890-1938. On the basis of the Deane estimates, it appears that per capita real output was falling during the mid-1930s. In view of the rapid growth of population and the decline in staple export prices after 1930, such a fall in the level of per capita real output is not very surprising. Indeed, similar reversals may well have occurred in the late 1890s and during the years of hurricane damage in 1903 and 1913.

These special years notwithstanding and due allowance being made for the crudeness of the estimates, there can be no serious doubt that real per capita income increased across the whole period 1890-1938. It was not of course an era of high prosperity, as was obvious to contemporary observers of the time.[3] In terms of aggregate income and on a per capita basis, however, it appears that Jamaicans were becoming marginally less poor during these years.

In order to better appreciate the structural features of this overall growth, it is useful to disaggregate the economy into the three broad sectors described in the previous chapter. The relative importance of these sectors is set out in Table 4.3.

Although the smallest in terms of contribution to real GDP, the staple export sector exhibited relatively rapid growth across the period. The proportion of real GDP originating in the staple export sector increased from 16% in 1890 to nearly 21% in 1930. In 1938 it is estimated that nearly one-quarter of Net Taxable Output arose from the export of agricultural products.[4] Domestic agriculture, on the other

TABLE 4.3

SECTORAL CONTRIBUTION TO GROSS DOMESTIC PRODUCT

JAMAICA, 1870-1930

(1910 PRICES)

	VALUE OF OUTPUT (£'000)				SECTORAL OUTPUT AS PER CENT GDP			
SECTOR	1870	1890	1910	1930	1870	1890	1910	1930
Staple Exports	928.1	1279.9	2430.3	3288.4	15.5	16.1	21.4	20.6
Domestic Agriculture	2365.3	2912.3	3805.3	4885.5	39.4	36.7	33.5	30.7
Non-Agriculture	2712.6	3733.1	5126.3	7795.1	45.1	47.2	45.1	48.7
TOTAL GDP	6006.0	7925.3	11361.9	15969.5	100.0	100.0	100.0	100.0

SOURCE: G. Eisner, *op. cit.*, Table 8.11, p. 119.

hand, declined as a percentage of real GDP over the period, although even in 1930 nearly 31% of real GDP was accounted for by domestic agriculture. The third sector of the economy, non-agricultural production, showed uneven growth across the period 1890-1930. Nonetheless, non-agricultural production represented a minimum 45% of real GDP during these years.[5]

In general the data in Table 4.3 suggest that non-agricultural production more or less kept pace with the overall rate of growth of real GDP. It further appears that the staple export sector expanded at the expense of the domestic agricultural sector during the period 1890-1930. Deane's estimates for 1929-1938 suggest a strikingly similar pattern of sectoral growth.[6] The differential rates of growth among agricultural sectors implies a shift in the economic structure of the island as a whole. The nature of that shift is made clear from a closer examination of each sector.

PATTERNS OF SECTORAL GROWTH

The Staple Export Sector

In the view of the colonial administration and the Jamaican oligarchy, the prosperity of the nation depended on the cultivation and export of sugar-based products, bananas, and a number of so-called minor staple commodities.[7] It was widely accepted that the value of staple exports directly determined the island's capacity to import, indirectly determined the level of public revenues, both directly and indirectly established the overall levels of employment and income, and ultimately guaranteed the stability of the social order.[8] Thus the composition

TABLE 4.4

COMPOSITION AND VALUE OF JAMAICAN STAPLE EXPORTS

FIVE YEAR TOTALS, 1885/1899-1940/1944

PERIOD	TOTAL VALUE OF STAPLE EXPORTS (£'000)	PER CENT OF TOTAL VALUE OF STAPLE EXPORTS ORIGINATING IN STAPLE SUB-SECTORS:		
		SUGAR & RUM	BANANAS	MINOR STAPLES
1885-1889	6366	37.2	15.2	47.6
1890-1894	8522	26.2	22.9	50.9
1895-1899	7325	19.5	29.2	51.3
1900-1904	8052	16.5	45.7	37.8
1905-1909	9685	14.2	53.8	32.0
1910-1914	11858	11.6	53.3	35.1
1915-1919	13612	36.4	18.3	45.3
1920-1924	20002	31.6	42.2	26.2
1925-1929	20026	18.7	51.1	30.2
1930-1934	15008	16.8	58.9	24.3
1935-1939	20932	23.9	57.8	18.3
1940-1944	15820	61.9	15.6	22.5

SOURCE: G. E. Cumper, "Estimates of Jamaican Commodity Trade", Social and Economic Studies, Vol. 6, No. 3 (September 1957), pp. 425-430.

and volume of staple exports were carefully studied and held to be the principal indicators of Jamaican economic performance.

As shown in Table 4.4 the total value of all staple exports increased by nearly 150% during the period 1885/89-1940/4. It is clear that during certain five year periods the value of staple exports declined substantially. For the period under investigation, 1890-1938, the total value of staple exports increased by nearly 250%. It would appear that the health of the staple export sector was more than satisfactory during that period.

This apparent growth conceals a significant shift in the composition of staple exports during these years. Apart from the peculiar conditions of the war years, the proportional contribution of rum and sugar exports to total staple export values declined across the whole period. A similar decline is evident with respect to the minor staples. By contrast, the importance of banana exports increased dramatically in most years. This shift in the composition of staple exports holds important implications for the structure of both national and parish economies. Hence it is worthwhile to examine the three staple export sub-sectors individually.

The Sugar Sub-Sector: As may be seen in Table 4.5, the production and export of sugar-based products declined across the period 1885-1914. Given declining market prices and a general unwillingness on the part of planters to invest in cost-reducing mechanization of field and factory operations,[9] the overall decline in the production of sugar and rum was to be expected.

TABLE 4.5

PRODUCTION, EXPORTS AND PRICES OF SUGAR AND RUM

FIVE YEAR PERIODS, JAMAICA, 1885-1944

	SUGAR			RUM	
PERIOD	SUGAR PRODUCTION (000 cwts)[a]	SUGAR EXPORTS (000 cwts)[b]	AVERAGE F.O.B. PRICE (s/cwt)[c]	RUM EXPORTS EXPORTS (Millions Gallons)[b]	AVERAGE F.O.B. PRICE (s/Gallon)[c]
1885-1889	1680	2103	12.4	9.2	2.3
1890-1894	2197	1986	12.6	8.4	2.3
1895-1899	1912	1747	9.3	8.0	1.5
1900-1904	1594	1491	9.5	7.3	1.7
1905-1909	1811	1051	10.4	6.8	2.4
1910-1914	1500	1404	12.7	5.4	1.8
1915-1919	3351	2796	24.3	6.8	4.6
1920-1924	3776	3256	34.3	3.8	3.9
1925-1929	5832	4435	14.4	4.2	2.7
1930-1934	6325	4653	9.4	2.1	3.2
1935-1939	10372	9020	8.7	3.8	5.8
1940-1944	15733	12400	12.5	2.9	14.1

SOURCES: (a) N. Deerr, The History of Sugar, Vol. I, p. 199.

(b) G. E. Cumper, "Estimates of Jamaican Commodity Trade", Social and Economic Studies, Vol. 6, No. 3, pp. 429.

(c) Ibid., pp. 429-30.

Some attempts were made to switch production away from sugar and towards rum since the latter's price in general declined less rapidly. But such efforts could at best save only the smaller and more highly specialized plantations.[10] Even the Brussels Convention of 1902, which removed the bounties on European grown beet sugar, did little to restore higher market prices or to renew confidence among Jamaican planters.[11]

The outbreak of the First World War dramatically increased sugar prices in world markets and Jamaican planters moved quickly to capture the profits of a distant war. Additional acreage was brought under cane cultivation and improved species of cane were planted. In a burst of enthusiasm, plans were laid for the construction of several modern and highly efficient central sugar factories, the completion of which was greatly hindered by wartime shipping restrictions and a general shortage of producer goods in Britain.[12]

When sugar prices began to decline after 1921 Jamaican output fell marginally. By the mid-1920s, however, the introduction of new factory and field production techniques and the widespread planting of improved varieties of cane had progressed so far that the level of output and exports continued to rise. By 1930 the operation of several central factories had begun and sugar production increased in spite of prices generally well below those prevailing before the war. Even during the worst years of the early 1930s when prices fell below ten shillings per hundredweight, the level of sugar production and sugar exports continued to rise. It is clear that production could not have expanded at such prices except as a consequence of an overall decline in the costs of production which virtually transformed the old structure of the sugar industry in Jamaica.[13]

This restructuring of the sugar industry was only in part the result of new production techniques. Alternative methods of management and a thorough reorganization of factor inputs were haltingly adopted during the period 1890-1934, and especially during the 1920s and 1930s played a critical role in the industry's rehabilitation. Perhaps the most important form of reorganization involved a reduction in the number of sugar factories as less efficient units were abandoned or consolidated into the new central factory complexes. Thus in the period 1885-1889 some 185 factories were actively producing sugar; by 1910-1914, some 75 were still in operation and during the years 1930-1934 a mere 40 factories continued to produce sugar products.[14]

Associated with this consolidation of factories was a pronounced increase in acreage under cane cultivation by the average sugar estate. In the years 1885-1889, acreage under cane on estates averaged 185 acres; by 1910-1914, that average had increased to 285 acres; in 1930-1934 estates on average cultivated 638 acres of sugar cane.[15] Thus while the total number of sugar estates was declining across these years, average estate acreage under cane cultivation was steadily increasing.

This amalgamation of sugar estates stemmed from three primary considerations. In the first place, the introduction of new factory equipment required initially large capital investment which could be more easily mobilized by large scale plantations. Secondly, the new factories required substantial amounts of cane on a regular and predictable basis in order to minimize unit costs of production. Thirdly, even the older type of sugar factory could be made to operate at lower costs if consistent supplies of fresh canes were delivered for processing. All these influences greatly encouraged the amalgamation of cane acreage into plantations of increasing size.

Even more indicative of the structural reorganization of the sugar sub-sector was the spectacular growth of cane cultivation on medium and small sized farms.[16] Since economies of scale were primarily confined to factory rather than field operations, a number of sugar manufacturers were content to rely upon canes supplied by independent farmers as supplements to cane production on estate cultivated land. While nearly 94% of all acreage under cane had been in the hands of estates in 1885-1889, that proportion had been reduced to 68% in 1910-1914 and had shrunk to 47% in 1920-24. Thereafter the estates increased their share of acreage under cane; in 1930-1934 they collectively cultivated 62%.[17]

The rise in estate controlled cane acreage during the 1930s highlights the major consequence of cane farming for small, independent producers. In periods of high sugar prices, sugar makers could expand output by purchasing additional canes from independent farmers. When market prices for sugar were declining, however, factories reduced output by using only the canes cultivated on estate owned land. Thus the burden of adjustment to variation in market prices for sugar fell most directly upon the small, independent cane farmers.[18]

A final aspect of the industry's reorganization during these years may be seen in the changing pattern of factory ownership. Before the

First World War, the consolidation of factories had largely proceeded through the private purchase of estates by individual entrepreneurs many of whom were resident in Jamaica. The introduction of new factory techniques required substantial capital investment and thus encouraged the emergence of corporate ownership of sugar factories. By 1928, for example, nearly one-third of all sugar produced in Jamaica came from the United Fruit Company's central sugar factories in the parishes of St. Catherine and Clarendon.[19] The joint stock company known as Jamaica Sugar Estates clearly dominated the industry in the parish of St. Thomas during the 1920s and after.[20] In 1937 the West Indies Sugar Company, a wholly owned subsidiary of Tate and Lyle, emerged as the single most important sugar producer in Jamaica when it purchased both Monymusk in Clarendon and Frome in Westmoreland. The emergence of these corporate sugar estates and the simultaneous demise of family plantations did much to revolutionize the industry, and established a system of industrial relations which has marked the industry to the present day.[21]

These structural changes tended to re-enforce the regional character of the sugar industry. Before the First World War, the cultivation of sugar cane was increasingly confined to the parishes of Westmoreland, Clarendon, and Trelawny. As may be seen in Table 4.6, these three parishes increased their share of island acreage under cane from 48% in 1885-1889 to 63% in 1910-1914. In other parishes previously given over to the production of cane (e.g., St. Thomas, St. Catherine, and St. James), planters either shifted to the cultivation of bananas or abandoned active cultivation altogether during the pre-War years.

TABLE 4.6

GEOGRAPHIC LOCATION OF SUGAR INDUSTRY, JAMAICA, 1885-1934

PARISHES	PER CENT TOTAL ISLAND ACREAGE IN SUGAR CANE (ANNUAL AVERAGE)			
	1885-1889	1910-1914	1920-1924	1930-1934
Westmoreland) Clarendon) Trelawny)	48.2	63.4	49.5	53.4
St. Thomas) St. Catherine) St. James)	29.6	19.6	33.9	31.3
Hanover) St. Ann) St. Mary)	17.3	9.9	12.9	9.7
St. Elizabeth) Portland) Manchester) St. Andrew)	4.9	7.2	3.7	5.5
TOTAL	100.0	100.1	100.0	99.9

SOURCE: Handbook of Jamaica, Annually, 1885-1935.

Highly attractive export prices during and immediately following the First World War enticed planters in other parishes to return to the cultivation of cane. The construction of central sugar factories in St. Thomas and St. Catherine, as well as the general reorganization of the industry described above, also worked to increase the share of island cane acreage in other parishes. Even after the export price of sugar declined precipitously in 1925, there was no systematic abandonment of cane cultivation as had been the case in the pre-War years.

In spite of the rejuvenation of the sugar industry in the parishes of St. Catherine, St. Thomas, and St. James after 1920, it is clear from Table 4.6 that in 1930-1934 the proportion of island cane acreage in these three parishes hardly differed from the proportion of 1885-1889. Considering the six major sugar producing parishes as a unit, the structural reorganization of the industry did little to disperse the sugar sub-sector during the period 1885-1934. Indeed, it appears that the cultivation of cane was more concentrated than ever before in these parishes. While these six parishes accounted for nearly 78% of total acreage under cane in 1885-1889, that proportion had increased to 85% in 1930-1934.

The Banana Sub-Sector: During the 1890s the total value of Jamaican staple exports was increasingly determined by the value of banana exports. Accounting for a mere 15% of total staple export value in 1885-1889, bananas surpassed in value the export of sugar and rum in 1895-1899. Except for the war years 1915-1919 and a period of readjustment in the early 1920s, the export of bananas consistently provided more than one-half of staple export earnings between 1905-1909 and 1935-1939.[22]

This meteoric rise in the value of banana export earnings was almost entirely the result of increased output. As seen in Table 4.7 the volume of banana exports during the period 1905-1909 exceeded that of the years 1885-1889 by some 625%. During the period 1910-1919 the volume of banana exports declined as a consequence of adverse weather and severe limitations of shipping during the war. Thereafter, the export of bananas resumed at a high level; in 1935-1939 the volume of banana exports was more than ten times larger than during 1885-1889.

TABLE 4.7

BANANA EXPORTS AND BANANA PRICES, FIVE YEAR PERIODS, JAMAICA, 1885/1889-1940/1944

PERIOD	QUANTITY EXPORTS (000 STEMS)	AVERAGE F.O.B. PRICES (SHILLINGS/STEM)
1885-1889	10,513	1.84
1890-1894	22,372	1.74
1895-1899	31,585	1.35
1900-1904	50,143	1.47
1905-1909	76,259	1.37
1910-1914	71,774	1.76
1915-1919	26,877	1.85
1920-1924	56,135	3.01
1925-1929	93,599	2.19
1930-1934	93,826	1.89
1935-1939	108,568	2.23
1940-1944	15,191	3.41

SOURCES: G. E. Cumper, "Estimates of Jamaican Commodity Trade," _Social and Economic Studies_, Vol. 6, No. 3, pp. 429-430.

G. Eisner, _op. cit._, Table XXII, pp. 242-243.

It appears from Table 4.7 that much of the expansion in the volume of banana exports occurred during periods of stable or even declining f.o.b. prices. This rather unexpected response on the part of producers was partly a consequence of the industry's newness. Relatively high prices were initially necessary to coax producers into the sub-sector. Thereafter, prices might be lowered and yet tolerated by producers since fixed capital costs, which in any case were small, had already been recovered. In short, producers were in a sense locked-in to the production of bananas, which often served as the principal source of cash income to peasants and small farmers who were therefore willing to accept the prevailing prices.

It is also probably true that f.o.b. prices generally understated the actual prices paid to independent producers by exporters. The United Fruit Company was able to cultivate bananas on its own estates for no more than one shilling per bunch. In order to gather sufficient quantities for profitable export however, United Fruit was often obliged to pay independent producers as much as three shillings per bunch.[23] Since no distinction was made between exported bananas on the basis of origin, the declared export value would likely understate producers' prices.

Finally, it is obvious that f.o.b. prices reflect local conditions of demand and supply rather than international market prices. Given a steadily expanding and manipulable demand in North America, exporting companies in Jamaica were able to adjust local prices to serve two ends. In the first place, exporters had to respond to local supply conditions. During periods of restricted local supply, as for example following the hurricanes of 1903 and 1911-1913, exporters were forced to offer higher prices to independent producers and hence the f.o.b. price increased. Conversely, the f.o.b. price tended to fall during periods of heavy local supply.[24] In the second place, local prices were adjusted to facilitate the long term strategy of exporters concerned with maintaining their dominant position in the Jamaica banana industry. Thus producers' prices were occasionally artificially raised in an effort to entice independent producers to break previous contractual agreements with rival exporters. This particular tactic was commonly employed by United Fruit in its efforts to disarm the Jamaica Banana Producers Association after 1927.[25]

This complex relationship between the volume of banana exports and f.o.b. prices emphasizes the need to enquire more closely into the organization of the sub-sector. At the outset it is important to distinguish clearly between the organization of banana cultivation and the organization of the export trade in bananas.

Ever since the banana export trade began in the 1880s, small settlers had been actively involved in the cultivation of the fruit.[26] Unlike the cultivation of sugar cane, coconuts, and certain other staple exports, the cultivation of bananas is admirably suited to the resources and requirements of small settlers. Banana cultivation requires little capital investment apart from access to land. Moreover, bananas do not require as much labour as does the cultivation of cane, and among small settlers practically all necessary labour was available within the immediate family. The cultivation of bananas is compatible with the soil, climate, and terrain of the mountainous regions in which the vast majority of small settlers held land. Further, bananas lend themselves to inter-planting with most domestic crops and thus their cultivation does not necessarily diminish the ability of small settlers to produce subsistence foodstuffs. On the contrary, since bananas could be sold for cash, their cultivation was an important factor ensuring the vitality of small settler agriculture.

In the early years small settlers supplied bananas to exporters on an ad hoc basis. As the North American market for bananas continued to expand and as more regular shipping services were introduced, it was clear that the supply of Jamaican bananas would have to increase and be put on a dependable basis. Thus in the 1890s exporters began to contract for the output of small settlers well in advance of the delivery date. But even this could not consistently provide an adequate volume of bananas for export on schedule.

Consequently the cultivation of bananas on plantations became common after the turn of the century. Once scorned by planters as a "backwood nigger business",[27] the cultivation of bananas was clearly lucrative and hence increasingly acceptable as an occupation of the local oligarchy. As abandoned sugar estates were brought under banana cultivation and new lands planted, a new set of planters emerged as the leaders of the local landed elite. To be sure sugar planters were not without influence; but it was the new banana planters who increasingly exercised decisive power in local affairs.[28]

In addition to these local entrepreneurs, powerful international corporations owned and operated banana plantations after the turn of the century. The most prominent of these was of course the United Fruit

Company. In 1910 United Fruit owned or leased 11% of all acreage under bananas in the island; in 1920, that proportion had increased to 25%; in 1930, United Fruit controlled some 21% of acreage under banana cultivation.[29] Thereafter, the company tended to specialize in the marketing of bananas so that in 1938 a mere 8% of acreage under bananas was controlled by United Fruit. It is hardly surprising that the opinions, representations, and political machinations of United Fruit were accorded respect and careful consideration by the Colonial Office in London.[30]

Plantations appear to have controlled between 60% and 76% of all acreage under banana cultivation in those years for which data are available during the period 1895-1943.[31] No doubt there is considerable inexactness in these estimates, but the overall picture is fairly clear.[32] From an industry in which small settlers had organized production in the 1880s, the production of bananas had increasingly fallen under the control of plantations. During the 1930s it is estimated that small settlers produced somewhat less than 30% of all banana exports.[33]

Whether cultivated by plantations or by small independent producers, bananas were marketed abroad by specialized commercial enterprises. These firms faced three primary tasks: the collection of marketable fruit in Jamaica, the provision of transport from Jamaica to metropolitan markets, and the disposal of Jamaican bananas in the markets of North America and the United Kingdom.

During the earliest years of the Jamaican banana trade, these three problems were handled directly by the independent sea captains who initiated the export of bananas.[34] As the volume of exports grew, it was impossible for any single individual to oversee all aspects of the trade. By the early 1890s a number of firms had been established to organize the marketing of bananas abroad. At the turn of the century, there were no independent banana exporters active in Jamaica.

The tangled tale of intrigue and conspiracy surrounding the formation of the United Fruit Company of Boston in 1899 need not be recounted here.[35] Suffice it to note that at the turn of the century United Fruit had established a virtual monopoly in the expanding North American market for bananas. Shortly thereafter United Fruit acquired indirect control of the British shipping firm of Elders & Fyffes which assured the Boston company a preeminent position in the British banana market. As a consequence of its monopoly position in the two principal markets for Jamaican bananas and through its absolute control of shipping services needed for the export of the island's fruit, the United Fruit Company acted as a monopsonist in the Jamaican market by 1910.

For nearly twenty years thereafter the United Fruit Company combined within one corporate structure the three principal functions of marketing banana exports. Through the operations of estates directly and by purchases of bananas from independent producers, United Fruit was able to export sufficient quantities to maintain its Jamaican operations at a level consistent both with short period profit requirements and long period considerations of market control. Through its monopolistic control of banana carrying ships, United Fruit was assured of reliable transport for its own exports, and was in a position to destroy any potential rival in the Jamaican market. Finally, by directly marketing bananas in both North American and British markets, United Fruit enjoyed an advantage which was painfully apparent to the few independent shippers who occasionally attempted to break into the Jamaican export market.[36]

The entrenched position of United Fruit was viewed by many Jamaicans as both a blessing and a burden. On the one hand, United Fruit's control over foreign markets provided a measure of security to the Jamaican banana industry which was normally assured outlets for its produce. United Fruit was also a major employer of labour in the island and provided probably the most important means by which small settlers were able to earn cash incomes. Given the position of the sugar industry in the early twentieth century, Jamaicans were thus relieved that the banana industry, under the suzerainty of United Fruit, had emerged as an important staple industry.[37]

At the same time, United Fruit was the source of considerable discontent among Jamaicans.[38] This was largely due to United Fruit's policies with respect to the purchase of bananas from independent growers. The volume of such purchases and the prices offered to local producers depended on the output of United Fruit's own plantations and on fundamental decisions regarding Jamaica's share in the metropolitan markets controlled by United Fruit. As both these factors were subject to change from time to time, United Fruit's purchases in the local market were highly variable. Consequently, independent producers could not accurately anticipate either the prices they would receive or the volume which United Fruit might be willing to purchase. Recognizing that such uncertainty was also detrimental to its own operations, United Fruit actively encouraged, often through the most outrageous coercion, long term contracting by small settlers. In exchange for rather lower prices, small settlers were to be guaranteed purchase of "marketable" bananas by United Fruit. Not surprisingly, the final arbiter of marketability was United Fruit itself, a situation which gave rise to frequent discontent on the part of independent producers.[39]

In 1927 a group of Jamaicans formed the Jamaica Banana Producers Association (JBPA) in an effort to mitigate the more objectionable features of marketing as undertaken by United Fruit.[40] With a good deal of initial enthusiasm, the JBPA set out to purchase bananas, to arrange for suitable transport, and to market bananas in the United Kingdom. In these efforts the JBPA enjoyed both moral and financial support from the Governor and the Colonial Office which had grown increasingly wary of the spectacle of an American corporation exerting significant economic control over a British colony.[41]

Operating no plantations of its own, the JBPA sought to purchase bananas from small producers on long term contracts. In an effort to reduce diversion of contracted fruit to other buyers, the JBPA successfully lobbied the colonial government to adopt legislation which made these contracts binding on the land under contract and further placed a criminal penalty on the illegal purchase of contracted fruit.[42] These efforts notwithstanding, the JBPA was plagued by the problem of unfulfilled contracts.

The JBPA showed some success during the first few years of its operation. By 1933 membership stood at some 15,000 and the Association held contracts on some 66,000 acres of land given over to the cultivation of bananas. In that year nearly 27% of banana exports were shipped on behalf of the JBPA.[43] Moreover, producer prices paid by the JBPA were at least equal to and often exceeded those offered by United Fruit. As 99% of JBPA contractees owned less than 50 acres of land, it is probably accurate to observe that "the Association's contracts assured much security to the banana-cultivating peasantry".[44]

The initial success was very short lived. Successive hurricanes and the appearance of botanical diseases greatly reduced output, and the JBPA found it extremely difficult to compete with the producer prices offered by United Fruit. After some hesitation the colonial government advanced additional financial aid to the JBPA in 1935, and in 1936 the Colonial Office dispatched a commission of enquiry to study the banana industry in Jamaica.[45] Under considerable pressure from United Fruit, Elders & Fyffes, and a number of local producers who had grown disenchanted with the JBPA, the commission recommended that the Association be reorganized as a joint stock company bereft of any co-operative pretence.[46] A formal quota system was established whereby the new JBPA was allowed to export 30% of the volume of banana exports; in turn, United Fruit was assured that government would no longer provide financial assistance to the JBPA.

At the end of the 1930s therefore the export of bananas had once more passed into the hands of specialized private enterprise. Co-operative marketing had been abandoned and small producers were once again at the mercy of exporters whose purchasing policies necessarily involved great uncertainty with respect to prices and volumes of sales.

The growth of banana exports and the changing organizational structure of the industry were accompanied by a significant shift in the geographic location of banana cultivation, as may be seen in Table 4.8.

TABLE 4.8

GEOGRAPHIC LOCATION OF THE BANANA INDUSTRY, JAMAICA, 1890-1943.

PARISH	PER CENT OF TOTAL ACREAGE UNDER BANANA CULTIVATION (ANNUAL AVERAGE) 1890-1894	1900-1904	1910-1914	1920-1924	1930-1934	Census of 1943
St. Mary	50.2	45.3	41.2	43.9	31.8	19.4
St. Thomas and Portland	28.0	23.9	20.3	23.0	18.9	24.3
St. Catherine and Clarendon	8.1	20.8	20.7	18.7	26.6	17.2
St. James and Hanover	3.3	3.9	8.5	9.6	12.3	15.7
All Other Parishes Combined	10.3	6.1	9.3	4.8	10.4	23.4
TOTAL	99.9	100.0	100.0	100.0	100.0	100.0

SOURCE: Handbook of Jamaica, Annually, 1880-1943, (Kingston: GPO).

During the earliest years for which data are available (1890-1894), the cultivation of bananas was largely confined to three parishes which together accounted for 78% of all acreage under banana cultivation: St. Mary, Portland, and St. Thomas. Thereafter those parishes declined in relative importance although total acreage under bananas in those parishes continued to increase absolutely until 1915-1919. In the period 1930-1934 these three parishes collectively contained 51% of the total island acreage under banana cultivation. In short, across the whole period 1890-1934, the primary centre of the banana industry was in St. Mary, St. Thomas, and Portland.

During the first decade of the twentieth century, the two southern parishes of St. Catherine and Clarendon emerged as an important secondary centre of banana cultivation. Together these two parishes contained between one-fifth and one-quarter of total island acreage under bananas. A third and much less important region of banana cultivation appeared in the parishes of St. James and Hanover around 1910.

The Minor Staple Sub-Sector: Prior to the turn of the century, approximately one-half of all staple export earnings was derived from the export of so-called minor staples. Although generally declining thereafter, the proportion seldom fell below one-third, and was never less than one-quarter before 1935.[47] In part this decline reflects the substantial growth in the value of banana and sugar exports. After the First World War and particularly during the depression of the 1930s however, minor staples were much less weighty in the export sector. In

1935-1939 the total value of all minor staple exports was only marginally greater than during the years 1895-1899.[48]

In order to appreciate the relative importance of individual commodities within this sub-sector, it is convenient to distinguish three classes of minor staples. Firstly, a certain group of minor staples was largely produced on estates. A second class of minor staples was produced both by plantations and by small settlers. Finally, a few minor staples were exclusively the produce of small settlers.

Included in the first class are logwood, pimento, and coconuts. Production of these staples required either extensive acreage freed from other cultivation (logwood and pimento) or substantial initial capital investment combined with a relatively long period of waiting until economic returns might be expected (coconuts). It is hardly surprising that the production of these commodities was generally undertaken on extensive estates, although small settlers were not unknown to produce small quantities of all three. During the period 1885-1944, these three commodities collectively accounted for 44% to 62% of the total value of all minor staple exports.

Coffee, cocoa, and citrus fruit comprise the second class of minor staple exports. The cultivation of these commodities does not necessarily require either extensive acreage or substantial capital investment. Since a relatively long period of waiting is involved between initial planting and economic production, plantations were in a somewhat better position than were small settlers to undertake the production of these commodities. On the other hand, these crops are admirably suited to mixed farming on small peasant plots. Thus small settler cultivation of citrus, cocoa, and especially coffee was widespread and reasonably profitable across the whole period under study.[49] Taken collectively these three commodities accounted for one-third to one-half of all minor staple export earnings in the period 1885-1944.

Ginger was the only important minor staple export cultivated almost exclusively by small settlers. Enjoying an excellent reputation in foreign markets, Jamaican ginger fetched consistently high prices for peasant producers who interplanted in with domestic foodstuffs.[50] Although ginger accounted for less than 10% of total minor staple export earnings during the period, it nonetheless represented an important source of cash income for peasant producers.

The international marketing of minor staples rested with local entrepreneurs in Kingston and the various port towns of the rural parishes.[51] These exporters faced two principal problems. First, sufficient quantities of a given minor staple had to be purchased and if necessary processed. Second, transport to overseas markets had to be arranged at economic costs and at regular intervals.

The first of these problems was handled in two main ways. Exporters travelled regularly to the major country markets in order to purchase minor staples directly from producers, especially from the small settlers. Alternatively, producers transported minor staples directly to the warehouses of exporters. In either case exporters were uncertain of the quantities which might be offered for sale at any given

TABLE 4.9

VALUE OF MINOR STAPLE EXPORTS BY CLASS, JAMAICA,

FIVE YEAR PERIODS, 1885/1889 - 1940/1944

PERIOD	VALUE OF MINOR STAPLE EXPORTS (£'000)	PERCENTAGE OF TOTAL VALUE OF MINOR STAPLE EXPORTS ARISING FROM: MINOR STAPLES PRODUCED ON ESTATES (LOGWOOD, COCONUTS, PIMENTO)	MINOR STAPLES PRODUCED ON ESTATES AND SMALL FARMS (COFFEE, COCOA, CITRUS)	MINOR STAPLES PRODUCED BY SMALL SETTLERS (GINGER)	ALL MINOR STAPLE EXPORTS
1885-1889	3033	52.0	44.8	3.2	100.1
1890-1894	4341	53.4	42.5	4.2	100.1
1895-1900	3763	44.2	50.0	5.8	100.0
1900-1904	3042	47.2	45.6	7.2	100.0
1905-1909	3097	47.5	46.2	6.3	100.0
1910-1914	4159	53.7	41.1	5.2	100.0
1915-1919	6170	62.3	32.9	4.9	100.1
1920-1924	5229	56.7	34.6	8.7	100.0
1925-1929	6051	48.7	45.6	5.7	100.0
1930-1934	3641	48.6	45.7	5.7	100.0
1935-1939	3823	46.8	45.2	8.0	100.0
1940-1944	3561	49.0	36.1	14.9	100.0

SOURCE: G. E. Cumper, "Estimates of Jamaican Commodity Trade", Social and Economic Studies, Vol. 6, No. 3. (1957), p. 430.

time, and producers were equally unsure of the prices which they could expect to receive.

Once minor staples had been purchased locally, overseas transport had to be arranged. Since most exporters were also engaged in the import business, the natural tendency was to place minor staples on ships which were delivering imported goods. This entailed the warehousing of minor staples until shipping space became available which in any event was always limited. Consequently the shipment of minor staples characterized by low bulk and non-perishability was in general much easier to arrange than was the shipping of minor staples of a bulky nature (e.g., coconuts and logwood), or which were highly perishable (e.g., citrus fruit). Not surprisingly, these latter staples suffered greatly during the war years when shipping services were curtailed.

In spite of these difficulties, Jamaican exporters managed to conduct a brisk trade in minor staples. It was largely through the entrepreneurial talents of these exporters that the minor staple sub-sector provided an important source of money income to producers during the whole period 1890-1940.

As with the cultivation of major staples, the production of various minor staple exports showed considerable geographic specialization. The cultivation of coconuts, for example, was most common in the three parishes of St. Thomas, Portland, and St. Mary which collectively accounted for approximately two-thirds of the total island acreage under coconut cultivation during the whole period.[52] The mountainous regions of St. Ann, St. Catherine, Manchester, Clarendon, St. Thomas, and St. Andrew appear to have been the areas of greatest coffee cultivation. Together these six parishes contained between 83% and 92% of total island coffee acreage during these years.[53]

In the early years of the twentieth century, cocoa cultivation was mostly confined to the parishes of St. Thomas, Portland, and St. Mary. Before the First World War, St. Mary alone contained approximately one-half of the island's total acreage under cocoa production.[54] As the cultivation of bananas spread to the parishes of St. Catherine and Clarendon following the First World War, these two parishes emerged as a major centre for the cultivation of cocoa which was frequently inter-planted with bananas. During the period 1930-1934 some 44% of total island acreage under cocoa cultivation was to be found in St. Catherine and Clarendon.[55]

Between two-thirds and three-fourths of total island acreage under oranges during these years was located in the parishes of St. Catherine, Clarendon, St. Elizabeth, and Manchester.[56] The cultivation of ginger seems to have been concentrated in the parishes of Clarendon, Manchester, and St. Elizabeth which together accounted for at least one-half and as much as three-fourths of total acreage under ginger cultivation.[57] Finally, based on data contained in the 1943 census, it appears that the pimento industry was mainly located in the parishes of Westmoreland, St. Elizabeth, and Manchester which collectively accounted for 51% of all pimento trees in the island; the parishes of St. Ann and Trelawny possessed an additional one-third of the island's pimento trees.[58]

No statistical data are available concerning the geographic location of the logwood industry. It is clear from contemporary accounts, however, that St. Elizabeth was the principal centre of logwood production.[59] The construction of a dyeworks in St. Elizabeth for the processing of logwood, and the regular shipment of logwood from the ports Black River in St. Elizabeth and Sav-la-Mar in Westmoreland lend further support to the view that St. Elizabeth, Westmoreland, and possibly Manchester were the most important centres of logwood production before the First World War.[60]

The geographic distribution of minor staple production has been summarized in Table 4.10. Since this table presents ordinal rankings of the most important parishes producing each minor staple, some caution is required in its use. Nonetheless, it does offer an indication of the manner in which the minor staple export sub-sector was regionally concentrated.

The Domestic Agricultural Sector

The domestic agricultural sector includes the cultivation of a wide variety of foodstuffs and the rearing of livestock exclusively for consumption in the island. As may be seen in Table 4.11, the former activity was far the more important, though the latter emerged as a substantial undertaking around 1930.

It has already been observed that the domestic agricultural sector expanded less rapidly than did the whole economy during the period 1870-1938.[61] There were at least three factors which ensured the declining importance of the sector as a whole, and of ground provisions in particular.

TABLE 4.10

GEOGRAPHIC LOCATION OF MINOR STAPLE EXPORT INDUSTRY, BY CROPS, JAMAICA, 1885-1943

ORDINAL RANKING OF PARISHES ON BASIS OF AVERAGE PER CENTAGE OF TOTAL ISLAND ACREAGE UNDER CULTIVATION OF GIVEN CROP LOCATED IN THE PARISH

ORDINAL RANK	LOGWOOD	PIMENTO	COCONUT	COFFEE	COCOA	ORANGES	GINGER
1	St. Elizabeth	St. Elizabeth	St. Thomas	St. Catherine	St. Mary	St. Catherine	Clarendon
2	Manchester	St. Ann	St. Mary	Manchester	St. Catherine	Manchester	Manchester
3	Westmoreland	Manchester	Portland	Clarendon	Portland	Clarendon	St. Elizabeth
4	---	Trelawny	St. Ann	St. Andrew	St. Thomas	St. Ann	St. Ann
5	---	Westmoreland	Hanover	St. Thomas	St. Ann	Portland	St. Catherine
6	---	St. Mary	Trelawny	St. Ann	St. Andrew	St. Elizabeth	Trelawny

SOURCE: <u>Handbook of Jamaica</u>, Annually, 1880-1943.

In the first place, land used for the cultivation of foodstuffs was generally suited to the cultivation of certain staple exports, especially bananas and some minor staples. Thus during periods of relatively high export prices, land was shifted out of domestic agriculture and into cash crop production.[62] The result was a decline in the rate of growth of output of domestic foodstuffs.

Secondly, in the face of modestly rising levels of per capita real income, consumers tended to favour certain imported commodities rather than domestic foodstuffs. On the one hand, this resulted in a desire for cash incomes on the part of domestic agricultural producers which in turn contributed to a reduction in the rate of growth of output of domestic crops.[63] At the same time, the local demand for domestic foodstuffs failed to expand as rapidly and hence encouraged still further shifting in the output of small settlers.

Thirdly, overall growth of population acted to reduce the availability of land suited to peasant cultivation. As rents and land prices rose, small settlers were increasingly forced to cultivate cash crops at the expense of domestic food.[64]

The actual production of domestic foodstuffs was almost entirely organized by small settlers who owned or rented land. Apart from land, labour was the most important factor input and was usually provided by unpaid family members. Domestic foodstuffs were primarily cultivated for direct consumption by the producing household. Small settlers located near to plantations or towns also sold foodstuffs for cash to landless labourers, but even then only foodstuffs surplus to family requirements were offered for sale.[65]

TABLE 4.11

COMPOSITION OF DOMESTIC AGRICULTURAL OUTPUT, JAMAICA,

SELECTED YEARS, 1870-1938

	ESTIMATED VALUE OF OUTPUT, 1910 PRICES (£'000)				ESTIMATED VALUE OF OUTPUT, 1938 PRICES (£'000)	PERCENTAGE DISTRIBUTION OF OUTPUT BY SUB-SECTION				
SUB-SECTOR	1870	1890	1910	1930	1938	1870	1890	1910	1930	1938
Ground Provisions and Other Food	2157.1	2648.8	3454.9	4125.8	2183	91.2	91.0	90.8	84.4	74.6
Animal Products	208.2	263.5	350.4	759.7	743	8.8	9.0	9.2	15.6	25.4
TOTAL	2365.3	2912.3	3805.3	4885.5	2926	100.0	100.0	100.0	100.0	100.0

SOURCES: G. Eisner, *op. cit.*, p. 119.

P. Deane, *op. cit.*, p. 125.

Livestock was reared on small settler plots and on extensive estates. Fowls, pigs, goats, and an occasional cow were raised by small settlers mainly for direct consumption or for sale in local markets. The grazing of cattle required a great deal of initial investment and extensive acreage, and so was generally confined to specialized estates known locally as "pens". These cattle pens produced virtually all the local beef sold in the markets of Kingston and the larger country towns.[66]

Geographic specialization in the cultivation of domestic foodstuffs does not appear to have been as pronounced as was the cultivation of staple exports. In part this is a consequence of deficiencies in the tax data which do not completely reflect the acreage actually devoted to the cultivation of ground provisions. In part the apparent lack of specialization is the result of the relative ease with which domestic foodstuffs could be cultivated in every parish of the island. Nonetheless, the parishes of St. Ann, Westmoreland, Clarendon, St. Catherine, Manchester, and St. Elizabeth seem to have been important domestic agricultural producers. Across the period 1894-1934, these six parishes accounted for at least half and as much as 60% of the island's total recorded acreage under foodstuff cultivation.[67]

The Non-Agricultural Sector

It will be recalled that between 45% and 53% of real national income was generated by non-agricultural activity during the period 1870-1938.[68] In light of the supposed importance of agriculture, the size of the non-agricultural sector may seem remarkably large. In fact this puzzle is more apparent than real for two reasons.

In the first place, it is necessary to distinguish size from strategic importance in evaluating sectoral contribution to national economic performance. As has been emphasized by others, it is not the direct contribution to national income which characterizes a leading sector, but rather the indirect influence such a sector brings to bear on the overall economy.[69] Operating through a variety of backward, forward, final demand, and fiscal linkages, the agricultural sectors of the Jamaican economy set the pace and determined the level of non-agricultural activity. The impact of the latter sector on agricultural output was virtually non-existent.[70]

Secondly, the estimation of non-agricultural output is necessarily imprecise during the period under study. Unavoidable but contentious assumptions have had to be made in order to compile even the crudest estimates. Eisner, for example, assumes that all persons recorded in the censuses as being artisans or servants were in fact employed at the prevailing wage rates.[71] Thus, if unemployment were high or if actual wages were less than official estimates, then Eisner's estimates will overstate the output of the non-agricultural sector. Similarly, Eisner estimates value added in commercial activity as a fixed proportion of the c.i.f. value of imports, a procedure which is frought with danger during periods of rapid inflation.[72] Value added in the transport sector is estimated by means of reference to very scattered cost data.[73] Finally, an estimate of the imputed value of owner-occupied housing is included in non-agricultural output.[74] On the whole, it is likely that the calculations of non-agricultural output are over estimated during these years.

Nonetheless, Eisner's estimates are the most thorough available and probably are reasonably accurate in tracing changes in the composition of non-agricultural activity over time. Moreover, by disaggregating the non-agricultural sector into a number of sub-sectors, Eisner has provided a useful framework for a discussion of the organizational structure of production within the sector.

It is clear from Table 4.12 that manufacturing was the single largest sub-sector during the period 1870-1930. It must be stressed, however, that manufacturing was not industrial in nature; the value of factory produced manufactured goods never exceeded 30% of total value added in the manufacturing sub-sector.[75] Between two-thirds and three-fourths of manufacturing output appears to have been produced by self-employed craftsmen. "Manufacturing" in Jamaica during these years should more properly be called craft enterprise.

Apart from the imputed value of owner-occupied housing, the service sub-sector was the second largest contributor to non-agricultural output. On the whole the service sub-sector appears to have grown at about the same rate as did total non-agricultural output. Professional services of doctors, lawyers, teachers, and the clergy accounted for approximately one-third of the sub-sector's value added; domestic servants gave rise to the remaining two-thirds. Except for the employment of a few professional and domestic servants by government, it was the private sector which employed servants, who obviously worked on own-account.

The construction industry, which is estimated to have accounted for approximately 10% of non-agricultural output, included residential housing, commercial and industrial building, and public works. Except for short periods following particularly destructive hurricanes or earthquakes, the construction of houses and business establishments was quite stable from year to year. The expenditures for public works depended upon the financial position of the colonial government. Not too surprisingly given the times, government expenditure almost invariably was pro-cyclical: public works spending was always drastically reduced at the first sign of a diminution in the level of government revenues.[76]

The construction sub-sector was organized in two ways. On the one hand, individual craftsmen (e.g., carpenters, bricklayers) organized the construction of private houses and, on occasion, the building of business facilities. On the other hand, larger construction projects such as road building and other public works, were organized by private firms or the colonial government. In this case, labourers were hired and paid on a daily basis; almost invariably the number of labourers seeking such employment far exceeded the number of jobs available.[77]

In Table 4.12, commercial activity refers exclusively to the distribution of imported goods. All marketing activity associated with agriculture, whether domestic or export, has been included under the value added of the relevant agricultural sector. All marketing associated with the sale and distribution of domestically produced non-agricultural goods is ignored altogether on account of an insufficiency of data.

Commercial activity associated with the distribution of imported

TABLE 4.12

COMPOSITION OF NON-AGRICULTURAL OUTPUT, BY SUB-SECTOR

JAMAICA, SELECTED YEARS, 1870-1930

	ESTIMATED VALUE OF OUTPUT, 1910 PRICES (£'000)				PERCENTAGE DISTRIBUTIONOF TOTAL NON-AGRICULTURAL OUTPUT (%)			
SUB-SECTOR	1870	1890	1910	1930	1870	1890	1910	1930
Commerce	247.1	426.5	512.3	672.6	9.1	11.4	10.0	8.6
Manufacturing	775.5	1068.1	1403.3	2147.4	28.6	28.6	27.4	27.5
Transport	28.0	96.0	148.3	323.3	1.0	2.6	2.9	4.1
Construction	246.7	355.4	489.4	798.1	10.9	9.5	9.5	10.2
Services	447.2	576.4	922.8	1329.8	16.5	15.4	18.0	17.1
Public Administration	236.3	321.0	434.5	846.4	8.7	8.6	8.5	10.9
Inputed Value of Home Ownership	681.6	889.7	1215.7	1677.5	25.1	23.8	23.7	21.5
TOTAL NON-AGRICULTURAL SECTOR	2712.4	3733.1	5126.3	7795.1	99.9	99.9	100.0	99.9

SOURCE: G. Eisner, *op. cit.*, p. 119.

goods may be divided into wholesale and retail trading. The wholesale trade was firmly in the hands of a few large, family controlled firms, many of which had connections with enterprises abroad. The retail trade was controlled on the whole by a large number of single family firms operating the ubiquitous shops of the countryside and of urban Jamaica. The wholesale trade employed a moderate number of wage labourers, especially in Kingston; retail merchants almost exclusively relied upon the unpaid labour of family members.

Within the public administration sub-sector are included all those services provided by the colonial government: the civil services, postal and communications services, various irrigation schemes, and the public utilities. Relatively small in its contribution to non-agricultural output, the provision of public services expanded roughly at the same rate as the overall non-agricultural sector before 1920. Thereafter, the sub-sector showed a slight increase as public utilities became more widespread and a reorganization of the medical services was undertaken.

Non-agricultural activity was generally concentrated in the two urban parishes of Kingston and St. Andrew, and to a lesser extent in the principal towns of the rural parishes. Kingston in particular was the site of virtually all manufacturing activity and of a disproportionate share of commercial activity since major wholesalers tended to locate in the capital city which also was the chief port. Although retail commerce, professionals, and domestic servants were to be found in every part of the island, they were clearly concentrated in the towns and especially in Kingston. Construction was similarly centred in the urban parishes, although major public works projects were from time to time undertaken in various country parishes. In short, the non-agricultural sector was for all practical purposes located in the two urban parishes of Kingston and St. Andrew.

PATTERNS OF EMPLOYMENT

Variation in the volume and composition of output naturally involves change in the level and composition of employment. In light of the previous discussion of production, it is to be expected that the patterns of employment underwent change during the period 1884-1943. In the absence of annual data on the level and composition of the employed labour force, it is necessary to rely on the various censuses of population. It is true that these data are sometimes "treacherous and unrewarding"[78] but when treated with caution and generosity, they do provide an insight into the level, distribution, composition, and spatial characteristics of employment in Jamaica during the period under study.

The Level of Employment

The level of employment at various census years is summarized in Table 4.13. Between 1881 and 1921 total employment appears to have grown at roughly the same rate as did total population. Thereafter employment expanded at a much slower rate. In 1943 about 39% of the total population was gainfully occupied as compared with approximately 50% at the time of the earlier censuses.

The inability of the economy to employ an increasingly large labour force after 1921 is also apparent in Table 4.13. Whereas nearly 90% of all Jamaicans aged between 15 and 64 years were employed in the period 1881-1921, that proportion had fallen to 66% in 1943. In part this is a result of an improved system of occupational classification employed in the 1943 census. Nonetheless, there is little doubt that the growth of employment was considerably less than the growth of the labour force after 1921.

TABLE 4.13

LEVEL OF EMPLOYMENT AT EACH CENSUS, JAMAICA, 1881-1943

CENSUS YEAR	TOTAL ISLAND POP-ULATION	NUMBER OF PERSONS OCCUPIED	POPULATION OF WORKING AGE (15-64 YRS)	% TOTAL POP-ULATION OCCUPIED	% WORKING AGE POP-ULATION OCCUPIED
1881	580,804	282,770	325,550	48.7	86.9
1891	639,491	373,521	366,750	58.4	101.9
1911	831,383	410,886	470,580	49.4	87.3
1921	858,118	443,937	488,006	51.7	91.0
1943	1,237,063	484,243	732,675	39.1	66.1

SOURCES: Tables A.1, A.7 in the Appendix and G. W. Roberts, The Population of Jamaica, p. 87.

Occupational Distribution of Employed Labour Force

As may be seen in Table 4.14 a significant shift occurred in the occupational distribution of the employed labour force across the period. Most obvious is the marked decline in the importance of

TABLE 4.14

OCCUPATIONAL DISTRIBUTION OF EMPLOYED LABOUR FORCE, JAMAICA, CENSUS YEARS, 1881-1943

OCCUPATIONS	LEVEL OF EMPLOYMENT (IN THOUSANDS)					PERCENTAGE DISTRIBUTION OF OCCUPIED LABOUR FORCE (%)				
	1881	1891	1911	1921	1943	1881	1891	1911	1921	1943
Agriculture	208.6	271.3	271.5	285.7	228.6	73.8	72.6	66.1	64.4	47.2
Commerce	7.4	10.9	19.8	20.6	52.0	2.6	2.9	4.8	4.6	10.7
Industry and Construction	47.1	57.6	72.4	73.6	123.1	16.7	15.4	17.6	16.6	25.4
Professional Services	4.7	7.0	9.2	11.4	20.0	1.7	1.9	2.2	2.6	4.1
Domestic Services	15.0	26.7	38.0	52.6	60.5	5.3	7.1	9.2	11.8	12.5
TOTAL	282.8	373.5	410.9	443.9	484.2	100.1	99.9	99.9	100.0	99.9

SOURCE: G. W. Roberts, The Population of Jamaica, Table 25, p. 87.

G. Eisner, Jamaica 1830-1930, Table XIX, p. 162.

agriculture as the principal employer of labour. While nearly 74% of all employed persons were to be found in the agricultural sectors in 1881, that proportion had fallen to 47% in 1943. Employment in agriculture was under greatest pressure in the period 1921-1943 during which the absolute number of agricultural labourers declined by 20%.

With the declining importance of agriculture as an employer of labour, non-agricultural activity naturally increased its share of overall employment. Commerce, industry, and construction together increased their share of employment from 19% in 1881 to 36% in 1943. The service sub-sector, which absorbed only 7% of the employed labour force in 1881, accounted for 17% of those occupied in 1943.

The decline in the level of agricultural employment, particularly during the period 1921-1943, was only partly relieved by increased employment in the non-agricultural sub-sectors. Although each of the latter showed significant increase in the absolute number of employees, they could not absorb all those who were released from the agricultural sectors. In short, it was the level of agricultural employment which largely determined the overall level of employment during the period 1881-1943.

Patterns of Agricultural Employment

In view of the critical importance of agriculture in the determination of aggregate employment, it is useful to examine the patterns of agricultural employment across the period. Employment by agricultural sub-sector at various census dates has been summarized in Table 4.15.

Given the official obsession with staple export production, it is

TABLE 4.15

DISTRIBUTION OF EMPLOYED LABOUR FORCE IN AGRICULTURE, BY SUB-SECTOR, JAMAICA, CENSUS YEARS 1881-1943

	LEVEL OF EMPLOYMENT (IN THOUSANDS)					PERCENTAGE DISTRIBUTION OF AGRICULTURAL LABOUR FORCE (%)				
SUB-SECTORS	1881	1891	1911	1921	1943	1881	1891	1911	1921	1943
Sugar	51.4	39.4	30.3	44.8	43.8	24.7	14.5	11.2	15.7	19.2
Bananas	---	6.8	43.2	30.1	31.5	---	2.5	15.9	10.5	13.8
Minor Staples	18.6	10.0	8.6	5.8	5.7	8.9	3.7	3.2	2.0	2.5
STAPLE EXPORTS	70.0	56.2	82.1	80.7	81.0	33.6	20.7	30.3	28.2	35.5
DOMESTIC AGRICULTURE	138.6	215.1	189.4	205.0	147.6	66.4	79.3	69.7	71.8	64.6
TOTAL AGRICULTURE	208.6	271.3	271.5	285.7	228.6	100.0	100.0	100.0	100.0	100.1

SOURCE: Censuses of Jamaica, 1881, 1891, 1911, 1921, 1943.

interesting to observe that between 65% and 79% of all agricultural labourers were employed in the cultivation of domestic crops. Even allowing that many of these labourers were also part-time or seasonal employees within the staple export sector, there is no reason to doubt that domestic agriculture was the principal employer of agricultural labour.

Employment levels within the various staple export sub-sectors followed closely the patterns of output previously described. The level of employment in the sugar sub-sector, for example, declined steadily during the period 1881-1911, and then made a partial recovery as the industry was reorganized and output expanded in the 1920s. Similarly, employment in the banana sub-sector moved sympathetically with output: peaking in 1911, declining slightly in the period 1911-1921, and partially recovering between 1921 and 1943.

The minor staples sub-sector appears to have employed a very small and generally declining proportion of agricultural labourers during the whole period. Since a substantial proportion of minor staples was in fact produced by small settlers, many of whom were probably enumerated under domestic agriculture, it is likely that the data presented in Table 4.15 underestimate the level of employment in the minor staples sub-sector.

Demographic Characteristics of the Work Force

Associated with the shift in the occupational distribution of the employed labour force, there was a marked tendency for employment of males to increase at the expense of female employment. Apart from the

TABLE 4.16

OCCUPATIONAL DISTRIBUTION OF EMPLOYED FEMALE LABOUR FORCE, JAMAICA, CENSUS YEARS, 1891-1943

	LEVEL OF FEMALE EMPLOYMENT (IN THOUSANDS)				FEMALES AS PERCENTAGE OF EMPLOYED LABOUR FORCE (%)			
OCCUPATIONS	1891	1911	1921	1943	1891	1911	1921	1943
Agriculture	133.7	113.1	125.4	45.6	49.3	41.7	43.9	19.9
Commerce	2.8	6.0	7.2	23.6	25.7	30.3	35.0	45.4
Industry and Construction	31.1	36.2	37.3	35.3	54.0	50.0	50.7	28.7
Professional Services	1.1	2.4	4.3	8.2	15.7	26.1	37.7	41.0
Domestic Services	21.4	32.5	45.4	51.2	80.1	85.5	86.3	84.6
All Occupations	190.2	190.3	219.6	163.9	50.9	46.3	49.5	33.8

SOURCE: Computed from G. W. Roberts, *The Population of Jamaica*, Table 25, p. 87.

census of 1921 which came at the end of a decade of sex-selective emigration that favoured female employment in Jamaica, the proportion of females in the employed labour force declined steadily from about one-half in 1891 to approximately one-third in 1943.

It is clear from Table 4.16 that the displacement of female by male labourers was most thoroughgoing in agriculture. Whereas nearly one-half of all agricultural employees were female in 1891, that proportion had declined to approximately one-fifth in 1943. Between 1891 and 1943, in fact, the absolute number of female labourers in agriculture declined by two-thirds, while the absolute number of male agricultural workers increased by one-third. It appears that the overall decline in the total number of agricultural labourers was accompanied by a massive shift in the sex-composition of agricultural workers.

In each of the non-agricultural occupations however, the absolute number of female workers increased between 1891 and 1943. Moreover, the female share of employment in each of these sub-sectors (except in industry and construction) rose significantly during the period. Female labourers were especially prevalent in commerce and in the professions, and in general retained their overwhelming position in domestic services.

As suggested previously, the growth of female employment in the non-agricultural sector only partly offset the reduction in the number of female agricultural labourers. Between the censuses of 1891 and 1911, it is true that the growth of female employment in non-agricultural activity slightly more than balanced the decline of female employment in the agricultural sectors. But in the period 1921-1943 nearly 56,000 female workers who had abandoned (or had been abandoned by) agriculture were unable or unwilling to find employment in the non-agricultural sector of the economy.

Associated with this overall decline in the level of female employment was a steadily declining female labour participation rate in all age groups.[79] By contrast, male labour participation rates appear to have declined among the younger age groups (15-19 years) and among older men (50-65 years). For the age group 20-49 years, the proportion of men actually employed "changed very little over the period 1891-1943".[80]

As might have been expected on the basis of previous discussion, both male and female labour participation rates in the various sectors showed marked shifts during the period. The most obvious was the shift out of agriculture by young men and by women of all ages, especially after 1921.[81] These young men appear to have been mainly attracted to commerce, industry, and construction; women sought employment primarily in commerce and domestic service.

Geographic Distribution of Employment

Allowing for differences in the size of parish working age populations, there appear to have been only minor variations in the overall level of employment across the parishes at any given census date. In general, the greater the working age population of a parish, the greater was the level of employment recorded in the census for that parish. Thus on the basis of parish labour force participation rates, it is impossible to

TABLE 4.17

PERCENTAGE OF NON-AGRICULTURAL EMPLOYEES RESIDENT IN KINGSTON AND ST. ANDREW PARISHES, JAMAICA, CENSUS YEARS, 1881-1943

CENSUS YEAR	COMMERCE	INDUSTRY AND CONSTRUCTION	PROFESSIONAL	DOMESTICE SERVICE	TOTAL NON-AGRICULTURAL
1881	33.4	23.6	44.2	25.4	26.2
1891	37.0	26.2	47.3	25.7	28.7
1911	40.0	30.0	46.5	29.8	32.5
1921	46.2	30.3	44.2	27.3	32.4
1943	49.0	30.9	51.3	36.6	37.5

SOURCE: *Censuses of Jamaica, 1881*, *1891*, *1911*, *1921*, *1943* (Kingston: GPO).

discern any geographic concentration in the total level of employment.

With respect to occupational status of the labour force, geographic concentration is apparent in the non-agricultural sector. As anticipated, non-agricultural employment was centred in the two urban parishes of Kingston and St. Andrew. Of all non-agricultural employees, those resident in these two parishes increased from 26% in 1881 to nearly 38% in 1943.[82] As may be seen in Table 4.17, employment in commerce and the service sectors appears to have been particularly concentrated in these parishes.

At the same time there is no obvious geographic concentration in so far as total agricultural employment is concerned. Excepting the two urban parishes, overall agricultural employment in the parishes at any given census date was roughly proportional to the size of parish working age population. Put slightly differently, the proportion of working age population enumerated as being employed in agriculture was nearly equal among all rural parishes at any given census date.

It does seem likely, however, that employment in the various agricultural sub-sectors was geographically concentrated. Direct statistical evidence of such concentration is impossible to obtain since the census data cannot be disaggregated with respect to employment by crop at the parish level. Nonetheless, it is obvious that the production of sugar requires sugar workers, the production of bananas requires banana workers, and so on for each particular crop. Given the marked geographic concentration of staple export production, it is therefore reasonable to suppose that employment connected with the cultivation of particular staples was also concentrated in the same parishes. Since the cultivation of domestic agricultural commodities was much less geographically concentrated, it is likely that employment in this sub-sector was correspondingly less concentrated.

PATTERNS OF INCOME DISTRIBUTION

During the years under study, comprehensive estimates of the factoral distribution of income are available for only two years, 1890 and 1930.[83] Based on crude averages with respect to wage rates, rents, and profits, these estimates no doubt embody considerable margins of error. Viewed with caution however, the data presented in Table 4.18 indicate the broad pattern of income distribution in 1890 and 1930.

It can be assumed that profits accruing to small settlers, professionals, and independent labourers (i.e., craftsmen) were in fact wages and salaries. On this basis it would appear that the factoral shares of income were roughly the same for 1930 as for 1890. Deane's estimate for 1938 shows almost identical results in that approximately four-fifths of the Net Taxable Output went to wages and salaries.[84]

Within the agricultural sectors it is possible to make crude estimates of the factoral distribution of income on estates producing sugar and rum, and on those producing bananas. Based on scattered data of costs per acre under cultivation, these estimates are necessarily crude and must be used with considerable caution. They are nonetheless indicative of important differences between the plantation production of sugar as opposed to bananas.

TABLE 4.18

FACTORAL DISTRIBUTION OF INCOME,

JAMAICA, 1890 AND 1930

FACTOR GROUPS	AGGREGATE CURRENT INCOME (£,000)		PERCENTAGE DISTRIBUTION OF AGGREGATE CURRENT INCOME (%)	
	1890	1930	1890	1930
Agricultural Labour	760.8	1861.7	8.7	9.3
Other Wages & Salaries	1708.9	4788.5	19.5	24.0
Sub-Total:	2469.7	6650.2	28.2	33.3
Small Settlers' Profits	3187.6	6945.2	36.4	34.8
Professional Profits	167.2	335.7	1.9	1.7
Independent Workers' Profits	982.7	1740.7	11.2	8.7
Sub-Total:	4337.5	9021.6	49.5	45.2
Planters' Profits	682.5	1331.7	7.8	6.7
Merchants' Profits	1256.9	2948.1	14.4	14.8
Sub-Total:	1939.4	4279.8	22.2	21.5
GRAND TOTAL	8746.6	19951.6	99.9	100.0

SOURCE: G. Eisner, Jamaica, 1830-1930, Table 8.IV, p. 121.

As seen in Table 4.19, labour's share of income appears to have been substantially higher on sugar than on banana estates. Since actual wage rates were nearly equal in the two sub-sectors, it may be concluded that the cultivation of cane was markedly more labour intensive than was the cultivation of bananas.[85] It is interesting to note that the share of income distributed as profits is much higher on estates producing bananas or sugar than in the economy as a whole. Indeed profits appear to be more than twice as great a share of income on estates producing major staple exports.[86] Such is of course what would be expected for plantation economies in general.

Table 4.19 further shows that, with respect to the estate production of bananas and of sugar, the factoral distribution of income was virtually the same in 1890 and 1930. It is not known with certainty that this pattern of distribution characterized estate production in the intervening years, but there is no evidence to suggest otherwise.

The organization of agricultural production by small settlers gave rise to a quite different pattern of income distribution. In so far as small settlers relied almost exclusively on the unpaid labour of family members and owned the land under cultivation, the producing household retained both labour and ownership shares of income. In a sense there was no factoral distribution of income arising out of small settler production: household income was simply consumed or otherwise distributed among family members according to non-economic criteria.

Within the non-agricultural sector, it is unlikely that the factoral distribution of income altered substantially during the period 1890 to 1930. Wage rates appear to have remained stable across those years and there were no significant changes in the techniques of production.[87]

TABLE 4.19

DISTRIBUTION OF INCOME ON SUGAR ESTATES AND BANANA ESTATES, JAMAICA, 1890 and 1930

FACTOR GROUPS	AGGREGATE CURRENT INCOME (£'000)				PERCENTAGE DISTRIBUTION OF ESTATE INCOMES (%)			
	SUGAR ESTATES		BANANA ESTATES		SUGAR ESTATES		BANANA ESTATES	
	1890	1930	1890	1930	1890	1930	1890	1930
Wage Labour	270.4	353.6	61.9	522.6	47.4	48.1	29.4	37.2
Salaried Labour	44.2	63.9	24.4	140.4	7.8	8.7	11.6	10.0
Other Factor Payments	78.7)	318.1	25.4)	741.4	13.8)	43.2	12.1)	52.8
Gross Profits	176.7)		99.0)		31.0)		47.0)	
TOTAL	570.0	735.6	210.7	1404.4	100.0	100.0	100.0	100.0

NOTE: All cultivations in excess of twenty acres are included as estates. "Other factor payments" includes estimates of wharfage charges, and purchased inputs such as fuel, seed and the like. "Gross profits" includes depreciation.

SOURCE: G. Eisner, Jamaica, 1830-1930, pp. 80-81, 110-112, 205-207.

Estimation of the size distribution of income is extremely difficult for the period under study. The only reliable data in this respect are for the year 1935.[88] In that year, according to a special report of the Nutrition Committee of the colonial government, slightly more than 200,000 individuals and companies paid income tax; that is, approximately 20% of the total population earned incomes sufficiently large to be subject to income taxation. Some 92% of these returns reported incomes less than £65. Since an income of £2 per week was considered a sign of distressed circumstances in 1939,[89] it must be concluded that the vast majority of Jamaicans were earning near-subsistence incomes. On the other hand, nearly 39% of total taxed income in 1935 accrued to persons or companies reporting more than £200 income; altogether this group represented approximately 3% of all taxpayers. It is beyond dispute that the size distribution of taxed income in 1935 was extremely skewed. There is little reason to suppose that this pattern was unusual across the period 1880-1938.

SUMMARY COMMENTS ON JAMAICAN ECONOMIC STRUCTURE, 1880-1938

This description of Jamaican economic structure has proceeded along two lines. On the one hand, it has stressed the relative economic performance of various sectors of the national economy. Particular attention was paid to the impact of individual sectors upon the levels of output, income, and employment. As each of these sectors became more or less expansive across the period under study, so they affected the overall performance of the economy.

At the same time, care has been taken to describe the geographic distribution of economic activity within Jamaica. We have attempted to show that activity within individual sub-sectors of the economy was concentrated in relatively few parishes. This is most obviously the case for the non-agricultural sub-sectors, but we have also seen that certain agricultural activity was highly concentrated geographically.

We have thus laid the basis for a classification of individual parishes according to the nature of economic activity prevailing within the parish at any given point in time. In so far as economic structure is associated with social organization, we are able to define operationally the concept of parish socio-economic structure, which is of such importance to the model developed in Chapter III. Before turning to the operational definition of parish socio-economic structure, it is useful to review the patterns of demogrpahic performance in Jamaica during the time period under study.

ENDNOTES TO CHAPTER IV

[1] G. Eisner, *Jamaica, 1830-1930*. (Manchester: 1961).

[2] P. Deane, *The Measurement of Colonial National Income: An Experiment*. (Cambridge: 1948), pp. 95-141.

[3] Lord Olivier, *Jamaica: The Blessed Island*. (London: 1936); W. M. Macmillan, *Warning from the West Indies*. (London: 1936); Evidence collected by the West India Royal Commission of 1938-1939, in C.O. 950.

[4] P. Deane, *op. cit.*, Table 96, p. 125.

[5] Estimates for 1938 suggest that non-agricultural output accounted for some 53% of Net Taxable Output. See, P. Deane, op. cit., Table 96, p. 125.

[6] P. Deane, op. cit., Table 101, p. 138.

[7] Minor staple commodities include pimento, ginger, coffee, cocoa, logwood, coconuts, and citrus fruits.

[8] See, for example, Sir David Barbour, Report on the Finances of Jamaica. (H.M.S.O.: 1899); E. F. L. Wood, Report on a Visit to the West Indies and British Guiana. (H.M.S.O.: 1922).

[9] R. A. Lobdell, "Patterns of Investment and Sources of Credit in the British West Indian Sugar Industry, 1838-97", Journal of Caribbean History, Vol. 4 (May 1972), pp. 31-53.

[10] G. Eisner, op. cit., pp. 298-300; Lord Olivier, op. cit., pp. 294-295; Annual Report of the Governor of Jamaica, 1917-18. (H.M.S.O.: Cmd. 1-3, 1919).

[11] G. Eisner, op. cit., pp. 250-251; Swettenham to Elgin, Dispatch of October 5, 1906, in C.O. 137/652; Swettenham to Elgin, Dispatch of February 23, 1907, in C.O. 137/656; Olivier to Elgin, Dispatch of July 4, 1907, in C.O. 137/658.

[12] Manning to Long, Dispatch of April 28, 1917, in C.O. 137/721; Annual Report of the Governor of Jamaica, 1918-19. (H.M.S.O.: Cmd. 508-8, 1920).

[13] G. Eisner, op. cit., pp. 206-209; Jelf to Passfield, Dispatch of October 5, 1930, in C.O. 137/791.

[14] Handbook of Jamaica. (Kingston: Annually, 1880-1938); G. Eisner, op. cit., pp. 202-204.

[15] Handbook of Jamaica. (Kingston: Annually 1880-1938).

[16] G. Eisner, op. cit., pp. 208-209; G. E. Cumper, "Labour Demand and Supply in the Jamaican Sugar Industry, 1830-1950", Social and Economic Studies, Vol. 2, No. 4 (December 1954), pp. 37-86.

[17] Handbook of Jamaica. (Kingston: Annually, 1880-1938); G. Eisner, op. cit., pp. 215, 226.

[18] G. E. Cumper, supra.

[19] Ibid., p. 78.

[20] Handbook of Jamaica. (Kingston: Annually 1880-1938).

[21] G. E. Cumper, *supra*; G. L. Beckford, *Persistent Poverty*. (Oxford: 1972), pp. 22-29.

[22] See Table 4.4 above.

[23] A. Hart, "The Banana in Jamaica: Export Trade", *Social and Economic Studies*, Vol. 3, No. 2 (1954), pp. 212-229.

[24] *Ibid.*

[25] Lord Olivier, *op.cit.*, pp. 377-398.

[26] The following discussion draws heavily upon: Lord Olivier, *op. cit.*, pp. 377-398; A. Hart, *op. cit.*; D. G. Hall, *Ideas and Illustrations in Economic History*. (New York: 1954), especially pp. 56-84.

[27] Lord Olivier, *op. cit.*, p. 379.

[28] A. Hart, *op. cit.*, pp. 216-217. The annual *Handbook of Jamaica* lists banana plantations by size and owner. A cursory glance through these lists reveals names hitherto unknown as part of the plantocracy: e.g., Pringle, Da Costa, Lindo, Cargill. It is not coincidental that as the banana industry expanded, these families grew increasingly influential in the nation's affairs. See, J. Carnegie, *Some Aspects of Jamaica's Politics, 1918-1938*. (Kingston: 1973), especially pp. 40-62, 96-127.

[29] *Handbook of Jamaica*. (Kingston: Annually 1880-1938).

[30] Wilson to Amery, Confidential Dispatch of May 29, 1935, in C.O. 137/777; File of Correspondence between the United Fruit Company, Elders & Fyffes, and the West India Committee, in C.O. 137/783; Stubbs to West India Department, Private Letter of September 14, 1930, in C.O. 137/790; Slater to Beckett, Private Letter of September 11, 1933, in C.O. 137/798; Minute by Mr. Emmens on Wilson to Clauson, Personal Letter of December 24, 1934, in C.O. 137/801.

[31] *Handbook of Jamaica*. (Kingston: Annually 1895-1934).

[32] A. Hart, *op. cit.*, pp. 213-214.

[33] G. Eisner, *op. cit.*, p. 234.

[34] D. G. Hall, *op. cit.*, pp. 62-63.

[35] Lord Olivier, *op. cit.*, pp. 377-398; D. G. Hall, *op. cit.*; A. Hart, *op. cit.*

[36] Lord Olivier, *op. cit.*; D. G. Hall, *op. cit.*

[37] E. F. L. Wood, Report...on a Visit to the West Indies and British Guiana, (London: 1922), pp. 40-42; Report of the West India Royal Commission, pp. 18-22, 263-265.

[38] Lord Olivier, op. cit., pp. 377-398; Memorandum of the West India Department, in C.O. 137/790; Stubbs to Cunliffe-Lister, Private Letter of February 7, 1932, in C.O. 137/795.

[39] A. Hart, op. cit.; D. G. Hall, op. cit.

[40] Among the more enthusiastic supporters of the JBPA was Lord Olivier; See, Lord Olivier, op. cit., pp. 390-398.

[41] Minute by Darnley on Manning to Law, Dispatch of August 10, 1916, in C.O. 137/716; Minute by Grindle, July 16, 1929, in C.O. 137/786; Minute by West India Department on File of Newspaper Clippings, in C.O. 137/795; Minute by Emmens on Slater to Beckett, Dispatch of September 11, 1933, in C.O. 137/798.

[42] Lord Olivier, op. cit., pp. 382-385; A. Hart, op. cit.

[43] A. Hart, op. cit., p. 221.

[44] Ibid.

[45] This commission was agreed to only after much debate within the West India Department. See, C.O. 137/805.

[46] A. Hart, op. cit., p. 222.

[47] See Table 4.4 above.

[48] G. E. Cumper, "Estimates of Jamaican Commodity Trade", Social and Economic Studies, Vol. 6, No. 3 (September 1957), pp. 425-430.

[49] Lord Olivier, op. cit., pp. 196, 209, 223-226; G. Eisner, op. cit., pp. 233-235.

[50] Lord Olivier, op. cit., p. 196.

[51] S. W. Mintz and D. G. Hall, "The Origins of the Jamaican Internal Marketing System," Yale University Publications in Anthropology, Vol. 57 (1960), pp. 3-26.

[52] Handbook of Jamaica. (Kingston: Annually 1880-1938).

[53] Ibid.

[54] Ibid.

[55] Ibid.

[56] Ibid.

[57] Ibid.

[58] The Handbooks do not report acreage under pimento or the number of pimento trees by parish. At the time of the 1943 census, however, such estimates were made. See, Census of Population (Kingston: 1943).

[59] Lord Olivier, op. cit., p. 292; Evidence of the Jamaica Imperial Association, West India Royal Commission of 1938-1939, in C.O. 950/926, especially p. 15.

[60] Jamaica Times, February 12, 1916; The Daily Gleaner, March 22, 1916; Jamaica Times, March 25, 1916.

[61] See Table 4.3 above.

[62] Report of the West India Royal Commission, pp. 43-45.

[63] G. Eisner, op. cit., pp. 233-235.

[64] See the evidence of W. Arthur Lewis to the West India Royal Commission, in C.O. 950/56.

[65] See the evidence of the Jamaica Imperial Association to the West India Royal Commission, in C.O. 905/926, p. 21.

[66] G. Eisner, op. cit., pp. 199-200, 305.

[67] Handbook of Jamaica. (Kingston: Annually 1880-1938).

[68] See Table 4.3 above.

[69] See, for example: M. Watkins, "A Staple Theory of Economic Growth", Canadian Journal of Economics and Political Science, Vol. XXIX (May 1963), pp. 141-158; D. C. North, The Economic Growth of the United States, 1790-1860. (New York: 1961), especially Chapter 1; J. Levin, The Export Economies. (Cambridge, Mass.: 1968).

[70] G. Beckford, op. cit., pp. 45-47, 198-223; L. Best, "Outlines of a Model of Pure Plantation Economy", Social and Economic Studies, Vol. 17, No.3 (September 1968).

[71] G. Eisner, op. cit., pp. 172-176.

[72] Ibid., pp. 18-19.

[73] Ibid., pp. 177-181.

[74] *Ibid.*, pp. 344-345.

[75] *Ibid.*, pp. 175-176.

[76] Lord Olivier, *op. cit.*, pp. 399-413; *Correspondence Relating to the Public Finances and Resources of the Island of Jamaica.* (H.M.S.O.: 1899); *Annual Report of the Governor of Jamaica, 1912-13.* (H.M.S.O.: Cd. 7050-24, 1914); *Annual Report of the Governor of Jamaica, 1916-17.* (H.M.S.O.: Cd. 8434-30, 1918); Slater to Cunliffe-Lister, Confidential Dispatch of January 1, 1934, in C.O. 137/801.

[77] G. Eisner, *op. cit.*, pp. 172-176; Lord Olivier, *op. cit.*, pp. 251, 402-406. See also the newspaper accounts of a minor riot resulting from the inability of public service construction to provide employment for all applicants in June, 1924; *The Daily Gleaner*, June 10, 1924; *Jamaica Times*, June 14 and 21, 1924.

[78] G. W. Roberts, *The Population of Jamaica.* (Cambridge: 1957), p. 85.

[79] *Ibid.*, pp. 95-96.

[80] *Ibid.*, p. 93.

[81] *Ibid.*, pp. 97-98.

[82] In 1881 these two parishes accounted for approximately 13% of the island's working age population; that portion had increased to 22% in 1943. In 1881 these two parishes together accounted for 13% of the island's total population; by 1943 that proportion had increased to slightly more than 19%. See, *Appendix*.

[83] G. Eisner, *op. cit.*, pp. 70-86, 98-116.

[84] P. Deane, *op. cit.*, Table 96, p. 125.

[85] Contemporary observers certainly held this view. See, for example: Lord Olivier, *op. cit.*, pp. 290-307; E. F. L. Wood, *op. cit.*, p. 49; *Report of the West Indian Sugar Commission.* (H.M.S.O.: 1930), pp. 112-120; *Report of the West India Royal Commission of 1938-39*, p. 27; R. L. Engledow, *Report on Agriculture.* (H.M.S.O.: 1945), pp. 28-29.

[86] Compare Table 4.19 and Table 4.18.

[87] G. Eisner, *op. cit.*, Appendix III, pp. 378-380.

[88] *Report of the Nutrition Committee.* (Kingston: 1937).

[89] *Report of the Cost of Living Survey.* (Kingston: 1940).

Chapter V

PATTERNS OF DEMOGRAPHIC PERFORMANCE, 1880-1943

This chapter describes the principal features of demographic performance experienced in Jamaica during the period 1880-1943. In keeping with the spirit of the model set out in Chapter III, special care has been taken to examine demographic performance at the parish level. By so doing we are better able to appreciate the regional nature of demographic performance and to generate statistical data useful in the testing of the economic-demographic relations derived in Chapter III.

It has been useful to divide this chapter into four main sections. The first examines the patterns of overall population growth during the period. Changing patterns of fertility, mortality, and hence of natural increase are described in part two of this chapter. The third section traces the patterns of migration which occurred in the period. Some ancillary aspects of Jamaican demography are briefly discussed in the fourth section.

PATTERNS OF OVERALL POPULATION GROWTH

The pattern of overall population growth is most easily discerned by examining the size of the island's population at successive census dates. Table 5.1 summarizes these data and shows the annual compound rate of growth for each intercensal period. Although the present study primarily focuses on the period 1881-1943, data for other periods are included for comparative purposes.

TABLE 5.1

CENSUS POPULATION AND ANNUAL COMPOUND RATES OF POPULATION GROWTH FOR INTERCENSAL PERIODS, JAMAICA, 1861-1970

CENSUS YEAR	TOTAL POPULATION AT CENSUS	ANNUAL COMPOUND RATES OF POPULATION GROWTH OF INTERCENSAL PERIODS, (%)
1861	441,264	
		1.38
1871	506,154	
		1.39
1881	580,804	
		0.97
1891	639,491	
		1.32
1911	831,383	
		0.32
1921	858,118	
		1.68
1943	1,237,063	
		1.56
1960	1,609,800	
		1.46
1970	1,861,400	

SOURCE: Table A.1, Appendix, and Census Research Programme, University of the West Indies.

During the sixty-two years separating the census of 1881 and the census of 1943, the population of Jamaica increased by 113%. It is quite clear however that population increased in rather erratic fashion during those years. Relatively low rates of intercensal population growth in 1881-1891 and 1911-1921 were followed by relatively high growth rates in 1891-1911 and 1921-1943 respectively.

This uneven pattern is also to be observed in the intercensal growth rates for individual parish populations. With the exception of Kingston, all parishes recorded relatively low rates of population growth during the two intercensal periods 1881-1891 and 1911-1921.[1] Indeed certain parishes recorded absolute decline in total population in one or both of these intercensal periods. Conversely, most of the fourteen parishes showed rapid rates of population growth in the period 1921-1943. In short, intercensal rates of population growth at the individual parish level appear to have fluctuated in a pattern analogous to that seen at the national level.

It is interesting to note that the extent of the fluctuations in, and the absolute levels of, intercensal population growth rates are quite diverse among individual parishes. This may be seen by comparing parish growth rates to the rate of growth of the island's population. Certain parishes consistently experienced rates of population growth in excess of national rates: e.g., Clarendon, Kingston, St. Andrew. Other parishes generally exhibited relatively low rates of intercensal population growth: e.g., Hanover, Trelawny. Perhaps of even greater interest, a few parishes (e.g., St. Mary, Portland) experienced much wider fluctuations in intercensal rates of population growth than did the nation as a whole.[2]

While the size of populations at various census dates provides a broad understanding of demographic performance, these data cannot reveal directly the sources of that growth. It is to that end that we turn attention to the patterns of natural increase during that period.

PATTERNS OF NATURAL INCREASE

The mandatory civil registration of births and deaths began in 1878 and appears to have been fairly comprehensive by 1881. Certainly there is no reason to suspect the basic validity of these data after 1891.[3] Thus, beginning in 1891 we have available annual statistics on registered births and registered deaths in each of the fourteen parishes of the island.[4] These data allow a detailed description of the patterns of natural increase and of its determinants, fertility and mortality.

Except for a few years centred on each census data, it has been necessary to employ crude birth rates and crude death rates as measures of fertility and mortality performance during the period 1891-1938. Official estimates of these crude rates are reported in the Annual Reports of the Registrar-General. Unfortunately, these estimates are inaccurate and generally unsuitable.[5] It has thus been necessary to revise the annual vital rates for each parish and for the island as a whole.[6] These revised rates are employed hereafter.

Patterns of Fertility

National fertility performance, as measured by the national crude birth rate, was highly variable during the period 1891-1943, ranging from a high of 44 per thousand in 1900 to a low of 31.5 per thousand in 1937.[7] Indeed the crude birth rate fluctuates so widely that it is difficult to perceive any obvious trend in fertility performance over time. Averaging these rates over five year periods however, provides a more comprehensive pattern of fertility performance as shown in Table 5.2.

TABLE 5.2

AVERAGE ANNUAL CRUDE BIRTH RATES, JAMAICA, FIVE YEAR PERIODS, 1891-1938

PERIOD	AVERAGE CRUDE BIRTH RATE, (PER 1000 POPULATION)	PERIOD	AVERAGE CRUDE BIRTH RATE, (PER 1000 POPULATION
1891/2-1895/6	38.9	1916-1920	36.7
1896/7-1900/01	40.0	1921-1925	36.3
1901/02-1905/06	40.9	1926-1930	36.0
1906/07-1910/11	39.0	1931-1935	33.8
1911/12-1915/16	38.5	1934-1938	32.8

SOURCE: Table A.2, in Appendix.

NOTE: In order to allow the computation of five year averages, the two periods 1931-1935 and 1934-1938 overlap.

Between 1891 and 1938 the national crude birth rate declined by approximately 18%. It is important to note that this decline was not spread evenly across the whole period. Between 1891-1895 and 1901-1905 the national crude birth rate actually increased. Thereafter it steadily declined, turned sharply downward during the war years, and was further depressed after 1930. In general, individual parish crude birth rates exhibit time trends very similar to those shown in Table 5.2.[8] Only the parishes of Kingston and St. James show any tendency for the crude birth rate to increase during the period 1891-1938. All other parishes experienced slightly increasing crude birth rates up to 1905, and thereafter exhibited steadily declining rates, especially after 1915.

Not unexpectedly, there is considerable diversity in the level of crude birth rates among the several parishes. Throughout the period 1891-1938 relatively high crude birth rates were consistently reported in the parishes of St. Ann, Clarendon, St. Elizabeth, and Hanover. Following the general decline in crude birth rates after the war, the parishes of St. James, Trelawny, and Westmoreland also experienced relatively high crude birth rates. On the other hand, the eastern parishes of Kingston, St. Andrew, and St. Mary regularly recorded crude birth rates far below the national average during the whole period 1891-1938.[9]

Crude birth rates are useful in describing the general pattern of fertility performance, but they are not accurate measures of fertility since neither the age- nor sex-composition of the relevant population is taken into account. It is thus uncertain to what extent inter-parish and inter-temporal comparisons of crude birth rates adequately reflect differences in fertility performance. Since the age- and sex-composition of each parish's population are known with accuracy only for the census years, a more refined measure of fertility is restricted to those years.

George Roberts has estimated joint gross reproduction rates for each parish during the five year period centred on each census date.[10] The patterns exhibited in Roberts' data are quite similar to those revealed in the parish crude birth rate data. Thus in the earlier intercensal periods, joint gross reproduction rates increased for nearly every parish, but after 1921 there was a uniform and significant decline in these rates. By 1943 all parishes except two exhibited substantially lower joint gross reproduction rates than they had in 1881.

As measured by these reproduction rates, the fertility performance of individual parishes was quite variable.[11] Consistently high levels of fertility were recorded in St. Ann, St. Elizabeth, Manchester, Clarendon, and Hanover. Fertility appears to have been quite low in the parishes of Kingston, St. Andrew, St. James, and St. Thomas. In short, while minor differences result from the use of joint gross reproduction rates as opposed to crude birth rates, the general pattern of fertility performance among the parishes remains essentially the same.

By way of summary, both national and individual parish fertility rates, whether measured by crude birth rates or by joint gross reproduction rates, in general declined during the period 1881-1943. This decline was most significant in the years following the First World War. While the time path of fertility performance was quite similar among the individual parishes, the level of fertility showed considerable diversity from parish to parish.

Patterns of Mortality

As indicated in Chapter III, it is useful to distinguish two measures of mortality performance: infant mortality and general mortality. The latter, of course, encompasses the former and hence the two are not independent. In so far as infant mortality is generally accepted as a more sensitive indicator of overall socio-economic well-being, it is worthwhile to enquire into the patterns of both measures of mortality.

Apart from relatively short periods of high infant mortality following earthquake (1907), influenza (1917-1918), and hurricane (1921), national rates of infant mortality were fairly stable from year to year.[12] During the late 1920s however infant mortality markedly improved as more comprehensive public health services came into operation.[13] Not unexpectedly, a similar pattern of general mortality performance, as measured by national crude death rates, is apparent during the period 1891-1938.[14] These patterns have been summarized in Table 5.3.

Within individual parishes, similar patterns of infant mortality rates and crude death rates over time are to be observed. Wide swings in these parish rates from time to time were largely the consequence of natural calamity or epidemic disease. Abstracting from these untoward circumstances, there appears to have been little change in the level of parish infant mortality or parish crude death rates before the mid-1920s. Thereafter, both rates declined dramatically in every parish.

As in the case of fertility, the absolute values of crude death rates and of infant mortality rates showed considerable variation from

TABLE 5.3

AVERAGE ANNUAL MORTALITY RATES, JAMAICA,

FIVE YEAR PERIODS, 1891-1938

PERIOD	AVERAGE CRUDE DEATH RATE (PER 1000 POPULATION)	AVERAGE INFANT MORTALITY RATE (PER 1000 LIVE BIRTHS)
1891/92-1895/96	22.2	171.1
1896/97-1900/01	22.8	174.8
1901/02-1905/06	23.7	174.1
1906/07-1910/11	25.4	193.2
1911/12-1915/16	23.1	179.3
1916-1920	27.2	174.2
1921-1925	23.4	176.3
1926-1930	19.4	160.0
1931-1935	18.5	142.8
1934-1938	17.1	129.5

NOTE: In order to allow the computation of five year averages, the two periods 1931-1935 and 1934-1938 overlap.

SOURCE: Tables A.3 and A.4 in Appendix.

parish to parish. Those reporting crude death rates consistently lower than the national rate include St. Ann, St. Elizabeth, Manchester, and Westmoreland. It is hardly surprising that the highest crude death rates were recorded in the urban parishes of Kingston and St. Andrew. Relatively high crude death rates were also recorded in the parishes of Hanover, Trelawny, and St. Thomas. With respect to infant mortality rates, an almost identical pattern across parishes is clear.

Patterns of Natural Increase

Patterns of natural increase are necessarily determined by the patterns of fertility and mortality.[15] For the island as a whole, the changing patterns of the rate of natural increase may be seen in Table 5.4.

During the period 1891-1906, the national rate of natural increase was relatively high and stable as a consequence of high rates of fertility and more or less stable rates of mortality. As mortality increased and fertility declined during the period 1907-1925, the rate of natural increase necessarily declined and was rather volatile, as a consequence of variation from year to year in the level of mortality. Sustained decline in mortality in the late 1920s resulted in an increase in the rate of natural increase, though generally declining fertility in those years depressed the rate of natural increase below pre-1906 levels.

TABLE 5.4

AVERAGE ANNUAL RATES OF NATURAL INCREASE

JAMAICA, FIVE YEAR PERIODS, 1891-1938

PERIOD	AVERAGE RATE OF NATURAL INCREASE (PER 1000 POPULATION)
1891/92 - 1895/96	16.8
1896/97 - 1900/01	17.3
1901/01 - 1905/06	17.2
1906/07 - 1910/11	13.6
1911/12 - 1915/16	15.4
1916 - 1920	9.5
1921 - 1925	12.9
1926 - 1930	16.7
1931 - 1935	15.3
1934 - 1938	15.7

NOTE: In order to allow the computation of five year averages, the two periods 1931-1935 and 1934-1938 overlap.

SOURCE: Table A.5, Appendix.

Rates of natural increase for individual parishes exhibit time trends similar to those shown in Table 5.4. For most parishes the rate of natural increase was relatively high in the period 1891-1906, declined sharply during the years 1907-1925, and recovered during the years following 1925.[16]

Variation in the rate of natural increase from parish to parish is of course a reflection of diversity in fertility and mortality performance. Parishes of relatively high crude birth rates and below average crude death rates were necessarily parishes of consistently high rates of natural increase: e.g., St. Ann, St. Elizabeth, Manchester, Clarendon. Parishes characterized by low birth rates and high or moderate death rates exhibited unusually low rates of natural increase: e.g., Kingston, St. Andrew, St. Catherine, St. Thomas, and Portland.

When viewed in relation to intercensal rates of population growth, these patterns of natural increase are suggestive of the overall pattern of demographic performance over the period 1891-1938. For example, of three parishes which generally exceeded the national rate of intercensal growth, only Clarendon recorded any marked tendency towards relatively high rates of natural increase. The other two (Kingston and St. Andrew) were very low in any ranking of parish rates of natural increase.[17] Conversely, many parishes which consistently reported below average intercensal population growth rates were also regions of relatively high rates of natural increase. This was especially striking for the parishes of St. Ann, St. Elizabeth, and Manchester. Even at the national level, there appears to be a wide disparity in the rates of natural increase and the rates of population growth during most intercensal years.[18] The obvious conclusion is that migration played an important role in the growth of the Jamaican population at both the national and parish level. It is to a fuller discussion of migration that we must now turn.

PATTERNS OF MIGRATION

It is almost impossible to find a commentary on Jamaica during these years which did not discuss migration. All manner of official publications, internal Colonial Office memoranda, and even the supercilious writings of tourists discussed Jamaican migration and frequently offered imaginative explanations of its causes and consequences.[19] Most of this discussion was uninformed by reliable data which even today, with all the advantages of historical hindsight, remain unsatisfactory. The Registrar-General annually reported figures purporting to show the volume and direction of external migration. These data are virtually worthless for the years proceeding 1921 and are generally thought to understate emigration throughout the whole period 1881-1943.[20] Annual data on migration within Jamaica are entirely non-existent, though there are data concerning such migration during the two intercensal periods 1911-1921 and 1921-1943. By far the most comprehensive and useful estimates of migration are those made by George Roberts.[21] The present discussion relies heavily on Roberts' data, modified as necessary by the work of others.

TOTAL 5.5

TOTAL NET MIGRATION AS PERCENTAGE OF NATURAL INCREASE, BY PARISH, JAMAICA, 1891-1911

(+ = Net In-Migration)
(- = Net Out-Migration)

PARISH	TOTAL NET MIGRATION AS % NATURAL INCREASE
Kingston	+ 62.6
St. Andrew	+ 88.4
St. Thomas	- 29.4
Portland	+ 41.6
St. Mary	+ 56.1
St. Ann	- 41.1
Trelawny	- 50.4
St. James	- 28.9
Hanover	- 49.6
Westmoreland	- 34.0
St. Elizabeth	- 48.0
Manchester	- 65.9
Clarendon	- 22.4
St. Catherine	+ 6.8

SOURCE: Table A.6, Appendix.

Patterns of Internal Migration

We have seen that during the period 1891-1943 those parishes which generally exhibited high rates of natural increase did not experience comparably high rates of overall population growth. Clearly, internal migration played an important role in the geographic redistribution of the Jamaican population during this period.

Evidence from the pre-1890 period strengthens the view that Jamaicans were willing and able to migrate from one part of the island to another. In the years following emancipation in 1838, former slaves in considerable numbers migrated to the "remoter parts of Jamaica",[22] and continued to do so until the 1880s. Thereafter, the towns and coastal regions increasingly attracted migrants from the mountainous areas of the island.[23]

This latter pattern appears to have continued during the period 1891-1911. Although it is impossible to distinguish net internal from net external migration at the parish level during this period, the overall pattern of net out-migration at the parish level may be seen in Table 5.5.

During the intercensal period 1891-1911, net in-migration was characteristic of the urban parishes (Kingston and St. Andrew), the banana producing parishes of St. Mary and Portland, and the parish of St. Catherine. Every other parish experienced considerable net out-migration during this period. Interestingly, the largest losers of population through migration were the domestic agricultural parishes of St. Ann, St. Elizabeth, and Manchester, and the sugar producing parishes of Westmoreland, Hanover, and Trelawny.

TABLE 5.6

NET INTERNAL MIGRATION AS PERCENTAGE OF NATURAL INCREASE, BY PARISH, JAMAICA, 1911 - 1921 AND 1921 - 1943

(+ = Net In-Migration)
(- = Net Out-Migration)

PARISH	NET INTERNAL MIGRATION AS % OF NATURAL INCREASE	
	1911 - 1921	1921 - 1943
Kingston	+ 792.3	+ 76.5
St. Andrew	+ 227.8	+ 443.9
St. Thomas	+ 22.2	+ 45.8
Portland	+ 25.5	- 18.2
St. Mary	+ 8.6	- 34.8
St. Ann	- 34.3	- 39.9
Trelawny	- 10.5	- 18.6
St. James	- 6.4	0.0
Hanover	- 16.3	- 24.3
Westmoreland	- 14.0	- 27.3
St. Elizabeth	- 46.6	- 51.9
Manchester	- 48.6	- 32.0
Clarendon	+ 5.5	- 6.5
St. Catherine	+ 6.5	- 2.8

SOURCE: Table A.6, Appendix.

Evidence for the two intercensal periods 1911-1921 and 1921-1943 tends to confirm this pattern of internal migration. Table 5.6

summarizes estimates of net internal migration at the parish level for these two intercensal periods.

The urban parishes of Kingston and St. Andrew were the primary destination of the vast majority of migrants after 1911. During the period 1911-1921, net in-migration was nearly eight times the recorded natural increase in Kingston; in St. Andrew, net internal migration was more than twice as large as natural increase. The migration to urban parishes is even more striking in the period 1921-1943: only one rural parish, St. Thomas, increased its population through net internal migration during these years.

Apart from these urban regions, certain rural parishes characterized by the cultivation of staple exports--particularly bananas--attracted migrants during these years. During the intercensal period 1911-1921, all rural parishes in which net internal migration was positive were dominated by the cultivation of bananas. During the period 1921-1943, only the parish of St. Thomas attracted net migration as the staple export sector contracted in the face of depressed international market conditions.

It will be noted in Table 5.6 that those parishes which consistently experienced substantial net out-migration in the period 1911-1943 were precisely those parishes which had experienced substantial net out-migration during the period 1891-1911. Thus the parishes of St. Ann, St. Elizabeth, and Manchester were the largest losers of population through net out-migration across the whole period 1891-1943.

Patterns of Immigration Into Jamaica

Following the abolition of the slave trade in 1807, Jamaica ceased to be a nation of substantial immigration. It is true that peoples of various nationalities settled in Jamaica during the nineteenth and early twentieth centuries. But as the numbers involved were relatively small, the demographic consequences of that immigration were on the whole insignificant.[24]

The overwhelming majority of immigrants into Jamaica in the post-emancipation period came from India as indentured labourers. As seen in Table 5.7, less than 39,000 East Indian immigrants landed in Jamaica during the entire period of indenture, 1845-1917. Of this number, slightly more than one-third arrived between 1890 and 1917. In view of the numbers of East Indians who were known to have been repatriated at the end of their contracts (approximately 12,000) and an undetermined number who emigrated elsewhere, it is generally believed that no more than 20,000 East Indians permanently settled in Jamaica during the period of indenture.

The numbers of East Indians landed in Jamaica varied considerably from year to year. Following experimentation with indentured East Indians in the late 1840s, the importation ceased altogether in the 1850s when planters reacted to the declaration of free trade in Britain. It was during the 1860s and 1870s that sugar planters, desperately seeking to reduce unit costs of production by insuring an adequate supply of labour, increased indentured immigration to record heights. During the 1880s however recruitment problems in India and the deepening depression in the sugar industry combined to limit severely the

TABLE 5.7

ESTIMATES OF EAST INDIAN INDENTURED IMMIGRATION INTO JAMAICA, 1845-1917

	ARRIVALS		DEPARTURES	
PERIOD	ROBERTS	EISNER	ROBERTS	EISNER
1845 - 1854	4551	5022	1520	1547
1855 - 1859	-	-	-	-
1860 - 1869	7662	7653	-	-
1870 - 1879	9401	9886	2921	2921
1880 - 1889	2217	2928	2905	2925
1890 - 1899	5062	4402	1401	1290
1900 - 1909	3308	3966	2235	2234
1910 - 1914	4209	4209	502	502
1915 - 1917	-	615	270	414
TOTAL	36410	33631	11880	11959

SOURCES: G. W. Roberts, _The Population of Jamaica_, Appendix II, pp. 334-338.

G. Eisner, _Jamaica 1830-1930_, Table IX, p. 144.

importation of indentured labourers.[25]

The rise of the banana industry in the 1890s and the modest revival of the sugar industry after 1910 gave rise to renewed interest in East Indian indentured labour. The planters and their supporters argued that without a regular and predictable labour force, the estate cultivation of staple exports could not be ensured. In the face of a general unwillingness on the part of Jamaicans to supply labour at wages acceptable to planters, the latter insisted that indentured immigration would have to be allowed. This view did not go uncontested, but in the end it was grudgingly supported by the Colonial Office which had always held that the economic and social stability of Jamaica depended on the well-being of the staple export industries.[26] It was only when the First World War disrupted shipping that the Indian government, long doubtful as to the desirability of the indenture scheme, forbade recruitment in 1917, after which date indentured immigration into Jamaica ceased altogether.[27]

Still, at no time was the East Indian community sufficiently large to influence measurably any element of Jamaican demographic performance.[28] By the time of the 1943 census, fewer than 27,000 were enumerated as being East Indian.[29]

The only other sizable immigrant group to enter Jamaica during these years was from China. A few hundred indentured Chinese arrived in Jamaica during the nineteenth century. On the whole, this venture proved disappointing to planters in that the transport costs involved were greater than for Indians, and Chinese immigrants tended to leave agricultural employment at the first opportunity.[30] Around the turn of the century and especially following the Chinese revolution of 1911, there appears to have been an increase in the number of Chinese immigrants arriving in Jamaica. Although there are no reliable data concerning the volume and exact timing of Chinese immigration, the various censuses of population shed some light on the minuscule numbers of Chinese in the island, as shown in Table 5.8.

TABLE 5.8

SIZE OF THE CHINESE COMMUNITY IN JAMAICA, 1881-1943

CENSUS YEAR	NUMBER OF PERSONS ENUMERATED AS "CHINESE"
1881	99
1891	481
1911	2111
1921	3696
1943	12394

SOURCE: G. W. Roberts, The Population of Jamaica, Table 14, p. 65.

Due to their small numbers, imbalanced sex ratio, and decided preference for racial cohesion, Chinese immigrants had little impact on the patterns of demographic performance already described.[31] Nonetheless, their strong predilection for urban as against rural residence, and their virtual domination of small retail enterprise gave to the Chinese of Jamaica a social and economic importance quite disproportionate to their numbers.[32]

In conclusion, immigration into Jamaica had little impact on demographic performance during the period 1891-1938. To be sure, immigration occasioned considerable discussion and dispute among colonial officials and ordinary Jamaicans. Almost without exception however the primary concern of such discussion was the economic, social, and political desirability of immigration rather than its demographic consequences.

Patterns of External Migration

The most spectacular and certainly the most visible feature of demographic performance during the late nineteenth and early twentieth centuries was the ebb and flow of external migration. Variations in overall fertility and mortality were difficult to discern and, apart from the few years of natural calamity, did not attract much general interest. By contrast, emigration was an extraordinary event which touched virtually every family in the nation as scores of thousands temporarily quit the island. During the period 1881-1943 the idea of emigration emerged as the great obsession of Jamaicans and to the present day remains a powerful feature of the nation's demography.

As noted previously, annual data on the direction and volume of Jamaican emigration are unavailable or deficient for the period 1881-1943. Comparing the intercensal natural increase with the size of the population at successive censuses, however, allows estimates of the volume of net emigration for Jamaica as a whole during each intercensal period. These estimates are presented in Table 5.9.

TABLE 5.9

NATURAL INCREASE AND NET EXTERNAL MIGRATION, JAMAICA,

INTERCENSAL PERIODS 1881 - 1943

(+ = Net Immigration)

(- = Net Emigration)

INTER-CENSAL PERIOD	NATURAL INCREASE	NET EXTERNAL MIGRATION	NET EXTERNAL MIGRATION AS % OF NATURAL INCREASE
1881 - 1891	83500	- 24800	29.7
1891 - 1911	235699	- 43807	18.6
1911 - 1921	102135	- 75398	73.8
1921 - 1943	353145	+ 25800	7.3

SOURCE: Table A.6, Appendix, and G. W. Roberts, "Notes on Population Growth", Social and Economic Studies, Vol. 7, No. 3 (1950), p. 29.

There is a wave-like nature to Jamaican net external migration during the period 1881-1943. Two intercensal periods, 1881-1891 and 1911-1921, show substantial levels of net emigration. The longer period 1891-1911 witnessed more moderate levels of net emigration. Most striking of all is the intercensal period 1921-1943 during which the numbers of returning Jamaicans significantly exceeded the number of emigrants.

Within any particular intercensal period, the level of external migration apparently varied from year to year. There is reason to believe, for example, that emigration during the period 1881-1891 was largely confined to the years before 1885.[33] Similarly, during the intercensal period 1891-1911, it was only after 1904 that large numbers of Jamaicans emigrated.[34] Even during the intercensal period 1921-1943, there appear to have been years in which emigration from the island was very high.[35]

The majority of emigrants were attracted to one of three destinations. By far the greatest number went to Panama or other of the Central American republics, especially before 1911. In later years, Jamaican emigrants tended to favour either Cuba or the United States. Although the data are imperfect, Table 5.10 summarizes what is known of the destinations and volumes of net emigration during the period 1881-1921.

Emigrants appear to have been drawn to these destinations by reports of high wages, steady employment, and by a general curiosity to see new places.[36] Emigration was further encouraged by the attitude of the Jamaican government prior to the 1920s. Foreign employers were allowed and even encouraged to recruit contract labourers in Jamaica, provided only that certain minimum conditions were fulfilled concerning wages and repatriation.[37] Finally, the monetary costs of emigration (essentially the cost of transport) were within the ability of many Jamaicans to pay, and hence provided another stimulus to emigration.[38]

Economic conditions in Jamaica also appear to have influenced the volume and timing of emigration. As noted in the previous chapter, the two periods of largest net emigration, 1881-1891 and 1911-1921, were also years of general economic dislocation. On the other hand, the

TABLE 5.10

ESTIMATES OF THE DIRECTION AND VOLUME OF NET MIGRATION

FROM JAMAICA, 1881-1921

PERIOD	TO U.S.A.	TO PANAMA	TO CUBA	TO OTHER PLACES	TOTAL
1881-1891)		17,000	)	)	69,000
)	16,000		)	10,000)	
1891-1911)		26,000	)	)	
1911-1921)	30,000	20,000	22,000	23,000	77,000

SOURCE: G. W. Roberts, *The Population of Jamaica*, Table 31, p. 139.

W. F. Maunder, "The New Jamaican Emigration", *Social and Economic Studies*, Vol. 4, No. 1, (March 1955) pp. 39-40.

intercensal period of moderate net emigration, 1891-1911, was a period during which the banana industry was expanding rapidly. It seems clear that if emigrants were pulled to overseas places, they were as well pushed by domestic conditions.

Data on net external migration from individual parishes are available only for the two intercensal periods 1911-1921 and 1921-1943.[39] As may be seen in Table 5.11, the several parishes exhibited much diversity in the degree to which net external migration occurred during both periods.

Consider first the pattern of parish net external migration during the years 1911-1921. Although every parish experienced loss of population through net emigration during these years, it is possible to classify individual parishes as having been characterized by heavy, moderate, or slight net external migration. The first class consists of those parishes which appear to have lost more than 100% of intercensal natural increase. These included the urban parishes of Kingston and St. Andrew, the northcoast banana producting parishes of St. Mary and Portland, and the chronically depressed parish of Trelawny. As a group these five parishes accounted for 46% of Jamaican net emigration during the period 1911-1921.[40]

A second set of parishes lost between 48% and 81% of intercensal natural increase through net emigration during the years 1911-1921. Included in this group of moderate net emigration parishes are St. Ann, St. Elizabeth, Westmoreland, St. James, and Hanover. Altogether some 44% of Jamaican net emigration came from these six parishes.

Finally, Table 5.11 shows a few parishes experienced a relatively

TABLE 5.11

NET EXTERNAL MIGRATION AS PERCENTAGE

OF NATURAL INCREASES, BY PARISH,

JAMAICA, 1911 - 1921 AND 1921 - 1943

(+ = Net Immigration)
(- = Net Emigration)

PARISH	NET EXTERNAL MIGRATION AS % NATURAL INCREASE	
	1911 - 1921	1921 - 1943
Kingston	- 576.9%	- 11.4%
St. Andrew	- 227.8	+ 144.9
St. Thomas	- 33.3	+ 5.8
Portland	- 133.3	- 10.3
St. Mary	- 123.8	+ 12.4
St. Ann	- 64.2	+ 10.3
Trelawny	- 113.2	+ 1.3
St. James	- 80.9	+ 6.9
Hanover	- 67.4	+ 1.7
Westmoreland	- 58.1	- 0 -
St. Elizabeth	- 48.9	+ 7.1
Manchester	- 62.9	+ 21.9
Clarendon	- 38.3	+ 5.8
St. Catherine	- 14.1	- 19.9

SOURCE: Table A.6, Appendix.

small amount of net emigration during these years. With net emigration representing less than 40% of intercensal natural increase, the three parishes of Clarendon, St. Catherine, and St. Thomas fall into this class. Taken collectively these parishes contributed approximately 10% of the island's net emigration in the period 1911-1921.

The period 1921-1943 witnessed an overall increase in the island's population through the return of many overseas residents. It would appear that slightly more than 107,000 Jamaicans returned to the island during these years.[41] The resettlement of these returning Jamaicans may be inferred from Table 5.11.

Most striking was the attraction which St. Andrew parish appeared to hold for returning Jamaicans. During these years net emigration increased the population of that parish by some 15,500, which was nearly half again the size of intercensal natural increase. Among the rural parishes, only Manchester, St. Ann, and St. Mary increased population to any significant degree through net immigration. This propensity to settle in selected parishes is the principal feature of external migration during the period 1921-1943.

In spite of this overall trend, three parishes (Kingston, Portland, and St. Catherine) appear to have lost population through net migration during these years. It is impossible to determine whether this was the result of large numbers of new emigrants from, or the consequence of few returning Jamaicans settling in these three parishes. In any case, the wide diversity of net emigration at the parish level is well established for the whole period 1881-1943.

ADDITIONAL ASPECTS OF JAMAICAN DEMOGRAPHY, 1881-1943

Age Structure

At any given point in time, the age structure of a population is determined by past performance with respect to fertility, mortality, and migration. As any of these change over time, the age structure of the population will alter. It is to be expected, therefore, that the age structure of the Jamaican population varied from one census to another. The age structure of the national population at census year is shown in Table 5.12.

TABLE 5.12

AGE COMPOSITION OF TOTAL POPULATION,

JAMAICA, CENSUS, 1881-1943

	PERCENT OF CENSUS POPULATION IN EACH AGE GROUP				
AGE GROUP	1881	1891	1911	1921	1943
0-9	26.0	25.3	28.0	27.1	25.3
10-19	21.9	23.8	21.4	22.5	20.7
20-29	18.9	18.2	18.5	17.6	18.0
30-39	12.6	12.2	12.0	11.4	14.1
40-49	8.2	9.5	8.6	9.6	9.6
50-59	4.6	5.1	5.6	5.7	5.8
60 and over	6.5	5.8	5.9	6.1	6.6
Not specified	1.4	0.2	0.1	0.1	-
TOTAL	100.1	100.1	100.1	100.1	100.1

NOTE: Columns do not add to 100.0 because of rounding.

SOURCE: Census of Jamaica, 1943, Table 25, p. 25.

Since demographic performance varied from one parish to another, it is to be expected that parish age structures would exhibit diversity. The nature of that diversity may be seen in Table 5.13 in which parish dependency ratios are shown for each census.

TABLE 5.13

DEPENDENCY RATIOS, BY PARISH, JAMAICA, CENSUS, 1881 - 1943

PARISH	DEPENDENCY RATIOS BY PARISH*				
	1881	1891	1911	1921	1943
Kingston	0.563	0.454	0.445	0.431	0.395
St. Andrew	0.721	0.660	0.668	0.654	0.510
St. Thomas	0.851	0.680	0.779	0.696	0.574
Portland	0.828	0.748	0.683	0.717	0.646
St. Mary	0.795	0.776	0.697	0.774	0.672
St. Ann	0.825	0.859	0.925	0.971	0.885
Trelawny	0.711	0.711	0.792	0.769	0.810
St. James	0.753	0.747	0.767	0.769	0.724
Hanover	0.757	0.671	0.814	0.817	0.823
Westmoreland	0.754	0.727	0.828	0.802	0.796
St. Elizabeth	0.859	0.800	0.917	0.873	0.876
Manchester	0.919	0.875	0.945	0.901	0.839
Clarendon	0.699	0.820	0.792	0.798	0.763
St. Catherine	0.686	0.762	0.728	0.704	0.661
Kingston + St. Andrew	0.634	0.537	0.542	0.526	0.454
JAMAICA	0.760	0.741	0.766	0.758	0.688

*Dependency ratio is defined as the total number of persons in the age groups 0-14 and 65 or over divided by the number of persons in all other age groups, excluding those not specified with respect to age.

SOURCE: Computed from Table 25, Census of Jamaica, 1943.

The value of the dependency ratio for any particular parish fluctuates over time. In general these fluctuations appear to follow no fixed pattern, though for many parishes the ratio peaks in either 1911 or 1921. This would seem to reflect the profound impact of migration on parish age structures. Perhaps most striking is the decline over time in the dependency ratios for the two urban parishes. This resulted from the substantial migration of adults into the urban centre and the common practice of sending children to live with relatives in rural parishes.

Table 5.13 shows an interesting consistency over time in the order of parishes ranked by the value of the dependency ratio. In light of the previously discussed patterns of fertility, mortality, and migration, it is hardly surprising that the urban parishes of Kingston and St. Andrew uniformly recorded the lowest dependency ratios in the island. Among rural parishes, the highest dependency ratios were usually reported in St. Ann, Manchester, and St. Elizabeth; relatively low dependency ratios were consistently recorded in St. Thomas, Portland, and St. Catherine.

Sex Composition

Since the abolition of the slave trade in 1807, the sex ratio of the Jamaican population has been substantially imbalanced in favour of females. As may be seen in Table 5.14, this imbalance increased during the period 1881-1921 and was only partly reversed once migration declined in the late 1920s.

The urban parishes of Kingston and St. Andrew reported consistently low sex ratios during the period under study. Although the number of males per thousand females in Kingston showed modest increase during 1881-1943, the population of St. Andrew was increasingly imbalanced in favour of females throughout that period. For the two parishes combined, the sex ratio declined from 882 in 1881 to 769 in 1921 and increased to 801 in 1943. In short, the urban population was even more imbalanced in favour of females than was the national population.

TABLE 5.14

SEX COMPOSITION OF POPULATION, BY PARISH AND BY CENSUS YEAR, JAMAICA, 1881-1943

	SEX RATIOS OF PARISH CENSUS POPULATIONS (MALES PER 1000 FEMALES)				
PARISH	1881	1891	1911	1921	1943
Kingston-St. Andrew	822	802	798	769	801
Kingston	704	708	723	721	775
St. Andrew	973	938	891	827	823
St. Thomas	982	936	923	932	1029
Portland	979	959	1013	942	1002
St. Mary	1016	982	1059	970	997
St. Ann	961	942	929	880	963
Trelawny	939	859	863	856	978
St. James	888	846	830	809	920
Hanover	965	923	889	884	956
Westmoreland	1003	934	917	897	964
St. Elizabeth	959	925	886	836	942
Manchester	952	961	903	857	943
Clarendon	1021	985	971	919	993
St. Catherine	963	940	969	975	984
JAMAICA	950	917	916	881	937

SOURCE: Census of Jamaica, 1943, Tables 24, 25, 26.

Among the rural parishes the number of females generally exceeded the number of males, although the sex ratios were far less imbalanced than for the urban parishes. Of the sixty sex ratios reported for rural parishes in Table 5.14, only seven have values in excess of 1000. Not too surprisingly, these divergent cases coincide with parishes which experienced substantial net in-migration during the periods concerned. On the whole however, rural parishes appear to have experienced a general decline in their sex ratios during the period 1881-1921; in the period 1921-1943, rural sex ratios increased without exception.

George Roberts has drawn attention to three factors which gave rise to the general imbalance of sex ratios in the Jamaican case. In the first place, the Jamaican population has been characterized by markedly low sex ratios at birth. Over the period 1878-1950, the sex ratio at birth is estimated to have been on average 1023, a figure which compares closely with estimates of sex ratios at birth for blacks in the United States and for non-Indians throughout the Caribbean.[42] Thus the overall imbalance of the sexes in Jamaica stems at least in part from the relatively low sex ratio among live births.

Secondly, marked differentials in mortality between the sexes in every age group have clearly contributed to the overall imbalance.[43] As elsewhere, female mortality was substantially lower than male mortality for every age group in Jamaica during the period under study. When combined with a low sex ratio at birth, relatively higher mortality among males necessarily results in a low sex ratio in the total population.

Thirdly, sex-selective migration clearly influences the population sex ratio.[44] It will be seen in Table 5.14 that periods of substantial net emigration (1881-1891) and 1911-1921) resulted in a marked lowering of the sex ratio. On the other hand, two decades of insubstantial net emigration (1891-1911) seems to have hardly altered the sex ratio. During the period of massive net in-migration (1921-1943) the sex ratio of the national population increased to a nearly normal level.

Marital Status

Historical demographers studying other societies frequently attach special significance to the marital status of the population.[45] On the one hand, variations in the marriage rate over time are supposed to reflect changes in general economic conditions which ultimately determine the ease with which new households can be formed. On the other hand, the marital status of a population is often taken as indicative of overall changes in the level of fertility in later periods. Both interpretations rest on a fundamental institutional assumption: formal marriage is the only socially acceptable means by which independent households are formed and procreation accommodated.

Marital status has never assumed a comparable degree of importance in the study of Jamaican historical demography. Although it may have been preferred as a social ideal, formal marriage was in fact only one of many accepted arrangements by which independent households were formed and within which women bore children. The diverse historical and social-psychological origins of this phenomenon need not be reviewed here.[46] Suffice it to observe in Table 5.15 that Jamaican marriage rates were extremely low, and illegitimacy extremely high, throughout the period 1881-1945.

TABLE 5.15

AVERAGE ANNUAL MARRIAGE AND ILLEGITIMACY RATES, JAMAICA

1881 - 1945

Years	Marriage Rate (per 1000 Population)	Illegitimacy Rate (% live births)
1881 - 1885	4.53	58.9
1886 - 1890	5.04	60.4
1891 - 1895	5.18	60.6
1896 - 1900	4.41	62.6
1901 - 1905	4.17	64.5
1906 - 1910	5.43	62.4
1911 - 1915	3.50	65.3
1916 - 1920	3.76	69.2
1921 - 1925	3.75	71.6
1926 - 1930	4.43	72.1
1931 - 1935	3.77	71.9
1936 - 1940	4.44	70.8
1941 - 1945	4.81	69.5

SOURCE: G. W. Roberts, The Population of Jamaica, Table 71, p. 288.

In many other societies, marriage rates have been observed to fluctuate from one period to another.[47] In Jamaica the average annual marriage rate appears to have been remarkably stable for the years shown in Table 5.15. The one notable exception was the huge increase in marriages following the earthquake of 1907. Although the religious zeal which motivated this behaviour had spent itself by 1909, the average annual marriage rate during the period 1906-1910 reached an historic high.[48] Apart from this peculiar quinquennium, it is doubtful that variations in the marriage rate were systematically linked to circumstances such as emigration or general economic prosperity.[49] It is more likely that these slight fluctuations represent nothing more than errors of registration and inconsequential changes in tastes and preferences.

As with other demographic features, marital status appears to have varied among the several parishes of Jamaica. Reliable data are unfortunately available only with respect to the 1943 census.[50] There is little reason to suspect that the patterns shown in Table 5.16 are significantly different from that obtained during the longer period 1881-1943.

From Table 5.16 it appears that relatively few women in the child-bearing ages were ever married in the parishes of St. Thomas, St. Catherine, St. James, and St. Mary, all of which were given over to the production of staple export crops by plantations. On the other hand, the parishes of St. Ann, Manchester, Kingston, and St. Andrew were characterized by relatively large proportions of married women among females of child-bearing ages. It would seem, therefore, that the anthropological literature which links family structure and marital status to economic structure finds some support in Table 5.16.[51]

TABLE 5.16

PROPORTION OF NEVER MARRIED FEMALES IN CHILD-BEARING AGE GROUPS (15-44 YEARS) BY PARISH, JAMAICA, 1943

PARISH	% FEMALES AGED 15-44 YEARS WHO WERE NEVER MARRIED AT TIME OF 1943 CENSUS
Kingston - St. Andrew	60.1
St. Thomas	74.2
Portland	66.1
St. Mary	70.4
St. Ann	58.2
Trelawny	65.5
St. James	70.8
Hanover	68.4
Westmoreland	61.8
St. Elizabeth	66.4
Manchester	56.7
Clarendon	63.4
St. Catherine	73.1

SOURCE: G.W. Roberts, The Population of Jamaica, Table 72, p. 290.

Inter-parish differences in marital status may have been one of several causes of variation in mortality and fertility across the parishes. It is generally accepted that infant mortality rates among illegitimately born children were fully fifty percent higher than among infants born to legally married women.[52] Almost certainly this was the result of the much less favourable economic conditions which unmarried mothers had to endure.[53] Since one prerequisite of formal marriage was economic security, it is hardly surprising that parishes in which a relatively large proportion of the female population in the child-bearing ages were married were also parishes in which infant mortality rates were relatively low.

Although it was common for unmarried women to bear children, it is clear that "the level of fertility is, by all available data, lowest among [unmarried women] and highest among married [women]."[54] At the time of the 1943 census, married mothers over forty-five years of age averaged 6.64 children, while common-law and single mothers of the same ages averaged 5.60 and 4.74 children respectively.[55] Since reproduction commenced at an earlier age in the case of unmarried women, a seeming paradox emerges: that is, "the level of fertility tends to vary inversely with the total length of the period of exposure to the risk of child-bearing."[56] However, single mothers spaced children over much longer periods than did married mothers.[57] In part this may have been the consequence of irregular exposure to risk; in part, the result of conscious avoidance of pregnancy by single mothers who had to bear the primary responsibility for their child's welfare.

At the parish level it is difficult to discern an empirical relationship between marital status and fertility. It is true that in 1943 St. Thomas parish exhibited a very low proportion of married females in the age group 15-44 years and also recorded the lowest joint gross reproduction rate of any parish. St. Ann was characterized by a relatively high proportion of married females and also by a relatively high fertility rate. However, there are significant exceptions to an intuitively positive relationship between marital status and fertility: in particular, the parishes of Kingston, St. Andrew, St. Elizabeth, Manchester, and Hanover do not seem to fit such a relationship.

Thus the impact of marital status on parish mortality and parish fertility performance appears to have been muted during the period under study. This is not surprising if one bears in mind the limited role which formal marriage played in the social organization of Jamaica and in view of the many other factors which undoubtedly influenced demographic performance at the parish level.

Urbanization

Heretofore Kingston and St. Andrew have been referred to as the only urban parishes during the period 1881-1943. All other parishes have consequently been classed as essentially rural. This simplification has unavoidably introduced an element of distortion into the discussion. On the one hand, there is no doubt that certain regions of St. Andrew were almost wholly rural in nature throughout the whole period. On the other hand, each rural parish contained at least one town which possessed something of an urban character. Since patterns of demographic performance appear to differ between rural and urban parishes, it is worthwhile to consider briefly the process of urbanization throughout the island.

The growth of individual towns during the period 1881-1943 cannot be accurately traced since enumeration districts varied from census to census.[58] However, the general process of urbanization during the period may be seen in Table 5.17. As a proportion of island population, the number of town residents showed modest growth up to the census of 1921. Thereafter, this proportion increased significantly so that in 1943 slightly more than 22% of all Jamaicans resided in towns with populations in excess of one thousand. Quite clearly it was the period 1921-1943 which witnessed the most rapid urbanization of the population.

Obviously the capital city of Kingston was the principal urban centre of the island. Moreover, Kingston expanded at a rate far in excess of that experienced by the total urban population of the island. While nearly 65% of the urban population resided in Kingston in 1891, that proportion had increased to nearly 74% in 1943. Apart from those living in Kingston, the urban dwelling population was widely dispersed. It was only in 1943 that two towns outside Kingston-St. Andrew recorded a population in excess of 10,000: Spanish Town in St. Catherine (12,000) and Montego Bay in St. James (11,500). By far the largest number of towns had fewer than 5,000 residents during the period 1881-1943. The growth of these small towns was quite unimpressive; the average population increased from 1,700 in 1881 to 2,663 in 1943.

Thus substantial urbanization was limited to Kingston up to 1943. Indeed it is doubtful that the other towns, with the possible exceptions

TABLE 5.17

URBAN POPULATION OF JAMAICA, 1881-1943

SIZE OF TOWN	1881			1891			1911			1921			1943		
	(1)	(2)	(3)	(1)	(2)	(3)	(1)	(2)	(3)	(1)	(2)	(3)	(1)	(2)	(3)
Less than 1000	2	872	1.1	2	1125	1.6	1	636	0.5	1	781	0.6	--	--	--
1000 - 5000	8	17029	22.5	9	19083	26.6	8	16998	14.3	8	16951	13.2	15	39947	14.4
5000 - 10000	2	12430	16.4	1	5019	7.0	3	20809	17.5	3	21546	16.8	2	11520	4.2
10000 - 25000	--	--	--	--	--	--	--	--	--	--	--	--	2	23554	8.5
More than 25000 (Kingston)	1	45534	60.0	1	47542	64.8	1	80701	67.7	1	89048	69.4	1	201911	72.9
TOTALS	13	75865	100.0	13	71769	100.0	13	119144	100.0	13	128326	100.0	20	276932	100.0

(1) Number of towns in size category.

(2) Total population of towns in a given size category.

(3) Percentage of total urban population residing in towns of given size.

SOURCES: Census of Jamaica 1881, 1891, 1911, 1921.

Data for 1943 is taken from G. W. Roberts, The Population of Jamaica, Table 40, p. 161.

of Spanish Town and Montego Bay, can reasonably be considered as urban centres at all. For the most part these small towns served as local markets and as transport and administrative centres for their immediate hinterlands, which in turn were almost exclusively agricultural. It is certain that these small towns were not significant centres of non-agricultural economic activity. In so far as these towns were centres for schooling and formalized health services and acted as clearing houses for information on conditions elsewhere in the island and abroad, it might be supposed that they did represent certain aspects of an urban environment which was conducive to social and political change.[59] Nonetheless, it is difficult to believe that these small towns served to alter the rural nature of the parishes within which they were located.

ENDNOTES TO CHAPTER V

[1] See Table A.1 in the Appendix.

[2] See Table A.1 in the Appendix.

[3] G. W. Roberts, The Population of Jamaica. (Cambridge: 1957), pp. 22-28.

[4] Annual Report of the Registrar-General for Jamaica, annually 1891-1938, in C.O. 140.

[5] A discussion of the deficiencies of the official data is presented in the Appendix.

[6] A discussion of the method of revision is presented in the Appendix.

[7] See Table A.2 in the Appendix.

[8] See Table A.2 in the Appendix.

[9] See Table A.2 in the Appendix.

[10] G. W. Roberts, <u>op. cit.</u>, Table 70, p. 281.

[11] See Table A.8 in the Appendix.

[12] See Table A.4 in the Appendix.

[13] G. W. Roberts, <u>op. cit.</u>, p. 193; G. Eisner, <u>Jamaica, 1830-1930</u>. (Manchester: 1961), pp. 138-139.

[14] See Table A.3 in the Appendix.

[15] See Table A.5 in the Appendix.

[16] See Table A.5 in the Appendix.

[17] See Table A.1 and Table A.5 in the Appendix.

[18] Compare Table 5.1 and Table 5.4 above.

[19] See for example: G. St.J. Orde-Browne, <u>Report on Labour Conditions in the West Indies</u>. (H.M.S.O.: 1939), p. 81; <u>Report of the West India Royal Commission</u>. (H.M.S.O.: 1945), pp. 10-12; <u>Report of the Unemployment Commission</u>. (Kingston: 1936), in C.O. 950/125; B. Pullen-Burry, <u>Jamaica As It Is, 1903</u>. (London: 1903); Olivier to Chamberlain, Dispatch of July 10, 1902, in C.O. 137/628; Olivier to Harcourt, Dispatch of April 21, 1911, in C.O. 137/684; Manning to Long, Dispatch of September 1, 1917, in C.O. 137/722; Probyn to Milner, Dispatch of January 24, 1920, in C.O. 137/737; Probyn to Churchill, Dispatch of June 8, 1921, in C.O. 137/748; Denham to Ormsby-Gore, Dispatch of March 29, 1937, in C.O. 137/817.

[20] A discussion of the defects of these data is presented in the Appendix.

[21] G. W. Roberts, <u>op. cit.</u>, pp. 101-164.

[22] British Parliamentary Papers, C. 709, as quoted in G. Eisner, <u>op. cit.</u>, p. 135.

[23] D. G. Hall, Free Jamaica, 1838-1865. (CARUP Reprint: 1969), pp. 212, 235; G. Eisner, op. cit., pp. 135-136, 182, 186; G. W. Roberts, op. cit., pp. 50-52.

[24] The return of Jamaican emigrants is considered in the section on emigration.

[25] G. W. Roberts, op. cit., pp. 116-121; G. Eisner, op. cit., pp. 143-147; D. G. Hall, op. cit., pp. 53, 89-90.

[26] Lord Olivier, Jamaica: The Blessed Island. (London: 1936), pp. 296-298; Olivier to Chamberlain, Dispatch of July 10, 1902, in C.O. 137/628; Olivier to Crewe, Dispatch of October 10, 1910, in C.O. 137/679.

[27] By 1917 some officials in London had come to believe that indentured immigration had outlived whatever benefits it might once have bestowed. Thus Mr. Green, a rising Colonial Office functionary, noted on a dispatch from Manning to Long, September 1, 1917, in C.O. 137/722: "....my view that the policy of Indian immigration has been the main, though not the only, factor in the industrial ruin of the British West Indies...."

[28] G. W. Roberts, op. cit., p. 130.

[29] Ibid., p. 65.

[30] D. G. Hall, op. cit., p. 107.

[31] G. W. Roberts, op. cit., pp. 73-74, 132.

[32] Probyn to Long, Confidential Dispatch of September 30, 1918, in C.O. 137/727; Probyn to Long, Dispatch of September 5, 1918, in C.O. 137/727; Probyn to Long, Dispatch of July 22, 1918, in C.O. 137/727; Evidence of the West India Royal Commission, C.O. 950/87.

[33] G. W. Roberts, op. cit., pp. 133-134.

[34] Ibid., p. 135; G. Eisner, op. cit., pp. 150-151; Swettenham to Lyttelton, Dispatch of December 10, 1904, in C.O. 137/642; Swettenham to Elgin, Dispatch of January 24, 1906, in C.O. 137/650.

[35] M. J. Proudfoot, Population Movements in the Caribbean. (Port-of-Spain: 1951), Table 20, p. 81.

[36] Lord Olivier, op. cit., pp. 299-300; W. M. Macmillan, Warning from the West Indies. (London: 1936), pp. 98-99; Probyn to Milner, Confidential Dispatch of December 9, 1920, in C.O. 137/743.

[37] For example, Jamaicans intending to emigrate were required to deposit an amount of money with the Jamaican government which would

be used to help pay for repatriation in the event of expulsion. This amount varied from £1.10.0 to £10.0.0 depending on the intended destination. For a summary of the provisions of the Emigration Protection Law see, Manning to Harcourt, Dispatch of July 15, 1914, in C.O. 137/704.

[38] G. W. Roberts, op. cit., pp. 136-137.

[39] See Table A.6 in the Appendix.

[40] See Table A.6 in the Appendix.

[41] It is estimated that at least 82,000 Jamaicans emigrated between 1921 and 1943. This implies that approximately 107,800 Jamaicans must have returned during the same period. See, M. J. Proudfoot, op. cit., p. 81.

[42] This compares with a sex ratio at birth of 1029 for black Americans as opposed to 1056 for white Americans over approximately the same time period. See, G. W. Roberts, op. cit., pp. 74-75.

[43] Ibid., pp. 200-204.

[44] Ibid., p. 76.

[45] See, for example: D. V. Glass and D. E. C. Eversley (eds.), Population and History. (London: 1965); F. Mendels, "Industry and Marriages in Flanders Before the Industrial Revolution", in P. Deprez (ed.), Population and Economics. (Winnipeg: 1970), pp. 81-94.

[46] M. G. Smith, "Introduction" to E. Clarke, My Mother Who Fathered Me. (London: 1966), pp. i-xliv; J. Blake, Family Structure in Jamaica: The Social Context of Reproduction. (New York: 1961); R. T. Smith, "The Family in the Caribbean", in V. Rubin (ed.), Caribbean Studies: A Symposium. (Jamaica: 1957).

[47] "Every study [in European demography] so far made shows that the number of marriages shows more violent fluctuations than those of births and deaths." D. E. C. Eversley, "Population, Economy and Society", in D. V. Glass and D. E. C. Eversley (eds.), op. cit., p. 44.

[48] "The great earthquake of 1907 so dislocated the psychical equilibrium of the population of Kingston that great numbers experienced conviction of sin and registered their good intentions in a rush of matrimony which sent up the marriage rate with a bound." Lord Olivier, op. cit., p. 373.

[49] Ibid., pp. 373-374; Annual Report of the Governor of Jamaica for 1901-1902. (H.M.S.O.: Cd. 788-43, 1902).

[50] G. W. Roberts, <u>op. cit.</u>, p. 289.

[51] See references in endnote [46] above.

[52] G. W. Roberts, <u>op. cit.</u>, Table 49, p. 187; G. Eisner, <u>op. cit.</u>, p. 139; <u>Annual Report of the Governor of Jamaica for 1895-1896</u>. (H.M.S.O.: C. 8279-41, 1897).

[53] G. W. Roberts, "A Note on Mortality in Jamaica", <u>Population Studies</u>, Vol. IV, No. 1 (June 1950).

[54] G. W. Roberts, <u>The Population of Jamaica</u>. (Cambridge: 1957), p. 298.

[55] <u>Ibid.</u>, Table 77, p. 297.

[56] <u>Ibid.</u>, pp. 298-299.

[57] <u>Ibid.</u>, Table 78, p. 299.

[58] <u>Ibid.</u>, p. 160.

[59] <u>Ibid.</u>, pp. 163-164; Denham to Cunliffe-Lister, Dispatch of May 25, 1935, in C.O. 137/806.

Chapter VI

AN EMPIRICAL TEST OF THE ECONOMIC-DEMOGRAPHIC MODEL

Having reviewed the main features of economic structure and demographic performance in Jamaica during the period 1880-1940, we are in a position to test empirically the economic-demographic model of Chapter III. The empirical testing of any set of hypotheses involves three distinct stages. First, it is necessary to define in an operational manner the theoretical concepts involved in the hypotheses. Second, adequate data must be collected which allow the operational definitions to be given empirical content. Third, acceptable statistical techniques must be applied to the data in order to evaluate the significance of the hypotheses.

This chapter is accordingly divided into a number of sections. In the first, operational definitions are established for the variables of the hypotheses of Chapter III. Part two examines the data which form the basis of the empirical test. The method of statistical analysis is set out in part three. The results of the analysis and an interpretation of those results are presented in part four. The chapter concludes with a few summary comments on the overall interpretation of the method employed and the results obtained.

OPERATIONAL DEFINITIONS OF THE VARIABLES

In historical research it is often the case that operational definitions of variables under study depend critically on the nature of available or derivable data. In many instances this imposes a significant constraint. For example, the operational definition of parish fertility or parish mortality would ideally include adjustments for the age- and sex-composition of parish population. Except for certain census years, however, the historical data for the Jamaican case do not permit such refinements. Similarly, a comprehensive operational definition of parish socio-economic structure would include some measure of cultural and psychological characteristics dominant within a given parish. To expect such elements to be included in the present case is an idle hope given the data available. In short, the operational definitions which follow are in a sense second-best, and are highly constrained by the nature of the historical data.

The Dependent Demographic Variables

The demographic variables of the present model measure the incidence of vital events among a specified population during some particular period of time, most commonly a year. With respect to the i-th parish during any given year, we may operationally define the concepts of infant mortality, general mortality, fertility, natural increase, and net out-migration in the following ways.

Infant Mortality: For the i-th parish in any given year, the level of infant mortality is operationally defined as the infant mortality rate

(IMR_i) as set out in Chapter V. The level of infant mortality experienced by the i-th parish over a given number of years is simply the arithmetic average of annual infant mortality rates during those years.

General Mortality: For the i-th parish, the level of general mortality may be defined operationally in one of two ways. First, for any given year the crude death rate (CDR_i) as set out in Chapter V may be taken as reflective of general mortality experienced by the i-th parish. The arithmetic average of annual crude death rates over a given number of years is defined to be the level of general mortality experienced by the i-th parish in that time period. Note however that this definition does not take into account the age- or sex-composition of the population; hence inter-parish comparisons of crude death rates may not accurately reflect differences in the true level of general mortality.

In order to mitigate this deficiency, we may operationally define the i-th parish's level of general mortality in a second way. The censuses provide age- and sex-compositions of individual parish populations at each census date.[1] Applying relevant life table[2] values to these data, it is possible to compute a standardize general mortality ratio for each parish at each census date. Thus for each census date (1891, 1911, 1921) we may define the general mortality experienced by the i-th parish to be these standardized mortality ratios (SMR).[3]

Fertility: The level of fertility experienced by the i-th parish may also be defined operationally in two different ways. In any given year, the crude birth rate (CBR_i) as set out in Chapter V may be employed as a measure of the fertility of the i-th parish. The level of fertility experienced by the i-th parish over a given number of years is defined to be the arithmetic average of the crude birth rates for each of those years. As is the case with general mortality however, this operational definition does not account for the age- and sex-composition of parish populations.

Accordingly, we may operationally define the level of fertility experienced by the i-th parish around the time of each census to be the joint gross reproduction rate ($JGRR_i$) estimated by George Roberts.[4] These estimates provide at least a measure of adjustment for variation in the structure of parish populations and hence facilitate inter-parish comparisons of fertility levels.

Natural Increase: For the i-th parish in any given year, natural increase is operationally defined to be the difference between the number of registered births and the number of registered deaths. Thus the rate of natural increase (RNI_i) is defined to be the crude birth rate minus the crude death rate, as set out in Chapter V. The rate of natural increase experienced by the i-th parish over a number of years is the arithmetic average of the annual rates of natural increase during that period.

Net Out-Migration: An operational definition of parish net out-migration is possible only for intercensal periods since there are no reliable annual estimates of the direction and volume of migration. For the i-th parish during a given intercensal period, let PG_i be the actual change in population between the two census dates, and let NI_i be the total number of registered births less the total number of registered deaths within the parish during the intercensal period. The level of net out-migration for the i-th parish ($LNOM_i$) is thus operationally defined to be the numerical difference between NI_i and PG_i as discussed in Chapter V.

The rate of net out-migration for the i-th parish during a particular intercensal period ($RNOM_i$) may be operationally defined as:

$$RNOM_i = \frac{LNOM_i}{EP_i} \times 1000$$

where EP_i is the estimated parish population midway between the two census. Note that $RNOM_i$ will be greater than zero whenever the i-th parish was on balance experiencing net out-migration; for those parishes which experienced net in-migration, $RNOM_i$ will be less than zero.

The Independent Socio-Economic Variables

As set out in Chapter III, the two fundamental socio-economic variables from which the characteristic features of parish socio-economic structure are derived include the organization of production and the composition of output. The hypothesized economic-demographic relations were specified in terms of two variables, denoted P_i and X_i respectively.

In Chapter III, P_i was described as a numerical measure of the organization of production within the i-th parish during a given period of time. The value of P_i is interpreted thus: the greater is the value of P_i the more completely was the i-th parish dominated by plantation organization of production; the smaller is the value of P_i the more completely was the i-th parish dominated by small settler or peasant organized production.

Having examined the organizational forms of production in Chapter IV, we now operationally define P_i to be the proportion of total cultivated acreage under the control of plantations in the i-th parish during a particular time period. Since agricultural production was organized either by plantations or by small settlers, it is necessarily the case that land not under the control of the former was under the organization of the latter. Hence, the value of P_i is directly related to the importance of plantations in the organization of production in the i-th parish during some specified time period.

As discussed in Chapter III, X_i is taken to be a numerical measure of the composition of agricultural output in the i-th parish during a given time period. The value of X_i is interpreted thus: the greater is the value of X_i, the more completely is the i-th parish given over to the cultivation of staple export crops; the smaller is the value of X_i, the more completely is the i-th parish given over to the cultivation of domestic crops.

We now operationally define X_i to be the proportion of total cultivated acreage under staple export crops in the i-th parish during some given time period. Since cultivated acreage was under staple export crops or domestic crops, it follows that cultivated land not used for the former was used for the latter. Thus the value of X_i is directly related to the importance of staple exports in the composition of agricultural output in the i-th parish during some specified time period.

It is important to note that these operational definitions of parish socio-economic variables apply only to rural, agricultural parishes. Using these definitions we cannot distinguish urban, non-agricultural parishes from rural parishes in which domestic crops were produced by small settlers: in both cases, the values of P_i and X_i would be very near to zero. It is necessary, however, to make such a distinction in light of our expectations concerning the pronounced differences between the socio-economic structures of these two classes of parish. Drawing on the discussion in Chapter IV, we operationally define the two parishes of Kingston and St. Andrew to be urban and non-agricultural. With respect to the demographic consequences of parish socio-economic structure, Kingston and St. Andrew are thus to be considered separately from all rural parishes.

THE DATA

The second step in an empirical evaluation of the hypothesized economic-demographic relations is the collection of statistical data compatible with the operational definitions of the variables of the hypotheses. Since much of this data has already been presented in Chapters IV and V, the major task here is the specification of the time period for analysis.

Although much of the previous discussion has dealt with the period 1880-1943, the availability of data has constrained the formal empirical examination of the hypotheses to the much shorter time period 1891-1935. This is naturally a disappointment, but there is no compelling reason to suppose that the shorter period is untypical of the entire period 1880-1940. Neither economic structures nor patterns of demographic performance appear to have differed substantially during the period 1881-1890 as compared with the latter period. Moreover, in spite of the turmoil of 1938 and the disruption of the early years of the Second World War, it is unlikely that Jamaica in 1935 differed significantly from Jamaica in 1943.[5]

For purposes of data collection, the years 1891-1935 have been divided into nine five-year periods: 1891-1895, 1896-1900, ..., 1931-1935. For each parish, five year averages of each demographic and socio-economic variable have been computed according to the previously discussed operational definitions. These five year averages have been employed in preference to annual estimates for a number of reasons. In the first place, it is anticipated that the registration of vital events was not always accurate with respect to time. The accuracy of estimates of infant mortality, for example, depends on the correct registration of live births and infant deaths during the calendar year in which they occurred. By averaging vital rates over five years, it is hoped that any distortions arising from the timing of registrations will be diminished. Secondly, there appears to have been irregular but not insignificant evasion of the annual land tax from year to year. Particularly during periods of drought, flooding, or hurricane, the annual returns of acreage under cultivation by crop and of acreage under the control of plantations are highly suspect.[6] By averaging these returns over five year periods, it is possible to eliminate wide annual fluctuations and hence to acquire a more accurate picture of the organization of production and of the composition of output within individual parishes.

Averaging these variables over five year periods greatly diminishes the significance of annual fluctuations. In so far as these fluctuations arose from error in the collection of the data, such a diminution is desirable. But, it is possible that wide annual fluctuations in these variables accurately reflect real changes in the phenomena being measured. Given the susceptibility of parish mortality and fertility to exogenous influences such as natural disaster, sharp annual fluctuations in parish demographic performance are to be expected. Nonetheless, such exogenous influences are not an integral part of the model under study. Since we are concerned primarily with the impact of parish socio-economic structure on the pattern of parish demographic performance, it seems appropriate to use five year averages which attenuate the impact of such exogenous influences.[7]

As discussed above, more sophisticated measures of parish fertility and mortality are available for a few years centred on the census years of 1891, 1911, and 1921. In order to employ these data in a test of the hypotheses, we have estimated the values of the two socio-economic variables (P and X) for each parish during a five year period centred on each of those census dates.[8]

The appropriate time periods of analysis for the net out-migration relationship are much different. Since annual data are not available, estimates of net out-migration for individual parishes are restricted to the three intercensal periods 1891-1911, 1911-1921, and 1921-1943. It is necessary therefore to estimate the values of both socio-economic variables for each parish in those intercensal periods.[9]

In conclusion, the periods under study are of three types. First, nine five-year periods are used to test the economic-demographic relationships dealing with fertility, mortality, and natural increase. Second, three time periods are defined around the time of each census in order to employ more refined measures of parish fertility and mortality. Finally, in order to test hypotheses of net out-migration, we have defined three intercensal time periods. In all cases, the values of the variables are estimated in accordance with the operational definitions of the preceding section.

For convenience the following notation has been adopted and is summarized in Table 6.1. The subscript i is employed to indicate the particular rural parish under study. Since there are twelve such parishes, i = 1, 2,...,12. The superscript t is employed to denote the time period being considered. In total there are fifteen different time periods so that t = 1, 2,...,15. As an example, it will be seen from Table 6.1 that P_8^2 refers to the proportion of cultivated acreage controlled by plantations in the parish of Westmoreland during the period 1896-1900.

TABLE 6.1

DATA NOTATION

SUBSCRIPT i	PARISH	SUBSCRIPT t	TIME PERIOD
1	St. Thomas	1	1891-1895
2	Portland	2	1896-1900
3	St. Mary	3	1901-1905
4	St. Ann	4	1906-1910
5	Trelawny	5	1911-1915
6	St. James	6	1916-1920
7	Hanover	7	1921-1925
8	Westmoreland	8	1926-1930
9	St. Elizabeth	9	1931-1935
10	Manchester	10	1891
11	Clarendon	11	1911
12	St. Catherine	12	1921
		13	1891-1911
		14	1911-1921
		15	1921-1943

METHODS OF ANALYSIS

The hypotheses developed in Chapter III concern the impact of the two socio-economic variables on each of the demographic variables across individual parishes during a given time period. Two separate approaches may be taken to the testing of these hypotheses.

The first approach may be considered a pure cross-section analysis. For a given time period t, it is supposed that:

$$(1) \quad V_i = f(P_i, X_i)$$

$$(i = 1, 2, \ldots, 12)$$

where

V_i represents the value of one of the demographic variables for the i-th parish during the relevant time period;

P_i represents the proportion of cultivated acreage under the control of plantations in the i-th parish during the relevant time period;

X_i represents the proportion of cultivated acreage under staple export production in the i-th parish during the relevant time period.

As set out in Chapter III, the specific hypotheses involve the signs of the partial derivates, $\delta V/\delta P$ and $\delta V/\delta X$.

The second approach involves pooling cross-section data over time. Temporal variation in the demographic variables is controlled for by the use of a dummy variable for time. The principal advantage of this approach is to increase substantially the number of observations and hence the number of degrees of freedom of the regression equations.

Symbolically, this approach may be summarized thus:

$$(2) \quad V_i = f(P_i, X_i, t)$$

$$(i = 1, 2, \ldots, 12 \text{ and relevant } t)$$

Once again, the specific hypotheses involve the signs of the partial derivative, $\delta V/\delta P$ and $\delta V/\delta X$.

These two approaches give rise to a number of multivariate regression equations designed to test the hypotheses. The most obvious form for the first approach is:

$$(1a)\ V_i = a + b_1P_i + b_2X_i + E_i$$
$$(i = 1, 2, \ldots, 12)$$

This set of multivariate regressions must be estimated for each appropriate time period, t. Thus, where V_i represents alternatively the infant mortality rate, the crude death rate, the crude birth rate, or the rate of natural increase, nine separate time periods must be considered, so that t = 1, 2,...,9. Where V_i represents the standardized mortality ratio or the joint gross reproduction rate, three separate time periods must be considered; that is, t = 10, 11, 12. Finally, where V_i represents the rate of parish net out-migration, three separate time periods must be examined: t = 13, 14, 15. The error term, E_i, will include all other determinants of V_i. Since (1a) is estimated for separate time periods, E_i will not include any time related variation in V_i. It is, therefore, a "pure" error of estimation.

It should be noted that for each time period, t, the number of observations is small since only twelve parishes are involved. Hence, the degrees of freedom are small (9), and consequently the statistical significance of the estimated coefficients may be difficult to establish. If it were possible to pool these cross-section observations across all relevant time periods, the number of observations would be greatly increased. As a first step in this direction, the multiple regressions to be estimated take the form:

$$(1b)\ V_i^t = a + b_1 P_i^t + b_2 X_i^t + E_i^t$$

$$(i = 1, 2, \ldots, 12 \text{ and relevant } t)$$

Adoption of (1b) introduces some confusion into the interpretation of the estimated coefficients b_1 and b_2. That is, since V_i, P_i, and X_i vary not only as i changes but also as t changes, the coefficients b_1 and b_2 no longer can be interpreted as the impact of P on V and X on V independent of time. If (1b) were to be used as a test of the hypotheses, it would be necessary to establish that the demographic variables show no significant time trend. That such time trends do exist is apparent from the discussion in Chapter V.

The problems of employing (1b) are highlighted by the nature of the error term, E_i^t. In addition to a "true" error of estimation presumed to be randomly distributed, E_i^t also contains an error of estimation due to unexplained variation of V_i for a given time period, and an error of estimation due to unexplained variation in V^t for a given parish. In short, there is no way of being confident that E_i^t is randomly distributed; hence, the interpretation of b_1 and b_2 is uncertain.

Although regression form (1b) is of limited value, the benefits of pooling cross-section observations may be obtained if the impact of time on the dependent demographic variables can be eliminated. This in essence is the approach set out in (2) above. The appropriate multiple regressions to be estimated take the form:

$$(2a)\ V_i^t = a + b_1 P_i^t + b_2 X_i^t + b_3 t + E_i^t$$

$$(i = 1, 2, \ldots, 12 \text{ and relevant } t)$$

In (2a) the value of V_i^t is expected to vary because different parishes are being considered and because different time periods are included. The variation of V_i^t which is time related will be picked up by b_3, the estimated coefficient of the dummy time variable. If there were no linear time trend in V_i^t, then b_3 will not be statistically different from zero. In such a case, regression form (lb) could have been employed in place of (2a).

The estimated coefficients b_1 and b_2 will reflect the statistical association between the organization of production and the composition of output on the demographic variable, respectively. That is, the signs of b_1 and b_2 will indicate the impact of parish economic structure on demographic performance across the parishes. Hence, these coefficients are the focus of the analysis, as discussed in Chapter III.

The error term, E_i^t, of (2a) requires some explanation. To the extent that either P_i^t or X_i^t are characterized by a strong time trend, E_i^t will include both a "true" error of estimation and a time related error of estimation. Thus it is necessary to examine the pair-wise simple correlations among the independent variables P_i^t,X_i^t, and t. As shown in Table 6.2, these variables are for the most part uncorrelated for the various time periods used in this study. P and X show some correlation during the periods 1926-1930 and 1931-1935; P and t show some correlation for the period 1891-1921. On the whole, however, the explanatory variables may be judged as statistically independent.

TABLE 6.2

SIMPLE CORRELATION COEFFICIENTS

BETWEEN INDEPENDENT VARIABLES

(r)

TIME PERIODS	P WITH X	P WITH t	X WITH t
1891-1895	+ .1267		
1896-1900	+ .1448		
1901-1905	+ .1262		
1906-1910	+ .1888		
1911-1915	+ .1838		
1916-1920	+ .2893		
1921-1925	+ .3018		
1926-1930	+ .4282		
1931-1935	+ .5441		
1891	+ .1436		
1911	+ .1988		
1921	+ .3534		
1891-1935	+ .1295	- .3733	+ .1793
1891-1921 (Census Year)	+ .0529	- .4940	+ .2006

RESULTS AND INTERPRETATION

The results of the cross-section regression analysis (form 1a) are summarized in Table 6.3.[10] It will be seen that the signs of the estimated coefficients of the independent variables are, by and large,

TABLE 6.3

SUMMARY OF RESULTS OF PURE CROSS SECTION ANALYSIS:

REGRESSION FORM (1a)

DEPENDENT VARIABLE	NUMBER OF REGRESSIONS ESTIMATED	ORGANIZATION OF PRODUCTION (P)		COMPOSITION OF OUTPUT (X)	
		NUMBER OF COEFFICIENTS OF HYPOTHESIZED SIGN	NUMBER OF COEFFICICENTS OF HYPOTHESIZED SIGN AND STATISTICAL SIGNIFICANCE	NUMBER OF COEFFICIENTS OF HYPOTHESIZED SIGN	NUMBER OF COEFFICIENTS OF HYPOTHESIZED SIGN AND STATISTICAL SIGNIFICANCE
I.M.R.	9	9	2	7	-0-
C.D.R.	9	9	3	9	-0-
C.B.R.	9	6	-0-	9	2
R.N.I.	9	8	2	9	5
S.M.R.	3	3	-0-	3	1
J.G.R.R.	3	3	-0-	3	2
R.N.O.M.	3	2	2	3	1

NOTE: Complete results of these regressions are reported in Table 6.6 and in the Appendix, Tables A.18-A.23.

Statistical significance is at the 0.10 level.

TABLE 6.4

SUMMARY OF RESULTS OF POOLED CROSS SECTION ANALYSIS:

REGRESSION FORM (1b)

DEPENDENT VARIABLE	NUMBER OF OBSERVATIONS	HYPOTHESIZED SIGN OF: b_1	b_2	ESTIMATED COEFFICIENTS OF INDEPENDENT VARIABLES: CONSTANT TERM (a)	ORGANIZATION OF PRODUCTION (P) (b_1)	COMPOSITION OF OUTPUT (X) (b_2)	SIGNIFICANCE OF REGRESSION (F-RATIO)	R^2
I.M.R.	103	+	+	+156.96	+ 34.21* (8.63)	+ 22.49 (17.88)	9.35*	0.1512
C.D.R.	108	+	+	+ 20.24	+ 3.99* (1.18)	+ 5.55* (2.43)	9.46*	0.1527
S.M.R.	36	+	+	+ 0.28	+ 0.01 (0.02)	+ 0.20* (0.05)	8.10*	0.3294
C.B.R.	108	-	-	+ 39.54	+ 0.88 (1.07)	- 8.09* (2.21)	6.78*	0.1143
J.G.R.R.	36	-	-	+ 3.09	- 0.32* (0.12)	- 1.41* (0.27)	17.68*	0.5172
R.N.I.	108	-	-	+ 19.30	- 2.93* (1.40)	- 13.82* (2.88)	15.23*	0.2249
R.N.O.M.	36	-	-	+160.77	- 48.29 (66.93)	-348.98 (120.98)	4.89*	0.2288

NOTE: Bracketed figures are standard errors of estimate.
*Indicates significance level of 0.05

as hypothesized. Note however that in most cases the values of the coefficients are not significantly different from zero, even at the .10 level of confidence. Given the small number of observations for each estimated regression, this latter result is not entirely unexpected. Nonetheless, the "correctness" of the signs is encouraging.

The results of the pooled cross-section regression analysis (form 1b) are reported in Table 6.4. With only one exception, the signs of the estimated coefficients of the independent variables are as hypothesized. Moreover in ten of the fourteen cases the values of those coefficients are statistically significant at the .05 level of confidence. Note also that in each case, the F-ratio for the entire regression is significant at the .05 level. Notwithstanding ambiguity in the interpretation of the coefficients, these results appear to support the hypotheses.

The results of the time controlled pooled cross-section regression analysis (form 2a) are shown in Table 6.5. Since time related variation in the demographic variable has been estimated by the use of a dummy variable, the coefficients of P and X measure the impact of each on the dependent demographic variable. As previously discussed, this regression form is more appropriate for a test of the hypotheses developed in Chapter III given the desire to employ as many observations as possible.

Before turning to an interpretation of these results, it is worthwhile to remark on two prominent features displayed in Table 6.5. In the first place, it will be observed that for each of the six regressions estimated, the F-ratio for the entire relationship is

TABLE 6.5

SUMMARY OF RESULTS OF TIME CORRECTED POOLED CROSS SECTION ANALYSIS:

REGRESSION FORM (2a)

DEPENDENT VARIABLE	NUMBER OF OBSERVATIONS	HYPOTHESIZED SIGN OF: b_1	b_2	CONSTANT TERM (a)	ORGANIZATION OF PRODUCTION (P) (b_1)	COMPOSITION OF OUTPUT (X) (b_2)	TIME DUMMY (t) (b_3)	SIGNIFICANCE OF REGRESSION (F-RATIO)	R^2
				ESTIMATED COEFFICIENTS OF INDEPENDENT VARIABLES					
I.M.R.	108	+	+	+167.66	+ 26.15* (9.35)	+32.02+ (18.15)	- 1.95* (0.92)	7.95*	0.1865
C.D.R.	108	+	+	+ 22.32	+ 2.42+ (1.24)	+ 7.40* (2.41)	- 0.38* (0.12)	10.05*	0.2247
S.R.M.	36	+	+	- 1.58	+ 0.03 (0.02)	+ 0.18* (0.05)	+ 0.001 (0.0006)	6.72*	0.3866
C.B.R.	108	-	-	+ 43.40	- 2.02* (0.95)	- 4.66* (1.84)	- 0.70* (0.09)	25.79*	0.4266
J.G.R.R.	36	-	-	+ 0.34	- 0.29* (0.14)	- 1.44* (0.29)	+ 0.001 (0.003)	11.57*	0.5203
R.N.I.	108	-	-	+ 21.11	- 4.30* (1.50)	-12.21* (2.92)	- 0.33* (0.15)	12.21*	0.2604

NOTES: Bracketed figures are standard errors of estimate.

*Indicates significance level of 0.05

+Indicates significance level of 0.10

significant at the .05 level. This suggests that variation in the dependent variable is systematically related to variation in the set of independent variables. Thus even though the multiple regression coefficients (R^2) are relatively low, the overall relationships are valid. Secondly, the signs of the estimated regression coefficients of the two socio-economic variables are as hypothesized in each case. Nine of the twelve coefficients are statistically significant at the .05 level, and two others are significant at the .10 level. Thus in general these results appear to support the hypotheses advanced.

Socio-Economic Structure and Mortality

As previously discussed, three separate measures of parish mortality have been employed in the empirical tests: infant mortality rates, crude death rates, and standardized mortality ratios. It was hypothesized that parish mortality (however measured) would vary directly with the values of both parish socio-economic variables.

The results report in Table 6.5 lend support to this hypothesis. Both crude death reates and standardized mortality ratios appear to have been significantly influenced by the proportion of cultivated acreage under staple export crops (X). Moreover, crude death rates were significantly influenced by the proportion of cultivated acreage under the control of plantations (P) if one accepts a confidence level of .10. In the case of infant mortality rates, the organization of production is significant at the .05 level; the composition of output is significant only at the .10 level.

It is clear that inter-parish differences in mortality are more adequately measured by infant mortality rates and by standardized mortality ratios. The results shown in Table 6.5 indicate a differential impact of parish socio-economic structure on parish mortality so measured. The organization of production (P) was perhaps a more important influence on infant mortality, while the composition of production (X) appears to have had a stronger influence on general mortality as measured by the standardized mortality ratio.

In short, the results suggest that parish mortality was significantly influenced by one or both of the two socio-economic variables. Given the relatively low R in each case however, caution must be exercised in concluding that mortality has been well explained by the independent variables.

Socio-Economic Structure and Fertility

Whether measured by crude birth rates or by joint gross reproduction rates, parish fertility was hypothesized to vary inversely with the values of both socio-economic variables. As reported in Table 6.5, the regression results support this hypothesis.

As previously discussed, the more accurate measure of inter-parish fertility differentials are the joint gross reproduction rates. Hence the results of regressions employing this measure of fertility are accorded special weight. The results reported in Table 6.5 show that parish joint gross reproduction rates are significantly and inversely related both to the organization of production and to the composition of output. If parish fertility is measured by crude birth rates, the regression results also support the hypothesis: crude birth rates appear to have been significantly and inversely related to both socio-economic variables.

Socio-Economic Structure and Natural Increase

The parish rate of natural increase was hypothesized to vary inversely with the values of both socio-economic variables. Given the regression results for fertility and mortality, it is not surprising to observe in Table 6.5 that parish rates of natural increase were significantly and inversely related both to the organization of production and to the composition of output.

Socio-Economic Structure and Net Out-Migration

It will be recalled that the rate of parish net out-migration during an intercensal period was hypothesized to vary inversely with the values of both socio-economic variables. Given the unequal number of years in each intercensal period, no attempt was made to pool the cross-sections. That is, each intercensal period has been analysed separately.

The results as set out in Table 6.6 appear to lend some support to the hypothesis. Rates of parish net out-migration seem to have been significantly related to the organization of production in two of the three intercensal periods, and were significantly related to the composition of output in one of the three periods. In each of these cases, the significant coefficient has the hypothesized sign. Note

TABLE 6.6

SUMMARY OF RESULTS OF CROSS SECTION ANALYSIS OF NET OUT-MIGRATION:

REGRESSION FORM (1a)

DEPENDENT VARIABLE	TIME PERIOD	NUMBER OF OBSERVATIONS	HYPOTHESIZED SIGN OF: b_1	b_2	ESTIMATED COEFFICIENTS OF INDEPENDENT VARIABLES: CONSTANT TERM (a)	ORGANIZATION OF PRODUCTION (b_1)	COMPOSITION OF OUTPUT (b_1)	SIGNIFICANCE OF REGRESSION (F-RATIO)	R^2
R.N.O.M.	1891-1911	12	-	-	+218.38	+ 73.27 (110.57)	-1086.45* (324.58)	5.64*	0.5563
R.N.O.M.	1911-1921	12	-	-	+174.51	- 199.34+ (95.90)	- 76.31 (112.73)	2.89	0.3911
R.N.O.M.	1921-	12	-	-	+147.43	- 262.38* (104.85)	- 134.35 (138.83)	5.87*	0.5659

NOTES: Bracketed figures are standard error of estimates.

*Indicates significance level of 0.05

+Indicates significance level of 0.10

TABLE 6.7

CROSS-SECTION ANALYSIS OF DISAGGREGATED NET OUT-MIGRATION:

REGRESSION FORM (1a)

DEPENDENT VARIABLE	TIME PERIOD	NUMBER OF OBSERVATIONS	HYPOTHESIZED SIGN OF: b_1	b_2	ESTIMATED COEFFICIENTS OF INDEPENDENT VARIABLES: CONSTANT TERM (a)	ORGANIZATION OF PRODUCTION (b_1)	COMPOSITION OF OUTPUT (b_1)	SIGNIFICANCE OF REGRESSION (F-RATIO)	R^2
R.N.E.M.	1911-1921	12	-	-	+ 97.49	- 105.12 (81.72)	+ 104.90 (96.06)	1.15	0.2041
R.N.E.M.	1921-1943	12	-	-	- 38.86	+ 19.29 (69.70)	+ 94.33 (92.29)	0.86	0.1606
R.N.I.M.	1911-1921	12	-	-	+ 77.03	- 94.22* (33.35)	- 181.21* (39.21)	18.87*	0.8074
R.N.I.M.	1921-1943	12	-	-	+ 51.47	- 281.67* (95.36)	- 228.67 (126.26)	10.52*	0.7004

NOTES: Bracketed figures are standard error of estimates.

*Indicates significance level of 0.05

R.N.E.M. is the rate of net out-migration to the rest of the world and is defined as,

$$\text{R.N.E.M.} = \frac{\text{Parish net external out-migration}}{\text{Estimated parish population at mid-intercensal point}} \times 1000.$$

R.N.I.M. is the rate of net out-migration to other parishes within Jamaica and is defined as,

$$\text{R.N.I.M.} = \frac{\text{Parish net internal out-migration}}{\text{Estimated parish population at mid-intercensal point}} \times 1000.$$

however that in no single intercensal period were both socio-economic variables significantly related to net out-migration.

It is important to recall that parish net out-migration includes both net out-migration to other Jamaican parishes and net out-migration to the rest of the world. The data allow a distinction between these two flows for only two intercensal periods, 1911-1921 and 1921-1943. An analysis of parish socio-economic structure and these two net migration flows is reported in Table 6.7.

Parish rates of net external out-migration (RNEM) during those two intercensal periods appear to be unrelated to parish socio-economic structure. This suggests that such migration was largely determined by events abroad rather than by the socio-economic structure of the parish of origin. Since parish socio-economic structure basically reflects the 'push' side of emigration, it may be supposed that external migration was primarily determined by 'pull' factors in place of destination.

The results reported in Table 6.7 suggest that parish rates of net out-migration to other Jamaican parishes (RNIM) were influenced by parish socio-economic structure as hypothesized. In both intercensal periods this net migration was significantly and inversely related to the organization of production. For the period 1911-1921, the composition of output was also a significant explanator. It will be noted that in both periods the explanatory power of the independent variables, as measured by R^2, is quite high.

In short, the general hypothesis finds strongest support when internal net out-migration is examined, but practically no support when external net out-migration is analysed. When both are combined in the overall rate of net out-migration (Table 6.6), the hypothesis finds only mixed support.

CONCLUDING COMMENTS ON THE INTERPRETATION OF RESULTS

On the whole, the multiple regression results tend to support the several hypotheses relating parish demographic performance to the nature of parish socio-economic structure. Thus parish mortality appears to vary directly either with the value of organization of production variable (P), or with the value of the composition of output variable (X), or with the values of both. In general, fertility, natural increase, and net out-migration appear to vary inversely with the values of either or both of the socio-economic variables.

Of course great care must be exercised in the interpretation of these broad results. The proportion of cultivated acreage under the control of plantations or under staple export crops did not directly determine parish demographic performance. These operational measures of the organization of production and the composition of output are but proxies for unmeasured, and perhaps unmeasurable, features of parish economy and society which are presumed to have influenced parish demographic performance. Furthermore, both measured variables are proxies for more than one of these presumed influences. Thus, the organization of production is taken to reflect the nature of income distribution and the character of parish social organization; the composition of output serves as a proxy for both aggregate income and income stability over time.

These considerations greatly complicate interpretation. For

example, the finding that parish joint gross reproduction rates vary inversely with both the organization of production and the composition of output implies a very complex, and to a certain extent insolvable, causal mechanism. On the basis of the partial correlation coefficients it might be possible to argue that variation in parish joint gross reproduction rates is somewhat better explained by differences in the composition of output (r = - 0.6406) than by differences in the organization of production (r = - 0.3603).[11] But it is impossible on the basis of the present analysis to determine what particular aspects of organization or composition were especially critical determinants of parish fertility. Similar types of indeterminacy are embodied in each of the relationships studied.

These complications notwithstanding, the empirical results show that parish demographic performance in Jamaica during the period 1891-1935 was systematically related to the organizational form of production and/or to the composition of output. It has long been argued that these two aspects of economic structure hold important implications for economic growth, economic welfare, social organization, and public policy. It may now be concluded that these features of socio-economic structure also influenced the pattern of demographic performance.

ENDNOTES TO CHAPTER VI

[1] As presented in Census of Population, 1943. (Kingston: 1943), Table 25, pp. 25-27.

[2] G. W. Roberts, The Population of Jamaica. (Cambridge: 1957), Table 56, p. 198.

[3] These standardized mortality ratios are presented in Table A.9 in the Appendix.

[4] G. W. Roberts, op. cit., Table 70, p. 281. These rates are also presented in Table A.8 of the Appendix.

[5] G. W. Roberts, op. cit.

[6] See, for example: Annual Report of the Governor of Jamaica for 1896-1897. (H.M.S.O.: C. 8650-23, 1898); Annual Report of the Governor of Jamaica for 1912-1913. (H.M.S.O.: Cd. 7050-24, 1914).

[7] Five year averages of the demographic variables are presented in Tables A.6, A.10, A.11, A.12, and A.13 of the Appendix. Five year averages of the socio-economic variables are presented in Tables A.14 and A.15 of the Appendix.

[8] See Table A.16 of the Appendix.

[9] See Table A.17 of the Appendix.

[10] Complete results are reported in Tables A.18-A.23 of the Appendix; see also, Table 6.6.

[11] Correlation matrices with respect to Table 6.5 are presented in Tables A.24 and A.25 in the Appendix.

Chapter VII

SUMMARY AND CONCLUSIONS

As discussed in Chapter II, the literature on Jamaican historical demography is reasonably comprehensive. This literature has been especially strong in the collection and verification of data and in the detailed description of demographic change over time. Nonetheless, this literature has been relatively weak in the examination of the determinants of demographic performance. In particular, little systematic attempt has been made to explain the striking variation in demographic performance among the administrative parishes of Jamaica. It is this latter task which the present study has attempted to undertake.

This study rests on the common presumption that demographic performance is dependent upon the nature of the economy and society within which demographic events occur. By "the nature of the economy and society" is meant those specific economic and social features which characterize a particular region at any given point in time. In order to describe these features, this study draws upon the literature of the staple theory of growth and the plantation interpretation of underdevelopment. The former approach lays special emphasis on the composition of economic activity; the latter approach is particularly concerned with the manner in which economic activity is organized.

As discussed in Chapter III, these two approaches provide a means by which to describe parish socio-economic structure in a number of specific ways. These include (i) per capita real income, (ii) stability of real income over time, (iii) distributions of real income, and (iv) the general nature of social organization. In the absence of concrete measures of these specific features of socio-economic structure, it has been necessary to employ broad proxies for each. Based on theoretical considerations and incomplete empirical evidence, the organization of parish production, as measured by the proportion of cultivated acreage under the control of plantations, has been used as a proxy for (iii) and (iv) above. The composition of output, as measured by the proportion of cultivated acreage under staple export production, has been used as a proxy for (i) and (ii) above. The model discussed in Chapter III proposes hypotheses which relate these two proxies to parish demographic performance in terms of mortality, fertility, and net out-migration.

The structure of the Jamaican economy during the period 1881-1938 is the subject of Chapter IV. Particular care has been taken to show the relative importance of different economic sectors and to describe the spatial distribution of economic activity over time. Patterns of demographic performance are described in Chapter V. Special attention has been paid to inter-parish differences in mortality, fertility, and net out-migration. Little in these two chapters will be new to those familiar with the economic and demographic history of Jamaica. However, the emphasis given to the experience of individual parishes does represent a departure from much of the literature. In addition, these two chapters illustrate the historical counterpart of the abstract model developed in Chapter III. Most important, these two chapters provide the data required for a statistical test of the hypotheses of that model.

In order to test the hypotheses against historical evidence, a number of least-square multiple regressions were estimated. Details of this analysis and an interpretation of the results are reported in Chapter VI. Overall the independent variables of parish socio-economic structure appear to have influenced the dependent demographic variables in the hypothesized manner and to a statistically significant degree. Thus, parish mortality appears to have been directly related both to the degree of staple export production and to the extent of plantation organized production. As hypothesized, parish fertility and parish net out-migration appear to have been inversely related to both variables of parish socio-economic structure. As detailed in Chapter VI, there are exceptions but overall the results tend to support the hypotheses.

No one can doubt that caution is a virtue in the interpretation of empirical results. It is therefore proper that throughout Chapter VI attention is drawn to the conceptual and data problems encountered in the analysis and to the limits which must be placed on inferences made from the results. But caution, if unchecked, may obscure the contribution and broader implications of empirical studies.

There are three general contributions which this enquiry makes to the study of Jamaican demographic and economic history. First, it provides one explanation of the marked variation in demographic performance among parishes during the late nineteenth and early twentieth centuries. This study thus helps to fill a conspicuous gap in the literature.

Secondly, this study has demonstrated that the staple theory of growth and the plantation interpretation of underdevelopment offer some insight into Jamaican demographic performance. These two interpretations of Jamaican history have focused on such economic variables as real income and its distribution, patterns of consumption, saving, and investment, and the rates of economic growth. This study strongly suggests that demographic performance be added to the list of variables influenced by staple export production and by plantation organized economic activity.

It is of interest that both the composition of output and the organization of production appear to have influenced demographic performance in the same direction. An important implication of this is that commercially oriented economic activity--whether in the form of exporting staple crops, wage employment on plantations, or the market orientation of the urban economy--acts to depress fertility, to increase mortality, and to attract net in-migration. In this sense, the empirical results of this study fit well with demographic patterns observed elsewhere.

Thirdly, this study is suggestive of areas in which future research may prove fruitful. One of these is the desirability of studying historical events at a local or regional level. Given the considerable regional variation in demographic performance, it may be reasonable to expect that other types of social behaviour also varied substantially from parish to parish in Jamaica. Another area of possible fruitful research is the impact of parish demographic performance on subsequent socio-economic structure. Although this study ignores this issue, it is to be expected that over fairly long periods of time, socio-economic structure would alter in response to demographic change. Any comprehensive understanding of economic-demographic relationships will require both types of analysis. Finally, further research needs to be done on non-economic consequences of staple export production and plantation organized production. As mentioned in Chapter III, the organization of production and the composition of output may have held important implications for such diverse phenomena as criminal behaviour, political organization, and technological change.

In conclusion, it must be stressed that this study makes no claim to have uncovered startling new demographic or economic data. Nor has this study radically modified the basic approaches of the staple theory or the plantation interpretation of Jamaican economic history. Although data have been structured at the parish level and additional consequences of staple production and plantation organization have been suggested, these can hardly qualify as major revisions of the historiography. The element of novelty here is the demonstration that the largely descriptive concepts normally used in Jamaican economic history may be successfully employed as explanators of Jamaican demographic experience. The most important contribution of this study does not lie with its empirical results so much as with its attempt to recast general theories of economic history into testable form, and thus to extend the analytic power of those theories. In this respect this enquiry may yet meet George Beckford's exhortation: "What we need most are studies pregnant with ideas, not studies full of sterile detail."[1]

---

[1] G. Beckford, Persistent Poverty. (London: 1972), p. vii.

APPENDIX

REVISION OF CRUDE BIRTH AND CRUDE DEATH RATES

The Annual Reports of the Registrar-General for Jamaica contains estimates of crude birth rates and crude death rates for each of the fourteen parishes and for the island.[1] The chief deficiency of these lies in the estimation of mid-year populations for the intercensal years. Unable to measure migration flows, the Registrar-General assumed that mid-year population could be approximated by adding cumulative natural increase to the parish population as given in the most recent census. Consequently, these mid-year population estimates are seriously in error for periods of substantial migration.

New estimates of mid-year population have been made in an effort to correct this bias. Data on the volume and direction of migration are inadequate to allow a direct revision of parish mid-year populations. Assuming that net migration was uniform across any given intercensal period, it is possible to estimate mid-year population of any given parish for any given year of an intercensal period. Thus,

$$P_2 = P_1 (1 + r)^n$$

where

P_1 is the parish population at a given census date;

P_2 is the parish population at the next consecutive census date;

r is the average annual intercensal compound rate of parish population growth;

n is the number of years in the intercensal period.

Values of r for every parish during each intercensal period are thus easily calculated, and are reported in Table A.1 of this Appendix. Using the appropriate value of r, an estimate of the population of any given parish in year t of the intercensal period is given by:

$$P_t = P_1 (1 + r)^m$$

where m is the number of years between the census and year t. In exactly the same fashion, estimates of national population in any given year of an intercensal period may be estimated.

It has been shown that the annual registration of live births and of deaths were reasonably accurate during the period 1890-1938.[2] Employing the population estimates derived in the above manner, revised vital rates for the i-th parish in the t-th year have been estimated as follows:

$$CBR_t^i = \frac{RLB_t^i}{P_t^i} \times 1000$$

$$CDR_t^i = \frac{RD_t^i}{P_t^i} \times 1000$$

$$IMR_t^i = \frac{RID_t^i}{P_t^i} \times 1000$$

where

CBR_t^i is the crude birth rate for the i-th parish during the t-th year;

CDR_t^i is the crude death rate for the i-th parish during the t-th year;

IMR_t^i is the infant mortality rate for the i-th parish during the t-th year;

RLB_t^i is the number of registered live births in the i-th parish during the t-th year;

RID_t^i is the number of registered deaths of persons aged 0-1 years during the t-th year;

RD_t^i is the number of registered deaths in the i-th parish during the t-th year;

P_t^i is the estimated population of the i-th parish during the t-th year.

The revised vital rates for each parish and for the nation are shown in Tables A.2, A.3, and A.4 of this Appendix.

Revised rates of natural increase are defined as the arithmetic difference between the revised crude birth rate and the revised crude death rate for the i-th parish during the t-th year. The revised rates of natural increase are shown in Table A.5 of this Appendix.

ESTIMATES OF INTERNAL MIGRATION

The census of 1943 tabulated the population on the basis of parish of birth and length of residence in the parish of enumeration. These data have been used to estimate the volume and direction of migration within the island during the two intercensal periods 1911-1921 and 1921-1943.[3] Summaries of parish net internal migration are set out in Table A.6 of this Appendix.

It is worthwhile to stress that these estimates almost certainly understate the volume of internal migration. The most important reason for this underestimation lies in the fact that only the survivors of those who actually migrated were enumerated in the census of 1943.[4] Secondly, the data in Table A.6 are underestimates of internal migration because an unknown number of Jamaicans first migrated to another parish before leaving the island prior to 1943. Thus the data do not include the internal migration of subsequent emigrants. Finally these data do not include migration within a parish, nor do they include circular migration. Migration from one part of a given parish to another part of the same parish is thus excluded, even though there is reason to believe that such migration was not insignificant. Nor is it possible to estimate the numbers of migrants who left a particular parish for a few years but who returned to their parish of birth before 1943.

These limitations notwithstanding, the data summarized in Table A.6 are the best available estimates of net internal migration. Treated with care and generosity, these data throw considerable light on the volume and direction of internal migration during the period 1911-1943.

ESTIMATES OF EXTERNAL MIGRATION

In view of the inadequacies of the annual data, estimates of net external migration are limited to the intercensal periods 1891-1911, 1911-1921, and 1921-1943. At the national level, net emigration may be estimated simply by deducting intercensal natural increase from intercensal population growth as recorded in the two censuses. Thus any change in island population size not explained by natural increase is assumed to be the result of net emigration during the intercensal period. As seen in Table A.6, Jamaican net emigration so estimated was 43,800 during 1891-1911, 75,400 during 1911-1921, and during the period 1921-1943 there was net immigration of some 25,800.

At the parish level, net external migration is assumed to be the residual of intercensal population growth not explained by natural increase and net internal migration. As these last estimates are available only for the intercensal periods 1911-1921 and 1921-1943, estimates of parish net external migration are possible only for those two periods. These estimates are shown in Table A.6.

Although these estimates of net external migration are the best available, even more caution should be exercised than is usual in the interpretation of historical data. In the first place, it must be recalled that these are residuals. Any substantial error in the estimation of intercensal natural increase or in the estimation of parish internal migration during intercensal periods, will give rise to substantial error in the estimates of national or parish net external migration. Secondly, these estimates of net external migration do not indicate the volume of gross emigration or gross immigration at either the parish or national level. To the extent that circular or return migration was significantly large, therefore, these estimates undervalue the level of external migration.

STANDARDIZED MORTALITY RATIOS

Standardized mortality ratios are intended to adjust estimates of general mortality for differences in the age- and sex-composition of parish populations. Since age- and sex-compositions are known with accuracy only for census years,[5] estimates of standardized mortality ratios are confined to those dates.

For any given parish in a particular census year, the standardized mortality ratio (SMR) is the ratio of the expected number of deaths to the actual number of deaths recorded in the parish. The number of expected deaths is derived from the application of age- and sex-specific life table values for the national population to the particular population of the parish. That is, we estimate the number of deaths that would have occurred in the parish during the census year if parish mortality had been exactly that of the island as a whole. The ratio of the expected to the actual number of births is thus a measure of parish mortality which has been adjusted for the particular sex- and age-composition of the parish population.

The appropriate life table values are those presented by Roberts for the appropriate census dates.[6] The actual number of deaths is that reported by the Registrar-General for a given parish during the census year. The estimation of SMR for the i-th parish is some census year c, is thus:

$$SMR = \frac{\sum_j (MM_j)(MP_j) + (FM_j)(FP_j)}{(RD_c)(1000)}$$

where

MM_j is the life table value for the j-th age group of males;

FM_j is the life table value for the j-th age group of females;

MP_j is the number of enumerated males in the j-th age group;

FP_j is the number of enumerated females in the j-th age group;

RD_c is the total number of registered deaths in the census year for the i-th parish.

ENDNOTES TO APPENDIX

[1] Annually, 1890-1938, in C.O. 140.

[2] G. W. Roberts, The Population of Jamaica. (Cambridge: 1957), Chapters 6 and 8; G. W. Roberts, "A Note on Mortality in Jamaica", Population Studies, Vol. IV, No. 1 (June 1950).

[3] G. W. Roberts, The Population of Jamaica. (Cambridge: 1957), Tables 33-36, pp. 145-148.

[4] Given the uncertainty of the age distribution of such migrants, Roberts concludes that it is inappropriate to attempt to correct the migration data so as to reflect this mortality. Ibid., p. 144.

[5] The age- and sex-composition of parish populations at each census date are conveniently summarized in The Census of Population. (Kingston: 1943), Table 25.

[6] G. W. Roberts, supra, Table 56, p. 198.

TABLE A.1

CENSUS POPULATION AND ANNUAL COMPOUND RATES OF POPULATION GROWTH FOR INTERCENSAL PERIODS, BY PARISH, JAMAICA, 1871-1943.

PARISH	CENSUS POPULATION						ANNUAL RATES OR INTER-CENSAL POPULATION GROWTH (%)				
	1871	1881	1891	1911	1921	1943	1871-1881	1881-1891	1891-1911	1911-1921	1921-1943
Kingston	34,314	38,566	48,504	59,674	63,711	110,083	1.18	2.32	1.04	0.66	2.52
St. Andrew	31,683	34,982	37,855	52,773	54,598	128,146	1.00	0.79	1.68	0.34	3.95
St. Thomas	32,673	33,945	32,176	39,330	42,501	60,693	0.38	-0.54	1.01	0.78	1.63
Portland	25,313	28,901	31,998	49,360	48,970	60,712	1.33	1.02	2.19	-0.80	0.98
St. Mary	36,495	39,696	42,915	72,956	71,404	90,902	0.85	0.78	2.69	-0.22	1.10
St. Ann	39,547	46,584	54,127	70,651	70,922	96,193	1.65	1.51	1.34	0.04	1.40
Trelawny	28,812	32,115	30,996	35,463	34,602	47,535	1.09	-0.36	0.68	-0.25	1.45
St. James	29,340	33,625	35,050	41,376	41,946	63,542	1.37	0.42	0.83	0.14	1.91
Hanover	26,310	29,567	32,088	37,432	38,240	51,684	1.17	0.82	0.77	0.21	1.38
Westmoreland	40,823	49,035	53,450	66,456	68,853	90,109	1.85	0.37	1.10	0.36	1.23
St. Elizabeth	45,200	54,375	62,256	78,700	79,281	100,182	1.87	1.36	1.18	0.07	1.07
Manchester	38,925	48,458	55,462	65,194	63,945	92,745	2.45	1.36	0.81	-0.19	1.71
Clarendon	42,747	49,845	57,105	73,914	82,555	123,505	1.55	1.37	1.30	1.11	1.85
St. Catherine	53,972	61,110	65,509	88,104	96,590	121,032	1.25	0.70	1.49	0.92	1.03
JAMAICA	506,154	580,804	639,491	831,383	858,118	1,237,063	1.39	0.97	1.32	0.32	1.68

SOURCE: Computed from G. W. Roberts, *The Population of Jamaica*, Table 9, p. 51.

TABLE A.2

REVISED CRUDE BIRTH RATES, BY PARISH, JAMAICA, ANNUALLY, 1891-1938

YEAR	KINGSTON	ST. ANDREW	ST. THOMAS	PORT-LAND	ST. MARY	ST. ANN	TRELAWNY	ST. JAMES	HANOVER	WEST-MORE-LAND	ST. ELIZ.	MAN-CHESTER	CLAR-ENDON	ST. CATHERINE	KINGSTON & ST. ANDREW	JAMAICA
1891/92	34.1	37.6	39.1	37.0	37.6	39.2	34.7	30.0	40.0	39.2	43.0	43.2	39.5	38.3	35.6	38.4
1892/93	30.5	36.1	36.2	37.0	38.7	39.3	36.2	29.5	36.5	36.6	42.4	41.8	36.9	40.9	32.9	37.5
1893/94	34.6	38.9	43.0	42.1	39.8	42.1	39.9	34.8	38.7	38.7	47.4	45.6	43.5	44.3	36.5	41.4
1894/95	33.1	33.3	37.5	38.1	33.7	39.9	38.9	31.4	41.4	39.6	42.5	43.3	35.9	37.1	33.2	37.8
1895/96	33.0	37.1	41.9	41.1	38.8	41.4	41.2	31.7	38.8	39.4	45.4	42.5	39.7	39.2	34.8	39.6
1896/97	36.2	35.3	40.4	37.0	36.8	41.6	40.2	33.7	40.6	38.5	40.8	43.7	42.7	40.3	35.8	39.4
1897/98	38.1	37.9	43.5	41.5	39.9	41.8	38.5	33.7	43.5	39.6	43.9	43.2	43.2	41.1	38.0	40.9
1898/99	33.9	33.9	40.8	39.5	37.8	43.3	39.3	34.0	40.2	38.8	41.9	43.1	41.9	37.6	33.9	39.2
1899/00	38.4	35.7	45.6	42.4	42.2	48.4	44.5	36.4	44.6	44.9	50.9	47.5	43.6	42.5	37.2	43.7
1900/01	30.3	31.5	35.9	38.1	36.9	40.8	35.4	31.5	41.1	36.6	41.1	41.9	39.2	36.5	30.8	37.1
1901/02	39.8	35.5	46.2	43.9	42.2	44.7	43.4	35.8	45.4	43.2	45.0	45.6	43.7	41.5	37.9	42.6
1902/03	35.5	34.9	39.7	42.9	42.2	45.2	39.7	32.7	41.0	39.6	45.9	47.9	42.6	40.3	35.2	41.2
1903/04	38.3	36.4	41.1	40.3	37.8	42.8	42.9	34.4	44.8	43.9	47.3	47.3	43.9	42.8	37.4	42.1
1904/05	36.2	32.5	35.4	34.5	33.7	40.1	39.5	31.9	39.7	40.5	43.1	46.0	39.3	35.6	34.5	38.0
1905/06	34.5	33.6	43.7	44.4	42.3	44.4	42.3	39.9	41.6	39.2	44.3	41.2	41.4	40.0	34.1	40.9
1906/07	32.5	33.9	35.8	36.7	38.1	45.0	42.2	37.8	44.3	41.9	43.4	44.7	42.0	41.1	33.2	40.3
1907/08	27.7	30.0	37.7	37.5	37.8	40.2	36.9	34.9	38.3	38.4	47.0	39.2	32.7	34.4	28.7	36.8
1908/09	38.0	37.4	40.5	36.9	38.7	41.4	40.9	36.1	38.6	38.4	39.1	39.8	42.3	42.2	37.7	39.5
1909/10	37.6	38.7	38.0	36.8	40.8	42.4	38.6	35.5	41.8	39.0	42.1	39.4	39.5	42.1	38.1	39.8
1910/11	33.2	33.6	38.3	37.3	38.8	42.9	39.8	37.7	42.8	37.9	40.7	39.7	39.5	39.0	33.4	38.6
1911/12	35.6	32.8	39.2	40.7	38.4	41.3	37.6	38.1	42.1	37.5	42.5	40.5	41.2	40.5	34.3	39.3
1912/13	37.2	36.0	37.4	37.8	38.8	43.2	38.2	40.0	43.9	41.0	37.8	40.5	42.6	40.1	36.7	39.7
1913/14	33.2	32.8	36.4	36.4	36.6	40.4	35.5	37.7	40.1	36.9	33.7	33.4	39.1	37.8	33.1	36.4
1914/15	36.6	37.9	40.6	43.5	43.9	44.0	38.9	35.3	38.6	36.4	41.4	39.7	43.4	43.6	37.2	40.4
1915/16	29.8	31.5	32.9	35.7	35.6	40.6	36.4	35.7	41.7	38.3	37.0	36.4	40.6	37.5	30.6	36.6

TABLE A.2 (Cont'd)

REVISED CRUDE BIRTH RATES, BY PARISH, JAMAICA, ANNUALLY, 1891-1938

YEAR	KINGSTON	ST. ANDREW	ST. THOMAS	PORT-LAND	ST. MARY	ST. ANN	TRELAWNY	ST. JAMES	HANOVER	WEST-MORE-LAND	ST. ELIZ.	MAN-CHESTER	CLAR-ENDON	ST. CATHERINE	KINGSTON & ST. ANDREW	JAMAICA
1916	27.5	30.0	32.8	34.8	34.9	39.9	36.6	35.1	37.8	35.2	36.7	36.3	38.7	36.6	28.7	35.4
1917	26.4	32.1	34.7	39.7	37.1	40.7	36.5	34.4	38.9	36.1	39.0	33.8	39.1	35.0	29.1	36.0
1918	28.8	35.6	36.1	33.6	35.0	38.6	35.2	35.6	40.1	36.2	37.4	33.3	39.7	37.1	31.9	36.0
1919	27.9	36.8	32.2	32.7	34.3	38.4	36.3	35.3	34.9	33.9	37.6	36.0	38.5	34.2	32.0	35.1
1920	35.5	48.7	38.8	40.3	40.0	42.0	41.5	40.7	41.6	41.7	41.9	37.5	43.2	39.0	41.6	40.8
1921	31.7	39.1	35.7	34.0	33.8	35.1	35.8	34.5	35.6	35.4	36.3	31.2	37.7	33.0	35.1	34.8
1922	37.3	36.1	34.2	33.1	36.2	40.7	38.0	36.9	38.1	37.5	39.1	36.5	37.3	35.6	36.7	37.5
1923	37.3	35.1	38.8	37.5	38.0	38.7	38.8	38.0	39.7	37.8	39.0	36.0	40.7	39.8	36.2	38.2
1924	36.5	30.5	36.0	39.9	36.0	36.7	37.9	39.1	39.8	37.4	36.8	33.2	37.3	38.1	33.5	36.6
1925	31.9	38.1	31.4	37.3	35.3	36.2	36.1	37.1	37.9	34.4	35.1	32.1	35.2	34.7	30.0	34.3
1926	37.7	30.2	37.0	39.8	33.7	39.3	39.7	38.0	41.4	38.3	41.5	39.4	40.8	39.6	33.9	38.2
1927	32.9	27.9	31.8	33.3	35.7	36.4	37.1	36.4	35.7	35.3	35.3	32.9	36.2	37.2	30.3	34.6
1928	34.8	27.0	35.6	36.8	35.1	36.1	37.4	36.1	36.9	34.2	40.4	36.8	38.8	36.1	30.9	35.8
1929	34.1	25.1	32.5	36.9	35.9	35.0	38.5	38.7	39.0	37.2	34.8	32.1	35.8	33.7	29.6	34.3
1930	36.7	30.5	34.7	38.6	37.2	38.2	40.6	41.0	38.7	37.0	38.4	37.4	40.3	37.1	33.5	37.3
1931	36.4	26.2	33.7	34.6	35.7	35.8	39.1	39.2	39.6	36.3	38.9	35.5	37.1	35.0	31.2	35.6
1932	31.9	24.0	31.2	32.2	31.4	34.2	32.5	41.6	37.4	35.4	36.9	35.3	34.6	30.7	27.8	33.1
1933	32.7	28.0	30.4	31.9	32.8	34.4	36.8	39.1	37.8	35.6	36.9	33.9	35.0	34.1	30.2	33.9
1934	31.3	24.5	28.9	31.0	32.6	33.1	32.7	40.3	35.0	32.5	34.8	31.8	33.2	31.7	27.7	32.0
1935	33.1	26.4	29.9	31.4	30.8	37.0	39.8	42.1	35.9	34.2	39.1	36.0	37.4	33.2	29.6	34.4
1936	32.5	24.3	27.6	31.1	30.1	34.8	38.9	43.6	37.1	36.4	36.4	33.5	34.5	30.8	28.2	33.1
1937	33.9	21.5	27.1	28.9	28.9	34.2	38.2	38.9	32.8	31.9	35.3	34.0	32.2	29.2	27.4	31.5
1938	37.9	20.7	28.5	28.2	29.1	34.9	37.5	38.8	38.3	35.1	39.1	34.4	35.4	32.2	28.8	35.2

TABLE A.3

REVISED CRUDE DEATH RATES, BY PARISH, JAMAICA, ANNUALLY, 1891-1938

YEAR	KINGSTON	ST. ANDREW	ST. THOMAS	PORT-LAND	ST. MARY	ST. ANN	TRELAWNY	ST. JAMES	HANOVER	WEST-MORE-LAND	ST. ELIZ.	MAN-CHESTER	CLAR-ENDON	ST. CATHERINE	KINGSTON & ST. ANDREW	JAMAICA
1891/92	26.1	25.9	24.7	21.9	20.7	17.8	26.5	24.0	27.9	24.0	21.8	18.6	20.2	25.1	26.0	22.9
1892/93	22.9	21.7	22.7	20.8	20.0	18.4	25.2	19.7	22.0	22.6	20.8	17.0	18.3	24.5	22.4	21.0
1893/94	24.0	26.2	26.5	22.1	21.7	19.2	28.5	22.0	23.4	20.9	22.7	17.4	20.9	25.1	25.0	22.5
1894/95	25.3	25.5	24.2	22.7	19.4	18.3	24.8	21.1	23.7	19.5	19.5	17.4	20.1	23.5	25.4	21.4
1895/96	28.6	27.4	24.4	27.7	22.3	19.4	23.9	22.4	25.2	25.2	21.1	17.4	22.1	23.1	28.1	23.2
1896/97	27.7	23.4	23.7	23.6	20.3	21.9	26.5	21.2	25.6	23.0	20.1	18.6	20.8	24.3	25.8	22.6
1897/98	28.7	26.7	27.5	23.2	19.4	19.7	26.3	22.2	24.8	23.5	22.1	19.5	24.8	26.2	27.8	23.7
1898/99	27.0	24.7	24.6	21.2	19.7	17.1	25.2	21.3	24.1	22.1	18.9	17.1	23.1	22.6	25.9	21.7
1899/00	27.3	26.7	28.7	24.6	19.6	21.9	27.9	24.1	23.7	23.0	22.0	18.1	23.7	25.0	27.1	23.6
1900/01	26.6	24.2	25.5	23.2	21.5	19.9	24.2	21.8	26.8	20.9	19.1	18.1	22.0	25.3	25.5	22.4
1901/02	26.9	24.3	25.3	21.2	21.2	18.3	26.6	21.2	26.3	24.7	21.3	18.6	22.3	25.3	25.7	22.8
1902/03	25.0	19.2	21.7	22.0	21.1	19.2	23.2	20.6	24.9	20.0	17.7	17.3	20.5	22.0	22.3	20.7
1903/04	29.1	28.8	31.4	30.6	29.0	23.9	29.0	23.9	27.5	22.8	21.1	18.4	25.0	29.8	29.0	26.0
1904/05	28.9	28.5	25.9	24.3	24.3	20.7	27.4	23.7	30.4	27.5	23.6	23.9	28.3	28.9	28.7	26.0
1905/06	27.4	26.7	26.7	21.5	22.4	17.4	23.6	21.4	27.5	23.0	21.3	20.1	23.6	24.9	27.1	23.1
1906/07	35.8	33.9	28.7	24.5	22.5	21.2	26.4	27.2	31.5	26.6	23.9	26.8	32.9	29.1	34.9	27.7
1907/08	34.0	32.1	29.3	31.7	24.5	25.2	33.6	27.7	34.1	29.6	26.8	27.5	32.6	32.7	33.2	29.8
1908/09	31.4	24.4	23.2	24.2	21.4	18.4	27.5	23.2	23.2	21.6	22.5	20.5	24.6	25.9	28.1	23.5
1909/10	30.2	25.5	25.3	21.8	20.7	18.3	22.4	20.6	22.0	20.5	20.3	19.4	26.6	26.4	28.0	22.9
1910/11	32.4	27.7	24.7	22.8	21.8	18.6	23.2	22.1	23.7	22.4	19.0	17.9	23.2	26.7	30.2	23.2
1911/12	27.0	26.2	24.1	23.8	20.8	19.1	25.9	22.0	24.7	23.0	19.0	16.6	21.9	24.3	26.6	22.4
1912/13	32.0	30.2	27.0	29.9	21.6	18.3	22.4	26.5	26.7	25.8	25.2	21.6	26.1	28.6	31.1	25.7
1913/14	28.6	26.2	22.6	20.8	18.7	18.4	23.6	25.3	28.8	26.0	19.1	18.8	20.1	23.0	27.5	22.4
1914/15	26.5	26.7	25.0	25.2	24.4	19.5	24.2	22.9	23.3	21.0	18.5	17.2	20.3	23.4	26.6	22.4
1915/16	24.6	29.2	25.1	26.0	21.9	19.9	22.5	24.7	24.4	22.8	19.3	18.0	21.4	24.9	26.7	22.9

TABLE A.3 (Cont'd)

REVISED CRUDE DEATH RATES, BY PARISH, JAMAICA, ANNUALLY, 1891-1938

YEAR	KINGSTON	ST. ANDREW	ST. THOMAS	PORT-LAND	ST. MARY	ST. ANN	TRELAWNY	ST. JAMES	HANOVER	WEST-MORE-LAND	ST. ELIZ.	MAN-CHESTER	CLAR-ENDON	ST. CATHERINE	KINGSTON & ST. ANDREW	JAMAICA
1916	28.5	28.5	26.2	24.0	23.1	23.7	24.7	23.2	24.5	23.3	21.0	18.7	22.9	25.0	28.5	23.9
1917	36.0	34.0	29.0	27.9	25.7	23.0	31.2	27.5	29.4	25.8	23.2	25.0	29.2	34.3	35.0	28.5
1918	34.0	44.2	41.9	40.1	30.6	30.0	38.0	34.8	35.3	33.4	28.7	26.9	33.3	42.2	38.7	34.8
1919	24.6	32.6	24.2	25.4	20.8	21.3	23.5	23.5	25.9	21.7	20.0	19.8	21.8	25.1	28.3	23.3
1920	32.5	39.3	24.8	26.9	20.7	21.6	27.2	23.7	26.2	22.6	21.7	21.5	23.2	27.6	35.7	25.4
1921	33.4	42.7	29.1	26.9	26.7	21.4	31.2	26.8	31.4	25.0	23.1	21.0	26.6	34.4	37.7	28.3
1922	24.5	27.9	23.2	22.9	21.7	21.7	26.4	22.0	25.0	25.4	21.4	20.0	22.0	22.1	26.1	23.0
1923	24.4	26.5	27.0	24.7	20.4	20.3	24.6	23.6	22.4	20.5	22.1	20.8	22.7	23.1	25.3	22.8
1924	24.9	23.7	24.3	25.2	20.3	16.8	22.0	21.8	22.6	20.7	18.7	17.1	22.0	25.3	24.2	21.6
1925	25.6	25.1	26.3	21.5	21.0	18.1	23.1	21.8	20.4	18.5	17.5	15.6	20.7	25.2	25.3	21.2
1926	22.1	21.3	20.8	22.7	20.3	18.3	20.3	23.5	18.0	19.1	19.5	16.9	20.3	23.0	21.6	20.4
1927	23.7	24.0	22.9	23.4	20.9	17.4	21.6	21.8	21.1	22.7	19.7	17.3	18.0	23.0	23.7	21.0
1928	22.9	21.2	21.5	20.0	18.7	16.8	20.7	22.3	20.6	19.7	19.6	16.8	18.0	20.5	22.0	19.7
1929	21.3	20.6	19.8	20.0	17.8	14.1	18.8	22.3	18.4	17.4	18.9	16.1	17.3	19.1	20.8	18.5
1930	18.7	19.2	19.2	17.9	17.0	14.9	18.8	21.3	17.9	17.9	16.6	14.7	15.5	16.3	18.9	17.2
1931	21.1	18.6	20.5	20.1	18.5	16.3	22.3	25.1	20.9	18.4	18.6	15.2	17.0	20.5	19.8	19.0
1932	21.5	18.6	18.4	18.1	18.0	16.0	17.1	21.1	19.9	17.9	17.1	13.8	15.8	17.4	20.0	17.7
1933	25.2	21.8	21.5	18.8	19.0	16.2	21.7	21.8	19.6	19.5	19.7	17.6	18.4	20.6	23.4	19.9
1934	20.9	18.3	19.7	17.7	19.7	13.9	18.2	17.7	17.8	17.1	17.1	15.2	15.7	18.5	19.5	17.5
1935	19.9	18.3	20.9	18.8	18.0	15.5	19.0	22.4	19.5	17.0	16.7	14.4	17.5	19.8	19.0	18.1
1936	19.5	17.9	20.0	17.5	17.6	14.1	18.1	22.2	20.1	17.0	17.8	13.3	17.0	20.1	18.6	17.8
1937	19.5	15.2	17.0	16.5	14.9	13.1	16.1	18.6	16.4	14.6	15.3	12.7	14.3	16.3	17.2	15.6
1938	19.0	15.6	17.9	17.1	18.0	14.5	18.2	19.6	18.0	16.5	17.2	13.8	14.4	17.8	17.2	16.7

TABLE A.4

INFANT MORTALITY RATES, BY PARISH, JAMAICA, ANNUALLY, 1891-1938

YEAR	KINGSTON	ST. ANDREW	ST. THOMAS	PORT-LAND	ST. MARY	ST. ANN	TRELAWNY	ST. JAMES	HANOVER	WEST-MORE-LAND	ST. ELIZ.	MAN-CHESTER	CLAR-ENDON	ST. CATHERINE	KINGSTON & ST. ANDREW	JAMAICA
1891/92	231.3	156.8	169.3	156.9	154.8	151.3	233.8	211.2	208.6	188.8	163.0	138.0	153.9	188.4	196.8	174.7
1892/93	218.0	137.2	177.0	164.3	168.3	150.8	197.7	177.5	184.1	172.0	166.3	133.4	133.6	177.1	179.0	165.4
1893/94	199.0	183.8	153.1	169.5	167.9	166.3	229.5	196.6	196.7	154.9	148.6	137.5	155.7	170.9	191.8	168.5
1894/95	227.2	170.0	153.6	177.8	168.7	148.8	218.0	188.0	173.1	148.7	150.3	131.8	165.0	148.6	201.7	168.2
1895/96	244.8	184.4	173.0	201.4	182.3	160.7	205.9	209.2	219.4	187.9	163.4	133.7	159.8	165.9	216.1	178.5
1896/97	239.5	170.9	175.7	185.8	178.1	182.3	222.9	190.3	209.1	154.3	152.1	139.0	148.9	177.9	209.3	175.8
1897/98	199.4	181.4	181.5	170.0	164.7	165.1	235.0	228.7	189.5	174.7	160.3	130.8	176.5	189.2	191.3	177.4
1898/99	230.2	166.6	205.4	173.6	176.4	148.1	216.1	197.8	211.7	175.3	154.1	125.5	177.5	179.0	201.5	175.9
1899/00	199.1	169.1	199.7	174.2	152.9	178.8	220.4	196.8	180.2	168.1	161.1	125.4	149.3	172.5	186.1	170.4
1900/01	228.1	163.9	173.7	169.1	167.2	168.6	208.7	223.4	203.5	172.6	156.0	128.4	157.5	188.7	198.4	174.3
1901/02	191.3	151.9	165.5	169.1	158.8	148.5	192.7	169.7	181.8	164.7	156.9	132.9	146.8	183.2	174.5	163.3
1902/03	229.8	126.8	141.0	178.8	154.1	145.6	211.1	194.9	196.8	175.7	147.4	128.6	149.6	156.1	183.2	162.0
1903/04	245.4	194.6	225.3	222.6	208.0	164.4	207.6	202.8	183.8	174.1	166.8	136.0	158.8	201.8	222.8	187.0
1904/05	235.5	206.8	254.2	183.8	182.1	161.3	233.8	220.6	213.7	193.0	171.4	166.0	186.7	217.8	223.1	192.9
1905/06	229.9	168.2	175.9	161.0	159.9	129.3	194.5	138.2	204.3	171.0	145.4	143.2	160.4	176.6	201.9	165.1
1906/07	267.8	195.8	233.1	199.4	185.5	149.2	203.7	211.5	209.4	204.3	173.9	177.8	210.5	205.1	233.8	204.3
1907/08	273.9	246.5	207.4	223.9	193.6	196.8	269.7	250.2	262.7	244.0	166.1	194.3	250.2	250.4	260.6	223.7
1908/09	262.1	171.1	156.5	202.6	182.1	140.6	213.7	204.2	175.7	164.1	165.2	141.3	153.5	170.9	243.9	175.1
1909/10	246.9	174.6	185.6	206.5	170.8	141.8	185.4	195.3	161.5	157.4	148.3	135.7	189.8	184.8	212.6	174.6
1910/11	295.6	223.8	176.7	190.7	179.6	131.8	205.3	184.8	202.5	183.6	159.5	151.8	194.7	211.6	261.7	188.5
1911/12	248.8	194.5	168.1	177.3	184.4	165.9	213.1	203.3	209.6	218.6	165.7	148.6	178.9	194.3	224.5	187.9
1912/13	268.7	217.2	187.1	226.5	175.9	133.6	193.9	244.9	193.6	202.8	197.4	152.5	173.2	198.7	245.0	193.6
1913/14	259.8	195.6	165.1	151.8	156.7	131.5	203.8	202.6	214.3	196.4	143.2	141.7	143.3	169.2	229.2	171.7
1914/15	236.6	181.1	153.5	195.9	189.6	131.7	198.1	171.8	188.1	158.3	152.0	128.7	136.7	170.4	210.2	167.3
1915/16	231.9	202.6	179.7	187.5	169.3	132.6	183.5	197.2	183.4	184.1	178.5	144.2	154.6	183.1	217.8	175.8

TABLE A.4 (Cont'd)

REVISED CRUDE DEATH RATES, BY PARISH, JAMAICA, ANNUALLY, 1891-1938

YEAR	KINGSTON	ST. ANDREW	ST. THOMAS	PORT-LAND	ST. MARY	ST. ANN	TRELAWNY	ST. JAMES	HANOVER	WEST-MORE-LAND	ST. ELIZ.	MAN-CHESTER	CLAR-ENDON	ST. CATHERINE	KINGSTON & ST. ANDREW	JAMAICA
1916	246.9	176.2	183.3	170.9	168.1	156.9	223.1	192.9	190.1	182.8	174.6	133.1	154.2	176.0	212.5	176.0
1917	295.8	205.2	184.2	163.8	176.2	138.1	209.6	205.3	212.3	193.1	161.6	145.2	170.1	203.2	249.3	184.7
1918	241.7	188.0	225.3	209.3	147.9	151.7	233.9	179.4	193.6	165.7	154.6	127.5	157.8	179.6	213.9	175.9
1919	208.0	161.3	162.1	184.9	148.7	133.3	192.7	196.8	200.3	162.2	153.7	125.7	142.9	166.0	183.2	161.7
1920	228.2	187.6	174.0	198.5	148.8	138.2	194.2	191.2	171.2	165.4	175.7	140.1	153.4	184.5	206.2	172.5
1921	272.3	219.5	223.2	209.5	197.9	141.8	223.5	207.4	239.9	169.5	174.7	150.6	164.9	226.0	245.1	197.0
1922	171.4	176.6	180.0	171.1	167.6	149.2	249.1	213.7	204.1	213.1	169.8	164.5	162.4	164.9	173.7	177.6
1923	182.0	201.1	193.1	201.7	158.8	164.8	206.5	189.8	173.9	156.8	153.3	146.2	152.3	173.8	190.7	171.7
1924	189.0	181.7	190.4	191.7	151.2	129.4	200.1	184.8	149.0	157.7	146.2	120.9	135.1	175.7	185.9	161.3
1925	221.3	208.8	222.2	178.6	158.9	127.6	211.8	181.6	180.5	170.3	153.5	140.2	153.3	186.9	215.8	173.7
1926	162.8	179.4	175.3	184.1	176.9	144.7	220.9	225.9	149.5	158.7	161.4	131.6	164.9	169.5	169.8	168.0
1927	179.0	207.6	183.8	201.3	159.2	143.7	216.9	210.0	182.1	185.2	178.8	144.9	130.7	175.0	191.6	173.4
1928	166.4	186.7	169.7	138.2	138.1	141.0	188.9	211.3	181.0	167.3	160.8	125.2	133.0	152.2	175.0	157.0
1929	159.5	194.4	198.0	162.3	163.6	126.4	191.5	207.6	152.7	156.8	153.8	141.6	141.8	153.0	173.9	160.2
1930	117.8	152.5	157.6	146.8	136.7	129.6	194.8	200.4	149.6	153.4	143.8	121.6	120.9	123.5	133.3	141.5
1931	129.0	160.3	161.5	147.0	142.1	127.3	200.6	219.2	173.8	258.9	162.2	130.1	144.0	151.7	142.0	153.9
1932	124.2	181.3	121.8	138.9	129.6	117.3	178.2	175.0	157.9	158.2	147.2	103.4	133.7	141.8	148.7	141.0
1933	137.7	160.8	150.4	149.6	144.3	126.5	185.0	179.1	159.3	158.9	163.4	133.3	133.4	147.1	148.4	149.8
1934	115.2	164.4	133.5	133.3	138.1	103.7	167.3	132.2	133.9	141.9	144.3	119.4	118.7	126.6	137.2	131.6
1935	114.3	158.3	144.8	158.9	135.1	120.5	174.1	163.2	169.2	141.1	127.7	106.3	124.2	145.3	134.2	137.6
1936	100.5	162.1	145.2	133.1	120.8	99.8	150.2	151.3	158.9	143.4	137.6	98.0	124.4	140.0	127.7	130.8
1937	94.1	144.7	136.4	121.9	103.4	110.6	140.0	141.2	136.7	123.8	127.6	89.4	102.6	128.3	114.6	118.5
1938	89.6	146.2	148.5	136.9	138.7	98.2	172.4	171.6	151.6	142.3	138.5	98.6	100.8	145.4	110.7	129.2

TABLE A.5

REVISED RATES OF NATURAL INCREASE, BY PARISH, JAMAICA, ANNUALLY, 1891-1938

YEAR	KINGSTON	ST. ANDREW	ST. THOMAS	PORT-LAND	ST. MARY	ST. ANN	TRELAWNY	ST. JAMES	HANOVER	WEST-MORE-LAND	ST. ELIZ.	MAN-CHESTER	CLAR-ENDON	ST. CATHERINE	KINGSTON & ST. ANDREW	JAMAICA
1891/92	7.9	11.7	14.4	15.1	16.9	21.4	8.2	6.0	12.1	15.2	21.2	24.6	19.3	13.2	9.6	15.6
1892/93	7.6	14.4	13.5	16.2	18.7	20.9	11.0	9.8	14.5	14.0	21.7	24.8	18.6	16.4	10.6	16.5
1893/94	10.6	12.7	16.5	20.0	18.1	23.0	11.4	12.8	15.3	17.8	24.7	28.2	22.5	19.3	11.6	18.9
1894/95	7.8	7.8	13.3	15.4	14.4	21.7	14.1	10.3	17.7	20.1	22.9	25.9	15.8	13.6	7.8	16.4
1895/96	4.4	9.7	17.5	13.4	16.5	21.9	17.3	9.3	13.7	14.3	24.3	25.2	17.6	16.1	6.7	16.4
1896/97	8.5	11.8	16.7	13.5	16.5	19.8	13.7	12.5	14.9	15.5	20.7	25.1	21.9	16.1	10.0	16.8
1897/98	9.3	11.2	16.0	18.3	20.5	22.1	12.2	11.5	18.7	16.1	21.8	23.7	21.2	14.9	10.2	17.2
1898/99	6.9	9.2	16.2	18.3	18.1	26.2	14.2	12.8	16.0	16.6	23.0	26.1	18.8	15.0	8.0	17.5
1899/00	11.0	9.0	16.8	17.8	22.6	26.4	16.6	12.3	20.9	21.9	29.0	29.3	20.0	17.5	10.0	20.1
1900/01	3.8	7.3	10.5	14.9	15.5	20.9	9.1	9.7	14.4	15.7	22.0	23.7	17.3	11.1	5.4	14.7
1901/02	12.9	11.2	20.8	22.7	21.0	26.4	16.8	14.6	19.1	18.4	23.7	27.0	21.4	16.2	12.1	19.8
1902/03	10.5	15.7	17.9	20.9	21.2	26.0	16.5	12.1	16.1	19.6	28.2	30.6	22.1	18.2	12.9	20.4
1903/04	9.2	7.6	9.7	9.7	8.8	18.9	13.8	10.5	17.3	24.3	26.2	29.0	19.0	13.0	8.5	16.1
1904/05	7.4	4.0	9.5	10.3	9.5	19.4	12.1	20.3	9.3	13.0	19.6	22.0	11.0	6.7	5.8	12.0
1905/06	7.1	6.9	17.0	22.9	19.8	27.1	18.7	18.5	14.2	16.3	22.9	21.1	17.8	15.1	7.0	17.8
1906/07	-3.3	-0-	7.2	12.2	15.6	23.8	15.9	10.6	12.7	15.3	19.5	17.9	9.1	12.1	-1.8	12.5
1907/08	-6.4	-2.2	8.4	5.8	13.3	14.9	3.4	7.2	4.3	8.7	20.2	11.8	0.1	1.7	-4.4	7.0
1908/09	6.6	13.0	17.3	12.7	17.3	23.1	13.5	12.9	15.4	16.9	16.6	19.3	17.7	16.3	9.6	16.0
1909/10	7.4	13.2	12.7	15.0	20.1	24.0	16.2	14.9	19.8	18.4	21.8	20.0	12.9	15.7	10.1	16.9
1910/11	0.7	5.9	13.7	14.5	16.9	24.3	16.6	15.6	19.1	15.6	21.7	21.7	15.3	12.3	3.1	15.5
1911/12	8.7	6.6	15.1	16.9	17.6	22.2	11.8	16.1	17.5	14.5	23.5	23.9	19.3	16.2	7.7	17.0
1912/13	5.3	5.8	10.3	7.9	17.2	25.0	15.9	13.5	17.2	15.2	12.7	18.9	16.5	11.5	5.5	14.0
1913/14	4.6	6.6	13.8	15.6	17.9	22.0	11.9	12.4	11.3	11.0	14.6	14.6	19.0	14.8	5.6	14.1
1914/15	10.1	11.2	15.6	18.2	19.5	24.5	14.7	12.4	15.4	15.4	22.9	22.5	23.1	20.1	10.6	18.0
1915/16	5.2	2.4	7.8	9.7	13.7	20.7	13.9	11.0	17.3	15.5	17.7	18.4	19.2	12.7	3.9	13.7

TABLE A.5 (Cont'd)

REVISED RATES OF NATURAL INCREASE, BY PARISH, JAMAICA, ANNUALLY, 1891-1938

YEAR	KINGSTON	ST. ANDREW	ST. THOMAS	PORT-LAND	ST. MARY	ST. ANN	TRELAWNY	ST. JAMES	HANOVER	WEST-MORE-LAND	ST. ELIZ.	MAN-CHESTER	CLAR-ENDON	ST. CATHERINE	KINGSTON & ST. ANDREW	JAMAICA
1916	-1.0	1.5	6.6	10.8	11.8	16.2	11.9	11.9	13.3	12.0	15.8	17.6	15.7	11.6	0.1	11.5
1917	-9.5	-1.9	5.7	11.8	11.3	17.7	5.3	7.0	9.5	10.3	15.8	8.8	9.9	0.8	-6.0	7.5
1918	-5.2	-8.6	-5.8	-6.6	4.5	8.6	-2.8	0.8	4.8	2.8	8.8	6.4	6.5	-5.1	-6.8	1.2
1919	3.2	4.2	8.1	7.3	13.4	17.1	12.8	11.9	8.9	12.2	17.5	16.2	16.8	9.1	3.7	11.8
1920	3.0	9.4	13.9	13.5	19.3	20.4	14.3	17.0	15.4	19.2	20.3	16.0	19.9	11.4	6.0	15.5
1921	-1.7	-3.6	6.6	7.1	7.1	13.8	4.5	7.7	4.2	10.4	13.2	10.1	11.1	-1.3	-2.6	6.6
1922	12.8	8.2	11.0	15.2	14.5	19.0	11.5	14.9	13.0	12.1	17.7	16.5	15.3	15.5	10.6	14.4
1923	12.9	8.7	11.8	12.8	17.6	18.4	14.2	14.4	17.2	17.2	16.9	13.9	18.0	16.7	10.9	15.4
1924	11.6	6.8	11.7	14.8	15.7	19.9	15.9	17.3	17.2	16.8	18.1	16.0	15.3	12.7	9.3	15.0
1925	6.3	2.9	5.2	15.8	14.3	18.1	13.0	15.3	17.5	15.9	17.7	16.5	14.6	9.5	4.7	13.0
1926	15.6	8.9	16.2	17.1	13.4	21.0	19.3	14.5	23.4	19.2	22.1	22.4	20.5	16.6	12.3	17.8
1927	9.2	3.9	8.9	10.0	14.9	19.0	15.5	14.6	14.6	12.6	15.6	15.6	18.2	14.2	6.6	13.6
1928	12.0	5.8	14.2	16.7	16.4	19.3	16.7	13.8	16.3	14.4	20.8	20.0	20.8	15.6	8.9	16.1
1929	12.9	4.5	12.7	16.4	18.1	21.0	16.7	16.4	20.6	19.8	15.9	16.0	18.6	14.6	8.8	15.9
1930	18.0	11.2	15.5	20.7	20.2	23.3	21.8	19.6	20.8	19.1	21.8	20.8	24.9	20.8	14.6	20.1
1931	15.3	7.6	13.2	14.4	17.2	19.6	16.8	14.1	18.7	17.9	20.3	20.3	20.1	14.5	11.4	16.5
1932	10.4	5.4	12.9	14.1	13.5	18.3	15.4	20.5	17.4	17.5	19.8	21.5	18.7	13.3	7.9	15.4
1933	7.5	6.2	8.6	13.1	13.8	18.2	15.1	17.2	18.2	16.2	17.3	16.3	16.6	13.5	6.8	14.0
1934	10.4	6.2	9.2	13.3	13.0	19.1	14.5	22.6	17.3	15.3	17.7	16.7	17.5	13.2	8.2	14.5
1935	13.2	8.1	9.0	12.7	12.9	21.5	20.8	19.7	16.3	17.2	22.4	21.6	19.9	13.4	10.6	16.3
1936	13.0	6.4	7.6	13.6	12.6	20.7	20.8	21.4	17.1	19.4	18.6	20.3	17.4	10.7	9.6	15.3
1937	14.4	6.3	10.1	12.4	14.0	21.1	22.1	20.2	16.4	17.4	19.9	21.3	17.9	13.0	10.2	15.9
1938	18.8	5.1	10.6	11.1	11.0	20.4	19.3	19.2	20.3	18.6	21.9	20.5	21.0	14.4	11.6	16.5

TABLE A.6

ELEMENTS OF INTERCENSAL POPULATION GROWTH, BY PARISH, JAMAICA, 1891-1943

PARISH	1891 - 1911[a]			1911 - 1921[b]				1921 - 1943[b]			
	NATURAL INCREASE	NET TOTAL MIGRATION	INTER-CENSAL GROWTH	NATURAL INCREASE	NET INTERNAL MIGRATION	NET EXTERNAL MIGRATION	INTER-CENSAL GROWTH	NATURAL INCREASE	NET INTERNAL MIGRATION	NET EXTERNAL MIGRATION	INTER-CENSAL GROWTH
Kingston	6870	+ 4300	+ 11170	1386	+ 10258	- 7607	+ 4037	28061	+ 21511	- 3200	+ 46372
St. Andrew	7919	+ 6999	+ 14918	1962	+ 4148	- 4285	+ 1825	10582	+ 47466	+15500	+ 73548
St. Thomas	10130	- 2976	+ 7154	3621	+ 782	- 1232	+ 3171	12038	+ 5454	+ 700	+ 18192
Portland	12262	+ 5100	+ 17362	5049	+ 1246	- 6685	- 390	16451	- 3009	- 1700	+ 11742
St. Mary	19241	+10800	+ 30041	10314	+ 937	-12803	- 1552	25075	- 8677	+ 3100	+ 19498
St. Ann	28063	-11539	+ 16524	13385	- 4676	- 8438	+ 271	35865	- 14294	+ 3700	+ 25271
Trelawny	9012	- 4545	+ 4467	3725	- 380	- 4206	- 861	15656	- 2923	+ 200	+ 12933
St. James	8894	- 2568	+ 6326	4623	- 250	- 3803	+ 570	20225	- 29	+ 1400	+ 21596
Hanover	10594	- 5250	+ 5344	4767	- 792	- 3167	+ 808	17308	- 4164	+ 300	+ 13444
Westmoreland	19712	- 6706	+ 13006	8377	- 1175	- 4805	+ 2397	29293	- 8037	---	+ 21256
St. Elizabeth	31613	-15169	+ 16444	13027	- 6236	- 6210	+ 581	37808	- 19607	+ 2700	+ 20901
Manchester	28574	-18842	+ 9732	10258	- 5139	- 6368	- 1249	31979	- 10179	+ 7000	+ 28800
Clarendon	21652	- 4843	+ 16809	12532	+ 649	- 4540	+ 8641	41200	- 2650	+ 2400	+ 40950
St. Catherine	21163	+ 1432	+ 22595	9107	+ 628	- 1249	+ 8486	31604	- 862	- 6300	+ 24442
TOTAL FOR JAMAICA	235699	-43807	191892	102135	---	-75398	+26735	353145	---	+25800	+378945

SOURCES: (a) Natural Increase computed from Annual Report of the Registrar General in C.O. 140.
Intercensal Population Growth computed from Census of Jamaica 1891 and 1911.
Net Total Migration = (Intercensal Growth)-(Natural Increase).

(b) Natural Increase computed from Annual Report of the Registrar General in C.O. 140.
Intercensal Growth computed from the Censuses of Jamaica, 1911 and 1921 and 1943.
Net Internal Migration computed from G. W. Roberts, The Population of Jamaica, p. 150.

TABLE A.7

PERCENTAGE DISTRIBUTION OF PARISH POPULATIONS, BY AGE GROUPS, JAMAICA, CENSUS YEAR, 1881-1943

CENSUS DATE AND AGE GROUPS	KING-STON	ST. ANDREW	ST. THOMAS	PORT-LAND	ST. MARY	ST. ANN	TRE-LAWNY	ST. JAMES	HAN-OVER	WEST-MORE-LAND	ST. ELIZ-ABETH	MAN-CHESTER	CLAR-ENDON	ST. CATHERINE	JAMAICA
1881:															
0 - 14	31.69	38.18	33.63	40.57	39.82	40.97	36.81	35.72	38.50	38.78	42.13	44.01	37.00	36.11	38.32
15 - 39	45.83	40.25	39.06	38.43	39.34	39.47	40.80	42.93	39.96	41.25	38.53	38.50	44.45	44.02	41.04
40 - 64	15.85	13.44	15.89	14.74	15.96	14.84	17.28	15.98	16.16	15.82	14.55	13.32	13.68	14.45	15.01
65+	4.33	3.72	3.69	4.72	4.46	4.25	4.75	4.62	4.59	4.02	4.08	3.86	4.14	4.58	4.25
Unknown	2.30	4.41	7.72	1.54	0.43	0.47	0.36	0.75	0.80	0.13	0.70	0.31	0.72	0.84	1.37
1891:															
0.- 14	28.27	36.02	36.35	39.65	39.82	42.39	37.26	38.77	35.80	37.86	40.46	43.22	41.33	39.91	38.71
15 - 39	50.03	43.37	40.04	40.10	39.90	38.33	39.64	39.39	42.83	40.59	39.11	38.15	38.44	41.78	40.76
40 - 64	17.66	16.77	19.39	17.00	16.31	15.15	18.77	17.80	17.00	17.17	16.42	15.03	16.42	14.80	16.59
65+	2.93	3.73	4.12	3.15	3.87	3.81	4.31	4.00	4.34	4.23	3.97	3.46	3.74	3.51	3.77
Unknown	1.10	0.12	0.10	0.09	0.10	0.32	0.02	0.04	0.02	0.15	0.03	0.14	0.08	---	0.17
1911:															
0 - 14	27.59	36.88	39.55	37.49	38.52	44.37	39.96	39.47	40.94	41.17	43.85	44.67	41.31	39.01	39.83
15 - 39	51.22	43.14	38.00	43.81	44.49	36.02	37.74	39.60	37.58	37.46	35.76	35.29	39.58	41.47	40.11
40 - 64	17.88	16.76	18.14	15.50	14.37	15.90	18.02	16.91	17.47	17.20	16.33	16.12	16.16	16.38	16.49
65+	3.19	3.17	4.25	3.08	2.54	3.69	4.24	3.94	3.93	4.14	3.99	3.92	2.88	3.12	3.51
Unknown	0.13	0.05	0.06	0.11	0.09	0.03	0.03	0.07	0.08	0.04	0.06	0.00	0.07	0.02	0.06

TABLE A.7 (Cont'd)

PERCENTAGE DISTRIBUTION OF PARISH POPULATIONS, BY AGE GROUPS, JAMAICA, CENSUS YEAR, 1881-1943

CENSUS DATE AND AGE GROUPS	KING-STON	ST. ANDREW	ST. THOMAS	PORT-LAND	ST. MARY	ST. ANN	TRE-LAWNY	ST. JAMES	HAN-OVER	WEST-MORE-LAND	ST. ELIZ-ABETH	MAN-CHESTER	CLAR-ENDON	ST. CATHERINE	JAMAICA
1921:															
0 - 14	26.71	35.92	36.82	38.52	40.84	45.29	39.12	39.56	40.98	40.13	42.05	42.90	41.19	38.34	39.35
15 - 39	50.97	41.45	40.22	39.92	39.36	34.04	37.92	38.16	36.76	37.66	35.79	34.81	38.93	41.65	39.18
40 - 64	18.74	18.80	18.73	18.22	16.95	16.67	18.58	18.36	18.25	17.80	17.58	17.67	16.67	17.04	17.69
65+	3.42	3.62	4.22	3.26	2.79	3.99	4.36	3.90	4.00	4.39	4.55	4.49	3.20	2.96	3.73
Unknown	0.16	0.13	0.02	0.08	0.05	0.02	0.02	0.01	0.01	0.02	0.03	0.13	0.01	0.01	0.05
1943:															
0 - 14	25.12	29.93	32.45	34.91	36.37	42.30	40.39	37.97	40.61	39.40	41.30	40.68	39.72	36.07	36.56
15 - 39	53.26	47.22	42.90	20.48	40.63	37.06	38.35	41.25	38.10	38.37	36.29	38.25	40.38	41.28	41.45
40 - 64	18.39	18.99	20.60	20.22	19.14	15.96	16.87	16.73	16.73	17.26	16.98	16.09	16.31	18.93	17.78
65+	3.19	3.83	4.00	4.35	3.84	4.66	4.35	4.02	4.54	4.93	5.39	4.95	3.57	3.71	4.18
Unknown	0.04	0.03	0.05	0.05	0.02	0.03	0.04	0.03	0.02	0.03	0.04	0.02	0.01	0.01	0.03

SOURCE: Computed from Census of Jamaica, 1943, Table 25.

TABLE A.8

JOINT GROSS REPRODUCTION RATES, BY PARISH

AND CENSUS YEAR, 1891-1921

PARISH	JOINT GROSS REPRODUCTION RATES		
	1891	1911	1921
Kingston-St. Andrew	1.99	1.99	2.15
St. Thomas	2.53	2.72	2.43
Portland	2.64	2.31	2.49
St. Mary	2.61	2.31	2.52
St. Ann	2.93	3.21	3.24
Trelawny	2.56	2.71	2.82
St. James	2.15	2.60	2.70
Hanover	2.49	3.03	2.83
Westmoreland	2.60	2.79	2.75
St. Elizabeth	3.13	3.07	3.09
Manchester	3.22	3.06	2.94
Clarendon	2.80	2.81	2.82
St. Catherine	2.79	2.60	2.39

SOURCE: G.W. Roberts, The Population of Jamaica, Table 70, p. 281.

TABLE A.9

STANDARDIZED MORTALITY RATIOS, BY PARISH AND CENSUS YEAR, 1891-1921

PARISH	STANDARDIZED MORTALITY RATIOS		
	1891	1911	1921
St. Thomas	.3445	.3317	.3382
Portland	.3196	.3615	.3302
St. Mary	.2971	.3298	.3398
St. Ann	.2679	.2620	.2584
Trelawny	.3358	.3154	.3712
St. James	.2570	.3094	.3404
Hanover	.2964	.3286	.3780
Westmoreland	.3041	.3064	.2948
St. Elizabeth	.2592	.2664	.2737
Manchester	.2857	.2527	.2513
Clarendon	.2856	.3422	.3309
St. Catherine	.3348	.3851	.4391

NOTE: Method of Computation as discussed in the text of this Appendix.

TABLE A.10

INFANT MORTALITY RATES, PER 1000 LIVE BIRTHS, FIVE YEAR AVERAGES, BY PARISH, JAMAICA 1891-1935

PARISH	1891-1895	1896-1900	1901-1905	1906-1910	1911-1915	1916-1920	1921-1925	1926-1930	1931-1935
St. Thomas	165.2	187.2	192.4	191.9	170.7	185.8	201.8	176.9	142.4
Portland	174.0	174.5	183.1	204.6	187.8	185.5	190.5	166.5	145.5
St. Mary	168.4	167.9	172.6	182.1	175.2	157.9	166.9	154.9	137.8
St. Ann	155.6	168.6	149.8	152.0	139.1	143.6	142.6	137.1	119.1
Trelawny	217.0	220.6	207.9	215.6	198.5	210.7	218.2	202.6	181.0
St. James	196.5	207.4	185.2	209.2	204.0	193.1	195.5	211.0	173.7
Hanover	196.4	198.8	196.1	202.4	197.8	193.5	189.5	163.0	158.8
Westmoreland	170.5	169.0	175.7	190.7	192.0	173.8	173.5	164.3	151.8
St. Elizabeth	158.3	156.7	157.6	162.6	167.4	164.0	159.5	159.7	149.0
Manchester	134.9	129.8	141.3	160.6	143.1	134.3	144.5	133.0	118.5
Clarendon	151.8	161.9	160.5	199.7	157.3	155.7	153.6	138.3	130.8
St. Catherine	170.2	181.5	187.1	204.6	183.1	181.9	185.5	154.6	142.5

SOURCE: Table A.4

TABLE A.11

CRUDE DEATH RATES, PER 1,000 POPULATION, FIVE YEAR AVERAGES, BY PARISH, JAMAICA 1891-1935

PARISH	1891-1895	1896-1900	1901-1905	1906-1910	1911-1915	1916-1920	1921-1925	1926-1930	1931-1935
St. Thomas	24.48	25.99	26.22	26.22	24.77	29.20	25.60	20.83	20.19
Portland	23.04	23.15	23.91	25.00	25.13	28.85	24.23	20.81	18.69
St. Mary	20.80	20.08	23.59	22.18	21.49	24.18	22.01	18.93	18.62
St. Ann	18.60	20.10	19.89	20.35	19.03	23.93	19.65	16.31	15.59
Trelawny	25.78	26.30	25.97	26.60	23.70	28.91	25.47	20.04	19.65
St. James	21.84	22.09	22.13	24.16	24.29	26.55	23.18	22.24	21.63
Hanover	24.43	24.99	27.29	26.90	25.56	28.27	24.37	19.18	19.54
Westmoreland	22.43	22.49	23.58	24.15	23.71	25.32	22.01	19.35	17.97
St. Elizabeth	21.16	20.42	20.99	22.50	20.20	22.91	20.54	18.87	17.82
Manchester	17.55	18.27	19.68	22.42	18.42	22.37	18.90	16.38	15.22
Clarendon	20.31	22.86	23.94	27.99	21.97	26.08	22.79	17.78	16.88
St. Catherine	24.24	24.68	26.20	28.15	24.83	30.84	26.01	20.38	19.37

SOURCE: Table A.3

TABLE A.12

CRUDE BIRTH RATES, PER 1,000 POPULATION, FIVE YEAR AVERAGES, BY PARISH, JAMAICA 1891-1935

PARISH	1891-1895	1896-1900	1901-1905	1906-1910	1911-1915	1916-1920	1921-1925	1926-1930	1931-1935
St. Thomas	39.52	41.23	41.22	38.07	37.30	34.90	35.20	34.33	30.82
Portland	39.05	39.68	41.19	37.03	38.80	36.19	37.37	36.97	32.21
St. Mary	37.71	38.71	39.64	38.83	38.65	36.25	35.88	35.53	32.66
St. Ann	40.38	43.18	43.43	42.37	41.90	39.92	37.47	37.01	34.91
Trelawny	38.17	39.18	41.54	39.70	37.32	37.21	37.28	38.05	36.17
St. James	31.48	33.84	34.93	36.40	37.36	36.23	37.11	38.04	40.44
Hanover	39.07	41.97	42.50	41.15	41.28	38.64	38.19	38.33	37.13
Westmoreland	38.70	39.65	41.27	39.12	38.01	36.61	36.49	36.37	34.78
St. Elizabeth	44.13	43.72	45.11	42.46	38.45	38.53	37.24	38.09	37.30
Manchester	43.29	43.87	45.60	40.55	38.09	35.36	33.77	35.71	34.48
Clarendon	39.08	42.13	42.17	39.00	41.38	39.83	37.64	38.38	35.44
St. Catherine	39.94	39.59	40.04	39.74	39.88	36.37	36.63	36.74	32.94

SOURCE: Table A.2

TABLE A.13

RATES OF NATURAL INCREASE, PER 1000 POPULATION, FIVE YEAR AVERAGES, BY PARISH, JAMAICA 1891-1935

PARISH	1891-1895	1896-1900	1901-1905	1906-1910	1911-1915	1916-1920	1921-1925	1926-1930	1931-1935
St. Thomas	15.04	15.24	14.99	11.84	12.53	5.70	9.25	13.49	10.56
Portland	16.02	16.54	17.27	12.03	13.67	7.34	13.14	16.17	13.52
St. Mary	16.92	18.62	16.05	16.65	17.16	12.07	13.87	16.60	14.04
St. Ann	21.77	23.08	23.54	22.02	22.88	15.99	17.82	20.70	19.32
Trelawny	12.39	13.15	15.57	13.11	13.62	8.31	11.81	18.01	16.52
St. James	9.64	11.75	15.21	12.24	13.07	9.68	13.93	15.80	18.82
Hanover	14.65	16.98	15.21	14.25	15.73	10.38	13.82	19.15	17.59
Westmoreland	16.27	17.17	18.32	14.97	14.30	11.29	14.48	17.02	16.81
St. Elizabeth	22.97	23.31	24.12	19.95	18.25	15.62	16.71	19.22	19.49
Manchester	25.74	25.59	25.92	18.13	19.67	12.99	14.61	18.94	19.26
Clarendon	18.76	19.84	18.23	11.02	19.42	13.75	14.85	20.59	18.55
St. Catherine	15.71	14.91	13.84	11.59	15.05	5.53	10.62	16.36	13.57

SOURCE: Table A.5

TABLE A.14

PROPORTION OF CULTIVATED ACREAGE UNDER PLANTATION CONTROL (P), FIVE YEAR AVERAGES, BY PARISH, JAMAICA, 1891-1935

PARISH	1891-1895	1896-1900	1901-1905	1906-1910	1911-1915	1916-1920	1921-1925	1926-1930	1931-1935
St. Thomas	.9325	.8304	.7267	.5504	.4340	.3747	.4208	.5747	.6128
Portland	.1052	.1342	.1379	.1581	.1583	.1137	.1031	.0829	.0792
St. Mary	.1521	.1426	.1663	.2009	.2460	.2361	.2213	.2328	.2618
St. Ann	.1294	.1140	.0539	.0518	.0464	.0492	.0530	.0508	.0666
Trelawny	.8999	.8150	.7537	.6599	.5109	.4948	.5247	.4157	.2407
St. James	.8369	.6610	.5013	.3150	.3965	.3349	.3488	.3278	.3974
Hanover	.4472	.4172	.3079	.2064	.1579	.0770	.0462	.0742	.0636
Westmoreland	.6906	.6720	.6056	.4020	.4012	.3138	.2203	.1396	.1477
St. Elizabeth	.5199	.3386	.2675	.1383	.1332	.1080	.1072	.1237	.1246
Manchester	.1405	.1122	.1117	.0904	.0665	.0609	.0372	.0332	.0271
Clarendon	1.0000	1.0000	.8484	.6608	.6366	.4386	.3848	.4177	.7591
St. Catherine	.5144	.3396	.3609	.3168	.3129	.2517	.2468	.3898	.3726

SOURCE: *Handbook of Jamaica*, Annually, 1891-1935 (Kingston: G.P.O.).

TABLE A.15

PROPORTION OF CULTIVATED ACREAGE UNDER STAPLE EXPORT CROPS (X), FIVE YEAR AVERAGES, BY PARISH, JAMAICA, 1891-1935

PARISH	1891-1895	1896-1900	1901-1905	1906-1910	1911-1915	1916-1920	1921-1925	1926-1930	1931-1935
St. Thomas	.2730	.3227	.3395	.3325	.3573	.3757	.3716	.3658	.4298
Portland	.2159	.2635	.2780	.3347	.3627	.3081	.3534	.3773	.3096
St. Mary	.2321	.2501	.2933	.3793	.5003	.4998	.4452	.4691	.4132
St. Ann	.0402	.0401	.0473	.0426	.0525	.0539	.0832	.0885	.0751
Trelawny	.1129	.1134	.1215	.1324	.1548	.1393	.1423	.1952	.1303
St. James	.1182	.1047	.1075	.1137	.1837	.1769	.2051	.1992	.2279
Hanover	.0691	.0618	.0718	.1125	.1219	.1187	.1453	.1335	.1502
Westmoreland	.0920	.1023	.0880	.0837	.1102	.0969	.0910	.1195	.1218
St. Elizabeth	.0302	.0225	.0353	.0254	.0253	.0199	.0170	.0164	.0207
Manchester	.1266	.1225	.1130	.1106	.0714	.0523	.0346	.0301	.0214
Clarendon	.1886	.1779	.1646	.1902	.1564	.1804	.1603	.1486	.2263
St. Catherine	.0972	.1329	.2303	.2735	.2427	.2477	.2886	.2597	.2173

SOURCE: Handbook of Jamaica, Annually, 1891-1935 (Kingston: G.P.O).

TABLE A.16

PROPORTIONS OF CULTIVATED ACREAGE UNDER PLANTATION CONTROL (P) AND UNDER STAPLE EXPORT CROPS (X), BY PARISH, JAMAICA, CENSUS YEARS, 1891-1921

PARISH	1891		1911		1921	
	P	X	P	X	P	X
St. Thomas	1.0000	.2636	.5515	.3720	.3701	.3619
Portland	.0864	.2189	.1715	.3758	.1119	.3350
St. Mary	.2012	.2462	.2151	.4184	.2443	.4742
St. Ann	.1480	.0409	.0492	.0444	.0461	.0677
Trelawny	.9135	.1124	.5685	.1397	.4930	.1420
St. James	.8550	.1259	.2684	.1251	.3028	.1813
Hanover	.4558	.0656	.2090	.1174	.0449	.1174
Westmoreland	.7511	.0925	.4036	.0862	.2606	.0944
St. Elizabeth	.5077	.0320	.1381	.0256	.1019	.0139
Manchester	.0862	.1315	.0805	.0931	.0544	.0434
Clarendon	1.0000	.2036	.7071	.1939	.3083	.1851
St. Catherine	.4863	.0923	.1938	.2767	.2387	.2608

SOURCE: *Handbook of Jamaica*, Annually, 1891-1935 (Kingston: G.P.O).

TABLE A.17

PROPORTIONS OF CULTIVATED ACREAGE UNDER PLANTATION CONTROL (P) AND UNDER STAPLE EXPORT CROPS (X), BY PARISH, JAMAICA, INTERCENSAL PERIODS, 1891-1943

PARISH	1891-1911		1911-1921		1921-1943	
	P	X	P	X	P	X
St. Thomas	.7600	.3163	.4044	.3665	.5361	.3891
Portland	.1336	.2730	.1360	.3354	.0884	.3434
St. Mary	.1657	.2887	.2411	.5001	.2386	.4425
St. Ann	.0873	.0426	.0478	.0532	.0568	.0823
Trelawny	.7846	.1201	.5029	.1471	.3937	.1559
St. James	.5786	.1110	.3657	.1803	.3580	.2107
Hanover	.3447	.0788	.1175	.1203	.0613	.1430
Westmoreland	.5926	.0915	.3575	.1034	.1692	.1108
St. Elizabeth	.3161	.0284	.1206	.0226	.1185	.0108
Manchester	.1137	.1182	.0637	.0619	.0325	.0287
Clarendon	.8773	.1803	.5376	.1684	.5205	.1784
St. Catherine	.3829	.1835	.2850	.2452	.3384	.2552

SOURCE: Handbook of Jamaica, Annually, 1891-1938 (Kingston: G.P.O).

TABLE A.18

RESULTS OF CROSS SECTION ANALYSIS WITH INFANT MORTALITY AS DEPENDENT VARIABLE:

REGRESSION FORM (1a)

DEPENDENT VARIABLE	NUMBER OF OBSERVATIONS	HYPOTHESIZED SIGN OF: b_1	b_2	ESTIMATED COEFFICIENTS OF INDEPENDENT VARIABLES: CONSTANT TERM (a)	ORGANIZATION OF PRODUCTION (P) (b_1)	COMPOSITION OF OUTPUT (X) (b_2)	SIGNIFICANCE OF REGRESSION (F-RATIO)	R^2
1891-1895	12	+	+	+163.47	+ 25.66 (20.23)	- 41.57 (89.51)	0.85	0.1590
1896-1900	12	+	+	+162.29	+ 35.94 (22.75)	- 13.99 (77.76)	1.25	0.2172
1901-1905	12	+	+	+154.59	+ 31.74 (20.49)	+ 53.19 (55.01)	1.89	0.2953
1906-1910	12	+	+	+163.49	+ 57.90* (24.16)	+ 45.33 (42.30)	4.07	0.4752
1911-1915	12	+	+	+159.91	+ 37.43 (35.73)	+ 28.26 (46.19)	0.88	0.1641
1916-1920	12	+	+	+155.25	+ 68.65 (44.07)	+ 9.06 (47.29)	1.44	0.2423
1921-1925	12	+	+	+150.58	+ 77.20+ (38.36)	+ 44.96 (44.95)	3.45	0.4338
1926-1930	12	+	+	+147.76	+ 53.72 (44.10)	+ 14.56 (55.89)	1.12	0.1987
1931-1935	12	+	+	+144.07	+ 0.58 (32.46)	+ 8.64 (55.41)	0.02	0.0044

NOTES: Bracketed figures are standard errors of estimate.
*Indicates significance level of 0.05
+Indicates significance level of 0.10

TABLE A.19

RESULTS OF CROSS SECTION ANALYSIS WITH CRUDE DEATH RATE AS DEPENDENT VARIABLE:

REGRESSION FORM (1a)

DEPENDENT VARIABLE	NUMBER OF OBSERVATIONS	HYPOTHESIZED SIGN OF:		ESTIMATED COEFFICIENTS OF INDEPENDENT VARIABLES			SIGNIFICANCE OF REGRESSION (F-RATIO)	R^2
		b_1	b_2	CONSTANT TERM (a)	ORGANIZATION OF PRODUCTION (P) (b_1)	COMPOSITION OF OUTPUT (X) (b_2)		
1891-1895	12	+	+	+ 19.85	+ 3.42 (2.15)	+ 2.93 (9.52)	1.40	0.2370
1896-1900	12	+	+	+ 19.70	+ 4.95+ (2.05)	+ 5.36 (7.00)	3.12	0.4095
1901-1905	12	+	+	+ 20.40	+ 4.24 (2.39)	+ 9.56 (6.40)	3.08	0.4060
1906-1910	12	+	+	+ 21.55	+ 7.85* (2.73)	+ 3.99 (4.78)	5.11*	0.5318
1911-1915	12	+	+	+ 20.19	+ 4.86 (3.76)	+ 5.92 (4.85)	1.93	0.3009
1916-1920	12	+	+	+ 23.96	+ 6.10 (5.34)	+ 5.49 (5.73)	1.56	0.2573
1921-1925	12	+	+	+ 19.95	+ 6.79+ (3.46)	+ 7.24 (4.06)	5.03*	0.5277
1926-1930	12	+	+	+ 17.50	+3.39 (2.89)	+ 4.74 (3.66)	2.66	0.3719
1931-1935	12	+	+	+ 17.00	+ 0.39 (2.70)	+ 6.81 (4.63)	1.72	0.2769

NOTES: Bracketed figures are standard errors of estimate.
*Indicates significance level of 0.05
+Indicates significance level of 0.10

TABLE A.20

RESULTS OF CROSS SECTION ANALYSIS WITH CRUDE BIRTH RATE AS DEPENDENT VARIABLE:

REGRESSION FORM (1a)

DEPENDENT VARIABLE	NUMBER OF OBSERVATIONS	HYPOTHESIZED SIGN OF: b_1	b_2	ESTIMATED COEFFICIENTS OF INDEPENDENT VARIABLES: CONSTANT TERM (a)	ORGANIZATION OF PRODUCTION (P) (b_1)	COMPOSITION OF OUTPUT (X) (b_2)	SIGNIFICANCE OF REGRESSION (F-RATIO)	R^2
1891-1895	12	-	-	+ 41.89	- 3.09 (2.79)	- 7.85 (12.33)	0.92	0.1699
1896-1900	12	-	-	+ 42.25	- 1.96 (2.81)	- 5.47 (9.59)	0.47	0.0953
1901-1905	12	-	-	+ 43.78	- 2.41 (3.07)	- 7.95 (8.25)	0.88	0.1640
1906-1910	12	-	-	+ 41.81	- 2.48 (2.27)	- 8.46+ (3.97)	3.42	0.4319
1911-1915	12	-	-	+ 39.98	- 1.54 (2.89)	- 2.55 (3.73)	0.46	0.0924
1916-1920	12	-	-	+ 38.23	- 0.01 (3.27)	- 5.60 (3.51)	1.39	0.2358
1921-1925	12	-	-	+ 36.77	+ 0.59 (2.59)	- 1.11 (3.04)	0.07	0.0163
1926-1930	12	-	-	+ 37.77	+ 0.35 (.233)	- 4.47 (2.95)	1.29	0.2234
1931-1935	12	-	-	+ 36.74	+ 2.72 (3.67	-12.87+ (6.28)	2.20	0.3284

NOTES: Bracketed figures are standard errors of estimate.
+Indicates significance level of 0.10

TABLE A.21

RESULTS OF CROSS SECTION ANALYSIS WITH RATE OF NATURAL INCREASE AS DEPENDENT VARIABLE:

REGRESSION FORM (1a)

DEPENDENT VARIABLE	NUMBER OF OBSERVATIONS	HYPOTHESIZED SIGN OF: b_1	b_2	CONSTANT TERM (a)	ESTIMATED COEFFICIENTS OF INDEPENDENT VARIABLES: ORGANIZATION OF PRODUCTION (P) (b_1)	COMPOSITION OF OUTPUT (X) (b_2)	SIGNIFICANCE OF REGRESSION (F-RATIO)	R^2
1891-1895	12	-	-	+ 22.05	- 6.52 (3.73)	- 10.76 (16.51)	1.91	0.2983
1896-1900	12	-	-	+ 22.47	- 6.28 (3.73)	- 10.77 (12.76)	2.02	0.3095
1901-1905	12	-	-	+ 23.68	- 6.14 (3.65)	- 19.12+ (9.81)	3.79	0.4569
1906-1910	12	-	-	+ 20.25	-10.32* (3.43	- 12.45+ (6.00)	8.15*	0.6444
1911-1915	12	-	-	+ 19.80	- 6.41 (4.75)	- 8.47 (6.14)	2.28	0.3367
1916-1920	12	-	-	+ 14.27	- 6.10 (6.44)	- 11.10 (6.91)	2.38	0.3459
1921-1925	12	-	-	+ 16.80	- 6.25+ (3.36)	- 8.43+ (3.93)	5.76*	0.5613
1926-1930	12	-	-	+ 20.16	- 2.91 (2.96)	- 8.98* (3.75)	5.39*	0.5422
1931-1935	12	-	-	+ 19.76	+ 2.29 (2.73)	- 19.75* (4.68)	10.43*	0.6986

NOTES: Bracketed figures are standard errors of estimate.
*Indicates significance level of 0.05
+Indicates significance level of 0.10

TABLE A.22

RESULTS OF CROSS SECTION ANALYSIS WITH STANDARDIZED MORTALITY RATIO AS DEPENDENT VARIABLE:

REGRESSION FORM (1a)

TIME PERIOD	NUMBER OF OBSERVATIONS	HYPOTHESIZED SIGN OF:		ESTIMATED COEFFICIENTS OF INDEPENDENT VARIABLES			SIGNIFICANCE OF REGRESSION (F-RATIO)	R^2
		b_1	b_2	CONSTANT TERM (a)	ORGANIZATION OF PRODUCTION (P) (b_1)	COMPOSITION OF OUTPUT (X) (b_2)		
1891	12	+	+	+ 0.27	+ 0.01 (0.02)	+ 0.16 (0.11)	1.26	0.2188
1911	12	+	+	+ 0.27	+ 0.04 (0.04)	+ 0.20* (0.07)	5.72*	0.5599
1921	12	+	+	+ 0.28	+ 0.12 (0.11)	+ 0.14 (0.11)	2.06	0.3141

NOTES: Bracketed figures are standard errors of estimate.

*Indicates significance level of 0.05

TABLE A.23

RESULTS OF CROSS SECTION ANALYSIS WITH JOINT GROSS REPRODUCTION RATE AS DEPENDENT VARIABLE:

REGRESSION FORM (1a)

TIME PERIOD	NUMBER OF OBSERVATIONS	HYPOTHESIZED SIGN OF: b_1	b_2	ESTIMATED COEFFICIENTS OF INDEPENDENT VARIABLES: CONSTANT TERM (a)	ORGANIZATION OF PRODUCTION (P) (b_1)	COMPOSITION OF OUTPUT (X) (b_2)	SIGNIFICANCE OF REGRESSION (F-RATIO)	R^2
1891	12	–	–	+ 3.02	- 0.37 (0.23)	- 0.84 (1.06)	1.74	0.2793
1911	12	–	–	+ 3.11	- 0.05 (0.26)	- 1.73* (0.40)	9.84*	0.6861
1921	12	–	–	+ 3.09	- 0.30 (0.35)	- 1.44* (0.36)	11.08*	0.7112

NOTES: Bracketed figures are standard errors of estimates.

*Indicates significance level of 0.05

TABLE A.24

CORRELATION MATRIX FOR TIME ADJUSTED POOLED CROSS SECTION ANALYSIS:

REGRESSION FORM (2a)

	P	X	t	IMR	CDR	CBR	RNI
P	1.0000						
X	.1295	1.0000					
T	-.3733	.1793	1.0000				
IMR	.3721	.1604	-.2816	1.0000			
CDR	.3327	.2464	-.3184	.7601	1.0000		
CBR	.0320	-.3296	-.5915	.0348	.1410	1.0000	
RNI	-.2353	-.4387	-.1762	.5836	-.7032	.6021	1.0000

TABLE A.25

CORRELATION MATRIX FOR TIME ADJUSTED POOLED CROSS SECTION ANALYSIS:

REGRESSION FORM (2a), CENSUS YEARS

	P	X	t	SMR	JGRR
P	1.0000				
X	.0529	1.0000			
t	-.4940	.2006	1.0000		
SMR	.0873	.5711	.2865	1.0000	
JGRR	-.3603	-.6406	.0834	-.5052	1.0000

BIBLIOGRAPHY OF WORKS CITED

MANUSCRIPTS CONSULTED AT THE PUBLIC RECORD OFFICE, LONDON

C.O. 137/496-835	Jamaica, Original Correspondence with the Secretary of State for the Colonies, 1880-1938.
C.O. 140	Jamaica, Annual Reports of the Governor of Jamaica and Departmental Annual Reports.
C.O. 950	West India Royal Commission, Written and Oral Evidence Presented to the Commission, 1938-1939.

OFFICIAL PUBLICATIONS

Parliamentary and Non-Parliamentary Papers

Report of the Royal West India Commission. (H.M.S.O.: C 8655-8657, C 8669, 1897).

Barbour, Sir David. Report on the Finances of Jamaica. (H.M.S.O.: C 9412, 1899).

Correspondence Relating to the Public Finances and Resources of the Island of Jamaica. (H.M.S.O.: C 9177, 1899).

Wood, E. F. L. Report...on a Visit to the West Indies and British Guiana. (H.M.S.O.: Cmd. 1679, 1922).

Report of the West Indian Sugar Commission. (H.M.S.O.: Cmd. 3517, 1930).

Orde-Browne, G. St.J. Report on Labour Conditions in the West Indies. (H.M.S.O.: Cmd. 6070, 1939).

Report of the West India Royal Commission. (H.M.S.O.: Cmd. 6607, 1945).

Engledow, R. L. Report on Agriculture. (H.M.S.O.: Cmd. 6608, 1945).

Jamaica Government Publications

Bluebook of Jamaica. (Kingston: G.P.O., annually 1880-1938).

Handbook of Jamaica. (Kingston: G.P.O., annually 1880-1938).

Report of the Unemployment Commission. (Kingston: G.P.O., 1936).

Report of the Nutrition Committee. (Kingston: G.P.O., 1937).

Report of the Cost of Living Survey Carried Out in Kingston, Jamaica, August-November, 1939. (Kingston: G.P.O., 1940).

BOOKS

Beachey, R. W. The British West Indian Sugar Industry in the Late Nineteenth Century. (Oxford: The University Press, 1957).

Beckford, George. Persistent Poverty. (London: Oxford University Press, 1972).

Best, Lloyd and Kari Levitt. Export Propelled Growth in the Caribbean. (Montreal: McGill University, mimeo., 1968?).

Blake, Judith. Family Structure in Jamaica: The Social Context of Reproduction. (New York: 1961).

Burn, W. L. The British West Indies. (London: 1951).

Carnegie, James. Some Aspects of Jamaica's Politics, 1918-1938. (Kingston: The Institute of Jamaica, 1973).

Clarke, Edith. My Mother Who Fathered Me. (London: George Allen and Unwin, second edition, 1966).

Clarke, John I. Population Geography. (London: Pergamon Press, 1965).

Comitas, Lambros. Caribbeana, 1900-1965: A Topical Bibliography. (Seattle: Institute for the Study of Man, 1968).

Craton, Michael and James Walvin. A Jamaican Plantation. (London: W. H. Allen, 1970).

Deane, Phyllis. The Measurement of Colonial National Income: An Experiment. (Cambridge: The National Institute of Economic and Social Research, 1948).

Deerr, Noel. The History of Sugar. (London: 1949-50).

Deprez, Paul (ed.). Population and Economics. (Winnipeg: University of Manitoba Press, 1970).

Eisner, Gisela. Jamaica, 1830-1930: A Study in Economic Growth. (Manchester: The University Press, 1961).

Eyre, L. Alan. Geographic Aspects of Population Dynamics in Jamaica. (Boca Raton: 1972).

Glass, D. V. and D. E. C. Eversley (eds.). Population and History. (London: Edward Arnold, 1965).

Hall, D. G. Free Jamaica, 1838-1865. (New Haven: Yale University Press, 1959).

Hall, D. G. Ideas and Illustrations in Economic History. (New York: Holt, Rinehardt and Winston, 1954).

Hart, Richard. The Origin and Development of the People of Jamaica. (Kingston: 1952).

Hollingsworth, T. H. Historical Demography. (London: Hodder and Stoughton, 1969).

Horowitz, Michael M. (ed.) Peoples and Cultures of the Caribbean. (New York: Natural History Press, 1971).

Innis, Harold. Essays in Canadian Economic History. (Toronto: University of Toronto Press, 1957).

Levin, Jonathan. The Export Economies. (Cambridge, Mass.: Harvard University Press, 1960).

Macmillan, W. M. Warning from the West Indies. (London: Penguin, 1936).

Mason, Karen O. and A. S. David. Social and Economic Correlates of Family Fertility. (Research Triangle Park, North Carolina, 1971).

Myint, Hla. The Economics of Developing Countries. (London: 1964).

North, Douglas C. The Economic Growth of the United States, 1790-1860. (Englewood Cliffs: Norton, 1961).

Olivier, Lord. Jamaica: The Blessed Island. (London: Faber and Faber, 1936).

Proudfoot, M. J. Population Movements in the Caribbean. (Port of Spain: 1950).

Pullen-Burry, B. Jamaica As It Is, 1903. (London: T. Fisher Unwin, 1903).

Redfield, Robert. Peasant Society and Culture. (Chicago: University of Chicago Press, 1956).

Roberts, G. W. The Population of Jamaica. (Cambridge: The University Press, 1957).

Root, W. The British West Indies and the Sugar Industry (Liverpool: 1899).

Sauvy, Alfred. General Theory of Population. (London: Methuen and Co., 1974).

Shanin, Teodor (ed.). Peasants and Peasant Societies. (London: Penguin, 1971).

Simon, Julian L. The Effects of Income on Fertility. (Chapel Hill: Carolina Population Center, 1974).

Tekse, K. Population of Jamaica in Numbers, 1844-1965. (Kingston: Department of Statistics, 1966).

Tekse, K. Internal Migration in Jamaica. (Kingston: Department of Statistics, 1967).

Tulloch, A. M. and H. Marshall. Statistical Report on Sickness, Mortality and Invaliding Among Troops in the West Indies. (London: 1838).

Wrigley E. A. Population and History. (London: Weidenfield and Nicholson, 1969).

Wrong, D. H. Population and Society. (New York: Random House, 1961).

ARTICLES

Adams, N. A., "Internal Migration in Jamaica: An Economic Analysis", Social and Economic Studies, Vol. 18, No. 2 (June 1969), pp. 137-151.

Baldwin, Robert E., "Patterns of Development in Newly Settled Regions", Manchester School of Economics and Social Studies, Vol. XXIV (May 1956).

Best, Lloyd, "Outlines of a Model of Pure Plantation Economy," Social and Economic Studies, Vol. 17, No. 2 (September 1968).

Bhattacharyya, Amit K., "Income Inequality and Fertility: A Comparative View", Population Studies, Vol. XXIX, No. 1 (March 1975), pp. 5-19.

Brunn, Stanley D. and Robert N. Thomas, "Socio-Economic Environments and Internal Migration: The Case of Tegucigalpa, Honduras", Social and Economic Studies, Vol. 21, No. 4 (December 1972), pp. 463-473.

Craton, Michael, "Jamaican Slave Mortality: Fresh Light from Worthy Park, Longville and the Tharp Estates", Journal of Caribbean History, Vol. 3 (November 1971), pp. 1-27.

Cumper, G. E., "Labour Demand and Supply in the Jamaican Sugar Industry, 1830-1950", Social and Economic Studies, Vol. 2, No. 4 (December 1953), pp. 37-86.

Cumper, G. E., "Population Movements in Jamaica, 1830-1950", Social and Economic Studies, Vol. 5, No. 2 (June 1956), pp. 261-280.

Cumper, G. E., "The Jamaican Family: Village and Estate", Social and Economic Studies, Vol. 7, No. 1 (March 1958), pp. 76-108.

Cumper, G. E., "The Fertility of Common Law Union in Jamaican", Social and Economic Studies, Vol. 15, No. 3 (September 1966), pp. 189-202.

Cumper, G. E., "Dependence, Development and the Sociology of Economic Thought", Social and Economic Studies, Vol. 23, No. 3 (September 1974), pp. 465-482.

DeCastro, Steve, "Theorems of the Open Economy", Social and Economic Studies, Vol. 19, No. 3 (September 1970).

Eaton, George, "Trade Union Development in Jamaica", Carribean Quarterly, Vol. 8, Nos. 1 and 2 (June 1962).

Ebanks, G. E., "Differential Internal Migration in Jamaica, 1943-1960", Social and Economic Studies, Vol. 17, No. 2 (June 1968), pp. 193-228.

Harris, J. R. and M. P. Todaro, "Migration, Unemployment and Development: A Two Sector Analysis", American Economic Review, Vol. LX, No. 1 (March 1970), pp. 126-142.

Harris, R. N. and E. S. Steer, "Demographic-Resource Push in Rural Migration: A Jamaican Case Study", Social and Economic Studies, Vol. 17, No. 4 (December 1968), pp. 398-406.

Hart, A., "The Banana in Jamaica: Export Trade", Social and

Economic Studies, Vol. 3, No. 2 (September 1954), pp. 212-229.

Higman, B. W., "Household Structure and Fertility on Jamaican Slave Plantations: A Nineteenth Century Example", Population Studies, Vol. 27, No. 3 (September 1973), pp. 527-550.

Kennedy, Charles, "Keynesian Theory in an Open Economy", Social and Economic Studies, Vol. 13, No. 1 (March 1964).

Lobdell, Richard A., "Patterns of Investment and Sources of Credit in the British West Indian Sugar Industry, 1838-97", Journal of Caribbean History, Vol. 4 (May 1972), pp. 31-53.

MacDonald, Leatrice and John, "Motives and Objectives of Migration: Selective Migration and Preferences Toward Rural and Urban Life", Social and Economic Studies, Vol. 18,No. 4 (December 1969), pp. 417-434.

Maunder, W. F., "The New Jamaican Emigration", Social and Economic Studies, Vol. 4, No. 1 (March 1955), pp. 38-63.

Mintz, Sidney, "The Caribbean as a Socio-Cultural Area", in M. M. Horowitz (ed.), Peoples and Cultures of the Caribbean, pp. 15-46.

Mintz, Sidney and D. G. Hall, "The Origin of the Jamaican Internal Marketing System", Yale University Publications in Anthropology, Vol. 57 (1960), pp. 3-26.

Nortman, Dorothy, "Population and Family Planning Programs: A Factbook", Reports on Population/Family Planning, No. 2 (6th Edition) (December 1974).

Phelps, O., "Rise of the Labour Movement in Jamaica", Social and Economic Studies, Vol. 9, No. 4 (December 1960).

Post, K. W. J., "The Politics of Protest in Jamaica, 1938", Department of Government, University of the West Indies, Mimeo., 1969.

Roberts, G. W., "A Note on Mortality in Jamaica", Population Studies, Vol. IV, No. 1 (March 1950).

Roberts, G. W., " A Life Table for a West Indian Slave Population", Population Studies, Vol. V, No. 3 (September 1951).

Roberts, G. W., "Notes on Population Growth", Social and Economic Studies, Vol. 7, No. 3 (September 1958).

Roberts, G. W. and J. A. Bryne, "Summary Statistics on Indenture and Associated Migration Affecting the West Indies, 1834-1918", Population Studies, Vol. XX, No. 1 (March 1966).

Roberts, G. W. and D. O. Mills, "A Study of External Migration Affecting Jamaica, 1953-1955", Supplement to Social and Economic Studies, Vol. 7 No. 2 (June 1958), pp. 1-126.

Seers, Dudley, "The Mechanism of an Open Petroleum Economy", Social and Economic Studies, Vol. 13, No. 2 (June 1964).

Sjaastad, L. A., "The Costs and Returns of Human Migration", Journal of Political Economy, Vol. LXX, No. 4 (October 1962), pp. 80-93.

Smith, M. G., "Community Organization in Rural Jamaica", Social and Economic Studies, Vol. 5, No. 3 (September 1956), pp. 295-312.

Smith, M. G., "Introduction" in Edith Clarke, My Mother Who Fathered Me, pp. i-xliv.

Smith, R. T., "The Family in the Caribbean", in Vera Rubin (ed.), Caribbean Studies: A Symposium. (Kingston: U.W.I., 1957).

Smith, R. T., "Social Stratification, Cultural Pluralism and Integration in West Indian Societies", in S. Lewis and T. G. Mathews (eds.), Caribbean Integration. (Puerto Rico: 1967).

Smith, R. T., "Culture and Social Structure in the Caribbean: Some Recent Work on Family and Kinship Studies", in M. M. Horowitz (ed.), Peoples and Cultures of the Caribbean, pp. 448-475.

Todaro, M. P., "A Model of Labor Migration and Urban Unemployment in Less Developed Countries", American Economic Review, Vol. LIX, No. 1 (March 1969), pp. 138-148.

Wagley, Charles, "Plantation America: A Cultural Sphere", in Vera Rubin (ed.), Caribbean Studies: A Symposium.

Watkins, Melville, "A Staple Theory of Economic Growth", Canadian Journal of Economics and Political Science, Vol. XXIX, No. 2 (May 1963), pp. 141-158.